BREADWINNERS

WOMEN IN
AMERICAN HISTORY

Series Editors
Anne Firor Scott
Susan Armitage
Susan K. Cahn
Deborah Gray White

*A list of books in the series appears
at the end of this book.*

BREADWINNERS

Working Women and Economic Independence, 1865–1920

LARA VAPNEK

UNIVERSITY OF ILLINOIS PRESS
Urbana and Chicago

Library of Congress Cataloging-in-Publication Data
Vapnek, Lara.
Breadwinners : working women and economic
independence, 1865–1920 / Lara Vapnek.
p.   cm. — (Women in American history)
Includes index.
ISBN 978-0-252-03471-8 (cloth : alk. paper)
ISBN 978-0-252-07661-9 (pbk. : alk. paper)
1. Women—Employment—United States—History.
2. Working class women—United States—History.
I. Title.
HD6095.V37   2008
331.40973'09034—dc22   2008047676

For Derek, Zoe, and Violet

CONTENTS

ACKNOWLEDGMENTS

It is a pleasure to thank the people who made it possible for me to write this book. Archivists and librarians at the Tamiment Library, the Schlesinger Library, Butler Library, New York Public Library, and St. John's University all provided invaluable assistance. My colleagues at St. John's generously offered their support and encouragement; the School of Liberal Arts and Sciences provided me with much-needed time and funds by granting me course reductions and summer support of research. Students in my women's history classes at Rutgers and at St. John's helped me learn to frame my arguments more clearly.

I first began thinking about the ideas at the heart of this book while I was a graduate student at Columbia, where I had three extraordinary mentors. My adviser, Eric Foner, introduced me to the radical potential of American democratic ideals. His scholarship and teaching continue to inspire me. Betsy Blackmar taught me to think critically about the boundaries between public and private property and labor. She posed questions that kept me thinking and she was always willing to read another draft. Even before she joined the faculty at Columbia, Alice Kessler-Harris read my work and generously shared her broad knowledge of women's labor history. Her belief in my project mattered to me immeasurably.

Numerous friends and colleagues read and commented on drafts of chapters, or conference papers drawn from this book. For their insightful comments, I would like to thank Nancy Berke, Hilary Botein, Eliza Byard, Cori Field, Maggie Garb, Linda Grasso, Vanessa May, Carol Quirke, and Andy Urban. Dana Frank sharpened my thinking about reformers' class identities and Lisa Tetrault helped me think critically about narratives of the women's rights movement. By sharing her "Reacting to the Past" game, "Greenwich Village 1913: Suffrage, Labor, and the New Woman," Mary

Jane Treacy gave me new insight into this historical moment. Over the past decade, I presented papers drawn from my research at numerous conferences, where I benefited greatly from discussion with my fellow panelists and with members of the audience.

Laurie Matheson at University of Illinois Press guided this manuscript on its twisting path to becoming a book. Her patience, persistence, and enthusiasm have been unfailing. Eileen Boris offered an insightful reading of my manuscript; in person, she shared her energetic inquiry into the social construction of domestic labor. Sue Armitage gave me the confidence to enliven my characters and leave the dissertation behind. Grey Osterud's searching questions and pointed comments enabled me to crystallize my argument and see the pieces of my story as a whole.

My family has been a tremendous source of support. My parents, Daniel and Dianne, and my sisters, Brett and Susanna, helped me keep my work in perspective. My husband, Derek Denckla, commented thoughtfully on nearly every draft. He and my daughters, Zoe and Violet, not only gave me time to write this book, they share my joy in its publication. I dedicate this book to them.

ABBREVIATIONS

AFL   American Federation of Labor
BSL   Bureau of Statistics of Labor
CAAIL   Church Association for the Advancement
         of the Interests of Labor
CLU   Central Labor Union
DRL   Domestic Reform League
ELSSW   Equality League of Self-Supporting Women
ILGWU   International Ladies' Garment Workers' Union
NAWSA   National American Woman Suffrage Association
NEWC   New England Women's Club
NYCL   New York Consumers' League
SRC   Social Reform Club
WEIU   Women's Educational and Industrial Union
WESL   Wage-Earners' Suffrage League
WPU   Women's Political Union
WSP   Woman Suffrage Party
WSPU   Women's Social and Political Union
WTUL   Women's Trade Union League
WWS   Working Women's Society

INTRODUCTION

In July 1848 a group of women, assembled in Seneca Falls, New York, re-wrote the Declaration of Independence. They began with the simple, but radical presumption that all "men and women" are created equal and went on to enumerate the many ways that men had conspired to deprive women of their "inalienable rights" to "life, liberty, and the pursuit of happiness." While their "Declaration of Sentiments" is best remembered for its contro-versial demand that women be granted the right to vote, this far-reaching statement of human rights linked women's "dependent and abject" state to their limited possibilities for self-support and called for women's full and "equal participation with men in the various trades [and] professions." Like most nineteenth-century Americans, these women linked political and economic rights, viewing both as necessary to achieve equality and attain independence. Historians have regarded the Declaration of Sentiments as a launching point for women's "century of struggle" to win full political rights. However, scholars have paid less attention to women's equally intense, if less well-documented struggle to win full economic equality.[1]

This book examines how working women pursued equality by claiming new identities as citizens and as breadwinners. The first signs of this move-ment appeared in the strikes of tailoresses in Philadelphia and New York in the 1820s, the protests of Lowell mill girls in the 1830s, and the words of the educated women who issued the Declaration of Sentiments in 1848.[2] However, the idea of female independence as linked to wage earning did not develop fully until after the Civil War, when industrialization acceler-ated to the point that older pieties about "women's place" in the home and women's "nature" as resting upon their dependence on men no longer made sense. These ideas did not disappear once and for all, but they underwent their first sustained challenge between 1865 and 1920, when women's labor reformers began making bold new claims for female independence.

I apply the term *women's labor reformer* to women of different classes who identified the reform of women's position in the labor market as the key to establishing women's domestic, social, and political equality. Women's labor reformers were a diverse group. Some were working women like Aurora Phelps, a single mother who worked as a domestic servant and a nurse before initiating a petition to gain free land from the state of Massachusetts so that women could become self-sufficient farmers. Others were upper-class women like Maud Nathan, a New York City society matron who urged affluent women to protect working women's health by shopping exclusively at department stores that treated their female clerks fairly. In between these two extremes stood female labor leaders, journalists, settlement house workers, and college-educated sociologists.

The class identities of women's labor reformers were complex and often hybrid, defined through a mix of family ties, education, work experience, organizational affiliation, and self-definition.[3] I use the term *working class* to describe women who earned wages through manual labor and identified themselves as workers, although some forged careers as reformers that gave them access to middle-class comforts, such as homeownership and savings accounts. I describe women whose chose to work as volunteers or professionals as *middle class*. By virtue of their sex and their social concern, these women viewed themselves as mediating conflict between capitalist employers and the working class. Some of these women came from elite backgrounds, but gender always inflected women's class position. Even women from privileged backgrounds might find themselves seriously short of cash when fathers died, marriages dissolved, or family businesses failed. Awareness of the economic insecurity all women faced motivated middle class women to organize to assist women of the working class. Women's class identities formed not just in relationship to work, but in relationship to each other.

This book examines how women's social class shaped their ideas of independence and their strategies for political transformation, revealing a series of conflicts, collaborations, and negotiations.[4] Middle-class women conceptualized independence as full intellectual and professional development, unhindered by the "family claim." Working-class women used the term to assert their right to take jobs that offered them respect, a decent wage, and the ability to care for dependent family members—children, aging parents, disabled siblings, ailing spouses. Both groups of women employed a mix of individual and collective strategies for seeking the economic and political independence they desired. Women of the upper middle class pushed for greater access to higher education and professional opportunities. They asserted themselves politically by forming numerous organizations devoted to social reform, from clubs to settlement houses. Acting individually, native-born white women of the working class staged what amounted to a massive walkout from domestic service. Some who took new industrial or retail positions joined working men in seeking collective power through organization.

During the Gilded Age, the labor movement asserted the dignity of labor and the primacy of "producers" as the backbone of the American republic. The Knights of Labor developed this ideology most fully. Like American socialists, however, the Knights took an ambivalent stance toward women's wage earning, viewing it as a sign of capitalist exploitation and family deterioration. Despite their affirmation of a domestic ideal, the Knights supported the principle of "equal pay for equal work" and opened the organization to women who worked as housewives, domestics, and industrial workers. The Knights peaked in 1886 and then declined dramatically, to be replaced by trade unions affiliated with the American Federation of Labor. While more enduring than the more expansive labor organizations that preceded them, trade unions were largely defensive and generally inhospitable to women. Wage-earning women who gained limited traction with organized men found stronger and more consistent support from organized middle-class and elite women who were excluded from formal politics, but eager to assert their power by addressing the social consequences of industrialization.[5]

The middle-class women who joined campaigns to reform working-class women's conditions of labor believed that women's progress rested upon their economic as well as political equality. The New England Women's Club (NEWC), which formed in Boston immediately after the Civil War, set the pattern for the organizations that followed. By focusing on the conditions of working-class women and children, it extended antebellum traditions of benevolence, justifying its members' own departure from the domestic sphere as necessary to protect society's weakest members and to mend the chasm of class that seemed to widen each year. The NEWC embraced social science as a technique for understanding social problems and believed that educated women must act on behalf of their less fortunate sisters. By the turn of the twentieth century, middle-class female labor reformers were increasingly likely to be college educated and to embrace a combination of state-centered and voluntary strategies for social change. Elite reformers' turn toward the state to protect working women from labor exploitation led them to emphasize women's dependence, a strategy that helped them pass protective labor legislation limiting the hours of women working in industry, but denied working women's broader aspirations for independence based on economic equality, political rights, and collective organization.[6]

By casting themselves as impartial mediators of class conflict, women such as Maud Nathan and Mary Putnam Jacobi, a physician who helped establish the New York Consumers' League (NYCL), affirmed their moral authority while denying the complexity of their own class position. This stance became particularly problematic in regard to domestic service, which remained women's largest category of paid employment outside of agriculture through 1930. Whether they belonged to the small female professional class, had inherited money, or relied on wealthy husbands for support, the well-to-do women who organized and financed women's labor reform organizations, such as the New England Women's Club, New York Consumers' League, the Women's Educational and Industrial Union (WEIU), and the Women's Trade Union League (WTUL) almost always relied on servants to take care of their households. This fact shaped their conception of "working girls," whom they defined through social investigation as young, single women working in factories or retail stores, producing or selling consumer goods. Elite female labor reformers' concerns about the health of young, white women in industry dovetailed with the anxieties of organized working men about losing their jobs to machines run by women and with politicians' imperialist promises to preserve "the future of the race."[7]

Although seldom more racist than the society to which they belonged, women's labor reformers focused on women who worked for wages outside of households and ignored the labor conditions of domestic workers, growing numbers of whom were European immigrants or African Americans. Women's labor reform took shape most visibly in Boston, New York, and Chicago, three cities on the cutting edge of capitalist industrial development, with strong traditions of labor activism and women's civic involvement. European immigrants flocked to these cities in the decades following the Civil War, but the African American population remained small until the turn of the twentieth century. Like recent European immigrants, African American women entered into public discussion of women's place in the labor question purely as negative examples of the problems affluent house-wives faced finding "good help" now that native-born white women were no longer willing to work as servants. Native-born commentators identified the Irish as a "race" of servants in the late nineteenth century. However, like other groups of groups of European immigrants, the Irish seldom spent more than a generation working as domestics before moving on to more desirable positions in factories, stores, and offices. African American women experienced no such mobility during this period.[8]

Patterns of occupational segregation, combined with the naturalization of women's domestic work, left African American women out of most public discussions of the positive and negative aspects of women's growing participation in the paid labor force. Since slavery, African American women had been expected to work outside the confines of their own families. After emancipation, African American men's limited prospects for earning a living gave most African American women no choice but to work for wages in order to help support their families. Their situation foreshadowed the eventual fate of most American families. However, dominant formulations of "working girls" and "working women" excluded African American women. This conceptual severance had enduring consequences. Nineteenth century understandings of the identity of working women set the agenda for twentieth century social policies. Early labor legislation applied exclusively to women working in industry, leaving out equal or greater numbers of women working in domestic and agricultural occupations. During the New Deal, white southern Democrats inscribed these preexisting patterns of exclusion into national labor policy.[9]

White working-class women demanded independence by rejecting positions as domestic servants and by organizing collectively to assert new social identities as breadwinners. The women whose voices are recovered here learned about the insecurity of male support through personal experience. Although exceptional in their decisions to speak out, organize, and express themselves publicly, they had experiences as orphaned daughters, widowed mothers, and supporters of aging parents that were typical for women of their social class. Using their own biographies as proof, women ranging from Jennie Collins, a native-born Massachusetts mill girl in the 1850s, through Mollie Schepps, an immigrant necktie maker in New York City during the 1910s, pointed to the class-bound nature of feminine ideals of dependence and protection within families. The fiction of "separate spheres" rarely fit working-class women, who typically combined care for family members with income-generating labor. Working-class women who became labor reformers and joined labor organizations sought social recognition for their status as breadwinners and collective power in their negotiations with employers.

Working-class women's ideas about independence and their chances of achieving it varied according to their age and family position. Girls forced into the labor market by family misfortune were underpaid and often mistreated by their bosses, but the wages they earned, however small, allowed them a new degree of self-assertion within their families. As female wage workers entered their teens and twenties, they used the money they earned to negotiate reduced domestic responsibilities with mothers, sisters, and in-laws. Those who lived at home could use any extra income to purchase "cheap amusements," thereby participating in a new commercial culture that promised freedom and collective identification through consumption.[10] Once women married and had children, they generally left the ranks of full-time wage earners and devoted most of their energy to housework and child care. Often, however, their withdrawal from the paid labor market was temporary. If a working-class woman's husband died, became disabled, or lost his job, she would have to find ways to support herself and her children, at least until they were old enough to go out and earn money themselves. Widowed mothers with young children faced a desperate struggle for survival, sometimes resorting to prostitution when their paltry earnings as outworkers or factory hands proved insufficient to keep food on the table and prevent their children from being scattered into orphanages. By asserting women's rights to be paid as individuals who supported other family members, working-class women's labor reformers asserted a new form of female independence, challenging long-held notions about women's dependence on men as irrelevant and dangerous.

With little to no capital, limited political rights, and widespread assumptions of female inferiority, working-class women did not make the world they lived in. But they tried tenaciously to change it, using the resources they had in their possession: their labor, their social networks, their claims to public sympathy, and their incisive reading of a national political ideology that promised equality to all people but had yet to deliver it to women.

Women's labor organizations were ephemeral and left behind few written records, but they provide the best evidence we have as to working-class women's own aspirations and self-definitions. By piecing together the stories of organizations such as the Working Women's League, the Working Women's Society (WWS), and the Wage-Earners' Suffrage League (WESL), as well as the story of women's participation in the Knights of Labor, we can appreciate wage-earning women's desires to be recognized as breadwinners entitled to full rights of citizenship. All of these organizations mixed together women working in different trades, uniting them in their common desire to be compensated fairly and treated respectfully by their employers. In establishing or joining labor organizations, these women sought many of the same goals as organized men: shorter hours, higher wages, and control over the pace and conditions of their labor. To these common objectives, they added demands for protection from sexual harassment and freedom from the draconian work rules and petty fines commonly imposed on female workers. Working women's notoriously low wages and limited free time made these independent organizations difficult to sustain. Finding limited support from working men, women's labor leaders formed alliances with elite female labor reformers, who offered financial support but cast themselves as the protectors of working-class women who were helpless to protect themselves. Class differences made it difficult for middle-class reformers to appreciate working-class women's desires for independence.

The case studies that form this book illustrate the meanings of independence to women of different social classes, revealing continuing conflicts over domestic service and showing the political circumstances under which social knowledge of working-class women was produced. Each of the five chapters traces a particular historical moment in which a group of wage-earning women demanded independence, bringing them into conflicts and alliances with elite advocates of women's labor reform. In some instances, laboring women allied with middle class labor reformers, as in the formation of the Women's Trade Union League (WTUL); in others, they clashed, as in working-class women's response to the attempts of the Domestic Reform League (DRL) to bring them back into positions as domestic servants. The biographies of working-class and middle-class women who devoted themselves to women's labor reform illustrate the personal meanings of independence for women, showing how individual experience shaped their political perspective and informed their strategies for social change. Although working-class women seldom achieved clear victories, their struggles reveal their determination to integrate their experiences as workers and as women into a coherent political identity.

As the Civil War drew to a close, northern working-class women began making new demands for independence, reflecting their increasing participation in the labor market and their patriotic service during the war. Chapter 1 uses the biographies of Jennie Collins and Aurora Phelps, the founders of the Working Women's League, to sketch out the meanings of independence for northern, native-born, white women in Boston during Reconstruction. Individually and collectively, these women defended their rights to seek jobs beyond domestic service and affirmed their place in a broad-based labor reform movement that included men and women organized into trade and labor unions, eight-hour-day leagues, and consumers' cooperatives. They rejected charity in favor of self-support and insisted on their right to speak for themselves. Under the auspices of the Working Women's League, Phelps spearheaded a campaign urging the commonwealth of Massachusetts to help working women become self supporting by granting them "garden homesteads" on which they could farm and raise their families, while Collins affirmed women's rights to be recognized as citizens and skilled wage workers. As the labor reform movement crumbled in the face of economic depression and a national backlash against the radicalism of Reconstruction, the Working Women's League dissolved. In contrast, the New England

Women's Club, an elite group of women committed to finding meaningful work for themselves as social reformers, endured. In a pioneering social-scientific study of Boston's needleworkers, they urged working-class women to solve the problem of their industrial exploitation by returning to positions as domestic servants.

From 1877 to 1886, the nation experienced an unprecedented degree of labor conflict. Chapter 2 focuses on four social investigations that placed women within the labor question: *The Working Girls of Boston* by Carroll D. Wright, the commissioner of labor statistics in Massachusetts; Leonora Barry's series of reports on working women for the Knights of Labor; *Prisoners of Poverty* by Helen Campbell, a reformer who advocated consumer organization; and *City Slave Girls,* a series of stories by undercover reporter "Nell Nelson" for the *Chicago Times.* In dialogue with the anonymous working-class women who responded to their interviews and questionnaires, each of these social investigators advanced a particular definition of the working girl and weighed in on a heated public debate as to whether the new groups of working women visible on city streets should be seen as symbols of female progress or as wage slaves. Each separated the struggles of women in industry from those of women in domestic service, despite the insistence of working-class women themselves that the problems of long hours, low wages, poor treatment, and sexual harassment spanned the entire field of women's paid employment.

Chapter 3 examines the early life of Leonora O'Reilly, whose activism illuminates the connections between gender, class, and consumption. Born in 1870 and raised on the Lower East Side of New York City by her widowed mother, an Irish immigrant who struggled to keep food on the table, O'Reilly left school to take a job in a collar factory at the age of eleven. By the time she was sixteen, she had joined a local assembly of the Knights of Labor and helped establish the Working Women's Society, an organization of women from various trades who proudly identified themselves as working women and who sought the same prizes being won by the city's organized working men. Many were veterans of the Knights of Labor, and they appealed to female consumers to consider the conditions of the women who made the clothes they wore. As the Knights declined, the city's trade union leaders showed less interest in organizing women, and the Working Women's Society pursued new alliances with bourgeois women seeking progress for their sex. These allies, who included Josephine Shaw Lowell, Maud Nathan, Helen Campbell, and Mary Putnam Jacobi, soon positioned themselves as impartial mediators in the battle between capital and labor by establishing their own organization, the New York Consumers' League.

While the League tried to protect women who worked as salesclerks and white goods workers (who made underwear and muslin garments) from industrial exploitation, its emphasis on protecting public health cast working women as the objects rather than the initiators of labor reform.

Most elite women's labor reformers preferred to keep their servants out of public discussions of women's place in the labor question. Chapter 4 examines the Domestic Reform League, a group of progressive Boston housewives who broke convention by investigating and seeking to reform domestic service. Their activities highlight the degree to which paid and unpaid domestic labor had become associated with dependence by the turn of the twentieth century. In contrast, work outside the household promised independence for women of different social classes. The Domestic Reform League undertook several initiatives designed to dignify domestic service. It opened a School of Housekeeping, established an agency devoted to day labor, and experimented with the delivery of cooked dinners. Aside from a registry, which placed full-time, live-in servants in the households of its members, the Domestic Reform League enjoyed little success. Its failure pointed toward the future: domestic work would continue to be marginalized as labor, and increasing numbers of women would have no choice but to go out and earn money in order to purchase goods and services previously produced in the home.

Chapter 5 returns to Leonora O'Reilly, whose suffrage activism during the first two decades of the twentieth century illustrates the connections working-class women drew between full citizenship and economic equality. Enlisting the support of women's clubs, trade unions, and socialist societies, she argued that wage-earning women needed labor organization and political rights in order to press the state for policies that served the interests of the entire working class, such as equal pay for equal work, an eight-hour day, and safe workplaces. O'Reilly envisioned wage-earning women as "citizen workers," who would speak on their own behalf and represent themselves politically, a dramatic departure from common characterizations of working women as helpless victims. She sought to realize this vision by establishing the Wage-Earners' Suffrage League, an organization composed exclusively of working women. Her necessary but difficult alliances with elite members of the women's movement and with men in the labor movement reveal the challenges working-class women continued to face in integrating their gender- and class-based interests and identities.

Women's labor reformers imagined themselves at the intersection of the women's movement and the labor movement. This story adds to historical understanding of both. Historians have generally seen the Gilded Age as a low point of agitation for women's rights. By expanding our field of inquiry beyond suffrage to include economic rights, we may instead see this period as a vital moment in considering the social, political, and domestic implications of women's increasing presence in the labor force. Furthermore, working-class women's activism is missing from most accounts of women's early twentieth-century campaigns to win the vote. While historians have offered compelling descriptions of working men's attempts to preserve their manliness and independence through labor organization during the Gilded Age and Progressive Era, less notice has been taken of the ways in which women who worked for wages demanded recognition as breadwinners.[11] To borrow the words of Josephine Casey, a streetcar conductor turned labor organizer, this book shows that working-class women had "that real American way of saying, 'I want to be independent.'"[12]

My study brings working-class women's daily experiences into dialogue with larger questions about the social and political meanings of women's wide-scale entry into the paid labor force, building on a generation of scholarship by women's labor historians, who have illuminated working-class women's experiences in particular cities and industries.[13] I add to this literature by explaining how working-class and middle-class women's desires for independence shaped their decisions about wage work and their programs for reform. Furthermore, I offer a critical examination of how and why domestic servants were excluded from public considerations of women's place in the labor question and I explore how working-class women contested this exclusion.

By looking at working-class women's individual decisions and collective strategies for organization in combination with middle-class women's programs for labor reform, we can begin to appreciate the complexities of class relations among women and to see how class shaped women's ideas of what was possible. Furthermore, we can recover a strain of women's movements for emancipation that went beyond the winning of formal political rights to address economic issues. As formal rights have become the norm for previously marginalized groups in American society over the course of the twentieth century, economic inequality persists, underlining the contemporary relevance of the stories told here. These case studies suggest the personal and social costs of failing to integrate paid and unpaid domestic labor into our understandings of work and social policy. As the vast majority of women now work for wages, these questions remain pressing in our own times.

Jennie Collins at Boffin's Bower. Visitors commented favorably on the homey decor. Published in Frank Leslie's *Illustrated Newspaper*, 26 June 1875, 256. Photo by E. R. Morse. Courtesy of Schlesinger Library, Radcliffe Institute, Harvard University

Working women eating lunch at Boffin's Bower. Note the care they put into their dress. Published in Frank Leslie's *Illustrated Newspaper*, 26 June 1875, 256. Photo by E. R. Morse. Courtesy of Schlesinger Library, Radcliffe Institute, Harvard University

Portrait of Leonora M. Barry, General Investigator of Women's Work for the Knights of Labor. Courtesy of T. V. Powderly Photographic Prints Collection, American Catholic History Research Center and University Archives, Catholic University of America, Washington, D.C.

Portrait of Helen S. Campbell, who ignited the midde-class consumers' movement. From *Woman of the Century* (1893), 148. Courtesy of Schlesinger Library, Radcliffe Institute, Harvard University

Lewis Wickes Hine, *Crowded Workroom on Broadway*. Women in employed in workshops in large cities across the country worked in similar conditions. Courtesy of Photography Collection, Miriam and Ira D. Wallach Division of Art, Prints and Photographs, New York Public Library, Astor, Lenox and Tilden Foundations

Shop girls, *Harper's Magazine,* 1880. Saleswomen's public visibility made them subjects for labor reform. Courtesy of Picture Collection, Branch Libraries, New York Public Library, Astor, Lenox and Tilden Foundations

"One firm in a new hygienically constructed store serves its saleswomen nourishing lunches at cost price." *Munsey's Magazine,* 1899. Merchants publicized their healthy working conditions in response to critiques from the New York Consumers' League. Courtesy of Picture Collection, Branch Libraries, New York Public Library, Astor, Lenox and Tilden Foundations

Hudson, "School of Housekeeping Scenes," *Boston Herald,* 27 December 1899, illustrate the work of the Boston Domestic Reform League. Courtesy of Wisconsin Historical Society, Image ID #WHi-60444

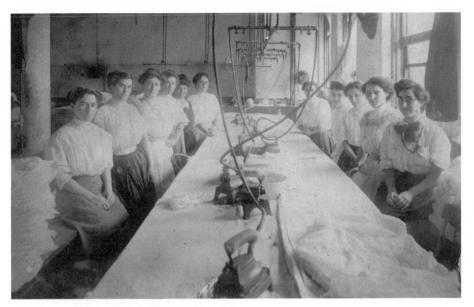

Women employees of the Reliance Waist Company pose around a work table, c. 1900. Shirtwaist makers' close working conditions facilitated labor organizing. Courtesy of International Ladies Garment Workers Union Archives, Kheel Center, Cornell University.

An informal family portrait of Leonora O'Reilly and her mother, Winifred, seated on the steps of a porch, c. 1910. Leonora is holding her adopted daughter Alice in her lap. Courtesy of Schlesinger Library, Radcliffe Institute, Harvard University

Votes for women. Women's growing presence as wage-workers added fuel to early twentieth-century suffrage campaigns. Courtesy of Prints and Photographs Division, Library of Congress, LC-USZ62-95344

CHAPTER I

The Daily Labor of Our Own Hands

In 1842, fourteen-year-old Jennie Collins set off from her home in Amoskeag, New Hampshire, to find a job in the textile mills of Lawrence, Massachusetts. Orphaned at the age of three, Collins had been raised by her Quaker grandmother, who gave her an unusual degree of liberty but left her with a limited education and no property. Like most girls, Collins must have learned basic domestic skills, such as sewing and cooking, in the expectation that she would marry and have a family of her own. When family support failed, however, Collins's domestic training had little market value. Like many girls and young women in New England, she made her way to the mills to take a position as a machine operative.[1]

When she reached Lawrence, Collins felt her loss of family protection, and she quickly realized that the popular sentimental view of young, white women stopped at the factory gate. In seeking out the employment agent, she was "treated neither with politeness nor consideration." She faced him on her own, and made "her own bargain with him." Earning "her own money," she was left to "hire her own board, buy her own clothes." She received no deference as a woman, and she knew that she "must work as hard and do her task as well as a man, or . . . be discharged, without ceremony or apology." Indeed, her sex entailed a burden, rather than a privilege; Collins earned only half of a man's wages and none of his "perquisites." She could never become eligible for a skilled position, since these were reserved for men.[2] Collins found herself outside the bounds of domesticity, yet compromised in her ability to negotiate the labor market.

By working in the mills, Collins violated middle-class ideas about the "separate spheres" of men and women. In the 1830s and 1840s, a flood of sermons, novels, and magazines popularized a new domestic ideal: girls and women would fulfill the dictates of God and nature by remaining at home, leaving men to negotiate the moral dangers of the marketplace. During this period, "home" took on a new cultural meaning as a repository of virtues under assault by the market revolution. This new ideology not only erased middle-class women's unpaid domestic labor as mothers, daughters, and housewives, but also excluded working-class women from the dominant, decorative feminine ideal.[3] African American women, the vast majority of whom were enslaved in the South, also stood outside the boundaries of domestic femininity, despite their performance of domestic labor for their own families and for their masters.[4]

As a young woman "cast on her own resources," Collins's situation anticipated that of hundreds and thousands of northern women forced to become self-supporting after the Civil War. Not only did many women lose sons, husbands, fathers, brothers, and prospects for marriage, but the intensification of industrialization after the war strained the viability of family farms and artisan workshops, increasing pressure on daughters and wives to find ways to earn money. By the early 1870s, daughters of farmers and craftsmen flooded into the labor force, joining orphaned girls and widowed mothers seeking employment in order to contribute to their family economy, or to support themselves if their families had dissolved. Finding few opportunities in the countryside, or in the prospect of westward migration, these women flocked to cities, where they formed an increasingly visible and impoverished class.

During the second half of the nineteenth century, the United States, imagined by its founders as a nation of property-owning men with dependent wives and children, became a nation of wage-earning men and women. Would this transformation lead to an upheaval in gender relations? If so, would the changes wrought by women's increasing presence in the labor force be positive, enabling women to develop new aspirations as individuals, or would they be negative, undermining family stability? The answers to these questions depended on whom you asked, and the stake he or she had in either preserving or transforming patriarchal gender and family relations. As the biography of Jennie Collins and hundreds of thousands of other women made clear, in many instances, the ideal that men supported women did not apply. Jennie Collins spoke for a small but growing number of women who used their new status as wage earners to claim formal and informal rights long denied to women, including wages sufficient for self-support, access to a wider range of occupations, and full political rights.

In Lawrence and in Lowell, where she soon moved, Collins became part of a group of factory operatives who saw themselves in collective terms. Like her, these women were young, white migrants from the New England countryside. They not only worked together, they lived together in company boardinghouses and spent their free time together, whether attending church, going to a hear a lecture, or reading aloud to each other in the evenings as they did their mending. Collins found that the women she worked with subscribed to "as many papers, and ha[d] as much interest in public affairs as any of the men who work[ed] beside her."[5] Despite the exhaustion of standing for twelve or thirteen hours and the pressure of keeping "pace with belts, drums, and cylinders, and other parts of the machinery," the girls and women Collins met in Lawrence and Lowell "retain[ed] their vivacity and spirit of independence" through their political engagement and their mutual concern.[6]

In Lowell, that spirit of independence manifested itself most clearly in the ten-hour movement, led by Sarah Bagley, the charismatic founder of the Lowell Female Labor Reform Association. In 1845 and 1846, thousands of workers from all over Massachusetts signed petitions demanding that the state legislature limit working hours in publicly chartered corporations to ten hours per day, to provide workers time for study, worship, and self-improvement.[7] As early as the 1840s, a link was forged between social investigation and social reform. In this instance, however, the legislature investigated but refused to take action, urging the women of Lowell to rely on the benevolence of their employers rather than on state intervention.[8] Members of the Lowell Female Labor Reform Association condemned the legislators for their sympathy with employers and their "lack of independence, honesty, and humanity."[9] As wages dropped, hours lengthened, and conditions worsened, single, native-born women like Collins began moving to larger cities in search of better work.[10]

Collins arrived in Boston in 1850. Possessing few transferable skills and lacking a family of her own to live with, she took a job as a domestic servant. In Boston, as in other large cities, such as Philadelphia and New York, 60 percent of female wage workers found positions in domestic service. Another 30 percent were employed in the garment industry, and the remaining 10 percent worked in the few trades open to women, including printing, bookbinding, and clerking at dry goods stores.[11] Educated women might find jobs as teachers, but they, too, earned only half of what men did. Depending on whether or not they had husbands present, children, or aging parents to care for, urban women engaged in a range of more casual forms of labor to generate income, such as taking in boarders, laundry, or sewing, or going out to work for the day scrubbing or washing. In difficult times, some women turned to prostitution to supplement their earnings.[12]

Collins may have worked as a general household servant before finding a position as a nurse in the family of John Lowell, an attorney, whose grandfather, Francis Cabot Lowell, had become extremely wealthy by establishing the textile mills in the town that bore his name.[13] While no direct record of Collins's work for the Lowell family survives, her time spent in this privileged household, which owed much of its wealth to the textile mill where she had once worked, may have sharpened her belief that workers were poor because they were deprived of a just share of the value they produced. Her time in the Lowell household also convinced her that "American girls" who valued their independence could not tolerate domestic service for long. While Collins had experienced the fast-paced labor and tight regulations of the Lowell mills as oppressive, she found the new limitations on her leisure time intolerable. Servants were not even allowed to "go out and buy a spool of thread until their appointed afternoon or evening."[14] Like other former servants, Collins complained of "incompetent mistresses" who knew nothing of housekeeping, but were determined to wring as much work as possible out of their household help.[15] To explain native-born white women's increasing rejection of domestic service, Collins quoted Patrick Henry's famous motto, "Give me liberty or give me death!"[16] By invoking Henry, Collins cast women's rejection of service in revolutionary terms.

Collins's critique of domestic service was widely shared. An 1869 investigation of the conditions of sewing women in Boston by the New England Women's Club revealed a strong animosity toward domestic service among the entire working-class community. Investigators reported that "poor girls" struggled "under a weight of debt and poverty" rather than work as servants. Native-born white women spoke with pride of the fact that they had "never had to live out yet." More shocking still, some chose prostitution rather than domestic service as a means of preserving their independence.[17] While middle-class women's labor reformers used the prostitute to symbolize the dangers of women's dependence on men, some working-class women used the trade to gain higher wages than they could earn from either service or sewing, and to free themselves from what they considered to be the oppressive conditions of living in someone else's household and being at their beck and call twenty-four hours a day. On a purely practical basis, prostitution offered women relatively high pay and flexible hours, making it an option for women with children or other dependent relatives who required their care.[18] For single women, who complained of their sexual vulnerability as live-in servants, sex work in boardinghouses or brothels offered some measure of control over the terms of their sexual encounters.[19] Some women judged prostitution preferable to living in as a domestic servant.[20]

The Lowell family's ability to find a white, native-born woman like Collins to work for them during the 1850s reflected their wealth and status. By that time, middle-class families with one "maid of all work" were far more likely to hire an Irish immigrant for the job. Young Irish women fleeing the potato famine (which began in 1845) often migrated alone, leaving behind parents and siblings in desperate poverty. The assurance of steady work, combined with employers' provision of room and board, appealed to Irish women who felt a strong obligation to save money to send back home. Acknowledging that many working women went hungry, Collins calculated the sole benefit of domestic service as having enough to eat. The promise of adequate food and shelter may have been enough to recommend the occupation to women who had faced starvation during the famine.[21] Some German women entered service, too, but those who did not speak English were considered less desirable household workers. German women were more likely to migrate with their families, which made them less likely to work as servants.[22] For mistresses seeking pliant household workers, however, the fix from immigrant labor proved temporary. As Catharine Beecher, a leading purveyor of domestic advice, complained in 1869, "the Irish and the German servants . . . become more or less infected with the spirit of democracy" and soon became as difficult to manage as native-born Americans.[23]

Radical members of the working class associated the growing demand for servants with the growth of a pretentious, parasitic managerial class that snubbed its nose at manual labor. Collins and other working-class labor reformers accused employers of skimping on food and wages for their domestic employees. A song titled "The Bell Goes A-ringing for Sairah," published in the *American Workman,* a Boston labor reform paper, recounted overwork, low pay, and stingy rations. The singer introduces herself as "the gener-al slave round the corner," with a wage of "a hundred a year." While her employer, a man who worked in a downtown office, earned "a thousand," the servant found her "own sugar and beer." Sarah described herself as "lady's maid, housemaid, and cook," explaining, "I do everything, honor, no joking; I scarcely have time to draw a breath, For she'll ring if the fire wants poking."[24]

Although Collins bristled at the subservience expected of domestic servants, she must have used her time in the Lowell household to gain the connections she needed to secure more satisfying employment. The Lowell family moved to an estate in Chestnut Hill in 1858. By 1860, Collins was working as a garment maker for a downtown Boston firm, and by 1861 she had gained a skilled position as a vest-maker at Macular, Williams & Parker, a Washington Street merchant known for its high-quality work.[25] Like many working women, she had difficulty securing lodging, but she appreciated her time off from work, spending some of it taking a class on English history at a Unitarian church.[26]

Within ten years of arriving in Boston, Collins had worked her way into a relatively secure position in the female labor market. Her ability to make this transition rested not just on her determination and ability, but on the fact that single, native-born white women had the widest degree of choice in the narrow field of female labor. By 1860 just one-third of native-born white women worked as servants, in contrast to 78 percent of foreign-born white women, most of whom were Irish, and 87 percent of African American women.[27] While Irish women took domestic jobs because they wanted to save money to send back home, African American women took domestic jobs because they could obtain no other work. While African Americans constituted only 1 percent of the population of Boston in 1860, their extremely constrained opportunities for earning a living reveal the racial segregation that structured the northern labor market.[28] As "A Colored Woman" explained in a letter to the *Philadelphia Morning Post* in 1871: "When respectable women of color answer an advertisement for a dressmaker . . . they are invariably refused, or offered a place to cook or scrub, or do housework; and when application is made at manufactories immediately after having seen an advertisement for operators or finishers, they meet with the same reply." Black women who refused to work as domestics were left to "eke out a scanty livelihood sewing at home."[29] An African American woman from Rhode Island complained that "colored females" were "compelled to accept the meanest drudgeries or starve," being excluded from places where native-born white women could find work, such as "the milliner, the dressmaker, tailor, or dry good store."[30]

Although the Civil War ended slavery, it did not fundamentally change the racial segregation of the labor market in the industrializing cities of the Northeast and Midwest. While white female workers became more class-conscious during the war, this consciousness did not extend to addressing racial inequality. The substitution of white working-class women for slave women in labor reform discourses invoked the degradation of women of color, only to erase them as real people with their own experiences of exploitation and resistance. African American women existed on the margins of labor reform as symbols of degraded womanhood, rather than as participants in postwar efforts to improve, or even transform, women's economic conditions.

Collins's hatred of slavery fueled her support for the Union cause. When the war broke out, she found new opportunities for action: organizing her fellow workers at Macular, Williams & Parker to make keepsakes to send to Union soldiers, volunteering in a Boston military hospital, and forming a soldiers' relief association.[31] Like the hundreds of thousands of other women who volunteered to sew, knit, or wrap bandages, Collins gained a new sense of the patriotic value of her labor during the war. Like many middle-class volunteers who went on to form women's clubs and organizations, she acquired significant organizational experience.[32]

Collins's perceptions of the war were strongly colored by her social class. Wealthy men's ability to buy their way out of the draft for $300 made many working-class men and women see the federal government as willing to spill a "poor man's blood for a rich man's money." These sentiments helped spark draft riots in New York City in 1863.[33] From returning soldiers, Collins heard stories of "everywhere the same great gulf between the rich and the poor." Together on the battlefield and in military hospitals, these soldiers from modest backgrounds "felt how much more they had to pay for their liberty than did the law-protected man of wealth, who sat in his home and smoked his cigar, while a hired substitute fought his battles."[34] Collins herself had been unprotected from the harshness of the labor market as a fourteen-year-old girl, but the situation was far worse for young men, who were exposed to mortal danger. Although she supported the fight against slavery, the war heightened Collins's sense that the government acted to protect corporations and property owners at the expense of workers. The war gave Collins a new sense of belonging to a national working class. Many workers around the country shared her new sense of class consciousness.

Numerous strikes flared during the war. Labor activity peaked in 1865 and continued at a high level until the depression of 1873. Workers' protest was concentrated in the industrializing towns and cities east of the Mississippi and north of the Ohio River and the Mason-Dixon Line, which contained three-quarters of the nation's factory workers and produced 70 percent of its manufactured goods through the early twentieth century.[35] The labor movement encompassed a diverse group of trade unions, working men's and women's associations, and leagues devoted to single issues, such as land reform or the eight-hour day (a continuation of the struggle for the ten-hour day). In addition to conducting strikes and promoting boycotts to raise wages and improve working conditions, these groups worked together to support other initiatives, such as establishing cooperatives of consumers and producers. Some sought political leverage to press for public distribution of land in the West.[36]

Like many former abolitionists, Collins saw the labor question as the next major political issue facing the nation. She first took the stage as a public speaker in 1868, when she was asked to present a working woman's point of view on the labor question during public debates at Washington Hall. The next year, she appeared at an Eight-Hour convention where, according to one contemporary, "she entered into leading political and social questions of the day in a remarkably intelligent manner, and from that time her reputation was made as a public speaker."[37] Collins soon joined the New England Labor Reform League, a mixed group of trade unionists, former abolitionists, and advocates of the eight-hour day led by Ezra Heywood, an anarchist who later became notorious for his advocacy of free love. Despite its dismissal by one historian as a motley group of "sentimental reformers," the New England Labor Reform League not only made room for women, it actively sought their participation and included them as officers.[38]

Organized in mixed, city-wide assemblies, the labor movement in Boston as in other industrializing cities articulated a strong sense of class identity. The Civil War had accelerated the development of national networks of transportation, production, and distribution, leading to the growth of large cities and speeding the integration of all Americans into a national market. The federal government had vastly, although temporarily, expanded its power by waging a successful war against the Confederacy, emancipating slaves, and embarking on Reconstruction. William H. Sylvis, a former iron molder, seized on these conditions to establish the National Labor Union, which embraced a broad ideal of worker solidarity. Espousing a viewpoint similar to that adopted later by the Knights of Labor in the 1880s, Sylvis envisioned a grand alliance of "producers" who would push the government to serve the needs of the majority by establishing an eight-hour day, supporting workers' cooperatives, and ensuring the wide distribution of land. These ideas received a limited implementation with the passage of the Homestead Act and the introduction of an eight-hour day for federal employees. Activists like Collins, however, saw far more to be accomplished for the United States to fulfill its promise of democracy.[39]

In April 1869 Jennie Collins joined Aurora Phelps and Elizabeth Daniels, whom she had met in the New England Labor Reform League, in establishing the Boston Working Women's League. Phelps, who had been a hospital nurse during the war, was known for her advocacy of free land for working women. Although her life had been "laborious," including stints as a servant and an outworker, she had attended college at Oberlin before moving to Boston. Phelps presented herself as having been briefly married in England, where she had borne a child. Daniels was married to a laborer but had no children; she had worked as a sewing machine operator and an artist before becoming a leader of Boston's eight-hour movement.[40]

Although the League lasted only a year, it provides a rare glimpse into working-class women's self-conceptions and political aspirations. The group presented themselves as "working women," claiming entitlement to participate in public debates on the basis of their status as self-supporting, productive citizens. They advocated homesteads for working women, higher wages for needlework, and establishment of a nonprofit employment bureau.[41] While supported by the larger movement for labor reform and receptive to alliances with elite women devoted to women's rights, members of the Boston Working Women's League expressed a determination to speak for themselves that reflected an independence of thought and action that many found surprising.

Aurora Phelps proposed the idea for Garden Homesteads in 1864, two years after the Homestead Act promised 160 acres of public land to any adult citizen who could pay a small registration fee and live on the land continuously for five years. While the offer of free land was supposed to ensure America's republican future by enabling men to leave wage work and become farmers, the costs of establishing homesteads were beyond the means of most working-class families, and even more out of reach for families without a male breadwinner. By establishing homesteads close to Boston, Phelps hoped to give women the means to become independent proprietors, while enabling them to remain closely connected to their families and their communities. Like most people at the time, Phelps believed that wages were governed by supply and demand, meaning that urban women's rates of pay would increase if a significant number of female workers left the city. Her advocacy of land reform reflected a long tradition of British, American, and Irish labor activists demanding rights to land as a means of restoring the independence lost through the deskilling of labor and the introduction of machinery. While most proponents of land reform associated the redistribution of land with the restoration of family values under threat from the pressures of industrialization, Phelps viewed Garden Homesteads as creating new opportunities for female independence.[42]

In the spring of 1869, the Boston Working Women's League circulated Phelps' petition for Garden Homesteads. The petition described everything women needed to become homesteaders, including "rations, tools, seeds and instruction in gardening, until such time as the women would be able to raise their own food, or otherwise become self-supporting." No rent would be due for the first three years. After that, each woman's rent would be applied to purchasing her plot, which could be passed along to her female heirs upon her death. Inspired perhaps by state homestead exemption laws, they asked that their property be protected from seizure for debt. The petitioners identified themselves as impoverished, overworked Boston women, "dependent for our daily bread upon the daily labor of our own hands."

The petition rhetorically cast the legislature as the protector of last resort for working women, pleading: "you should think for us, and take counsel from your own kind ears to do for us better than we know how to ask."[43]

Although the tone of the petition played off familiar narratives of female dependence, it mixed these more traditional appeals with a new consciousness of citizenship gained by patriotic sacrifice during the Civil War. Not only had many Boston working women lost fathers, brothers, and husbands in the conflict, thousands had worked "on contract army shirts at eight cents each, from dawn to midnight." Given their sacrifice of love and labor, Phelps believed, the commonwealth and "the nation" owed these women "a debt it [could] never pay."[44] From this perspective, a demand for state provision of land and simple homes might not seem so radical, especially when the federal government was giving away large tracts out West, not only to homesteaders but to railroad corporations.

In discussing her proposal for Garden Homesteads at a labor reform convention, Phelps argued that working women had a "righteous claim" on the government for relief. If, indeed, democratic government was instituted "for the people," then it should aid in "protecting all [of its] . . . citizens in the enjoyment of life, liberty, and happiness."[45] Virginia Penny, a former teacher who addressed women's limited options for earning a living in her popular book *Think and Act* (1869), insisted the government play a more active role in addressing the problem of women's economic inequality. Penny advocated laws mandating equal pay for men and women doing equal work; taxing unmarried men to support single women; and providing support for "worthy industrious" women unable to support themselves.[46]

In demanding Garden Homesteads, women who signed the petition rejected the popular advice that eastern workers improve their conditions by heading west. Since the 1850s Horace Greeley, the editor of the *New York Tribune*, had been exhorting, "Go west, young man, go west." After the Civil War, Mary Livermore, a leading advocate of suffrage and temperance, used her Chicago paper, the *Agitator*, to encourage women to join the migration. In a letter to a Boston labor paper, she promised "a very great demand in the West for the labor of women, especially on farming settlements and in smaller towns."[47] Virginia Penny, who had sought opportunity as a teacher by moving from Kentucky to Ohio, advised women in the "crowded thoroughfares of the eastern United States, who by their hard labor scarce earn a pittance, that they might do much better by going into the plenteous West, and engaging in the capacity of seamstresses in families, dairy maids, and similar offices."[48] While Penny focused on women's prospects for self-support, other commentators suggested that the "excess" women of the

East would have an easier time finding husbands if they headed west. Jennie Collins responded with annoyance to the suggestion that Boston working girls migrate to improve their prospects for marriage, noting that she had yet to meet a New England working woman "who would forego the dignity of self-support . . . for allurements so invitingly set forth to them in the West."[49] When someone suggested western migration to Elizabeth Daniels, she retorted that working-class women from Boston might just as easily "go to the moon, with scarcely a penny, or even clothing sufficient to keep them warm."[50]

Equally bold as these women's request for land was their demand that they be allowed to speak for themselves. Rebelling against elite assumptions that working-class women needed "thinking women" to act on their behalf, the Working Women's League asked in its petition that "no one will be allowed, except at our own express desire, to speak before your committee in our name."[51] The petition called for independence for working-class women on several levels. By living in homes that they owned, on land where they could grow food to support themselves, these women would fulfill the Jeffersonian dream of a republic populated by independent proprietors. By owning this property themselves, women would upend republican ideology, which posited women, like children, as dependent on men. They would escape their dependency on employers for an insecure livelihood, and they would no longer have to seek charity or take recourse to prostitution, each of which implied a morally compromising dependence.[52] Through their petition, these women claimed political independence, including the right to think and to speak for themselves and to make new claims as citizens.[53]

Collins, Phelps, and Daniels called a meeting to discuss the petition for Garden Homesteads and to introduce the Boston Working Women's League to the public on Wednesday, 21 April 1869. Parker Pillsbury, who attended the convention and wrote about it for the *Revolution*, Elizabeth Cady Stanton and Susan B. Anthony's women's suffrage newspaper, considered the gathering in "every way peculiar." Not only was it called by "working women, in the severest sense of the word," it was called primarily *for* working women.[54] An equally surprised correspondent from the *American Workman*, a Boston labor paper, noted that the meeting was managed by the working women themselves, "and the gentlemen or [ladies] other than working-women were not allowed to take up time, except by their permission." The journalist found it "quite amusing to see how some of the old stagers among the men were snubbed by the application of this rule so opposed to ordinary usage."[55] He did not comment on the "ladies." They may have been reticent to voice their opinions in a public meeting of men and women, preferring to limit their discussions to private forums, such as the New England Women's Club.[56]

The working women's meeting, held in a basement room, began in the morning with about twenty-five people. By noon, the crowd reached a hundred, and in the evening, when women were released from work, it rose to three hundred. Adopting the novel idea of using social investigation as a platform for social reform, the morning session focused on "eliciting facts," while the evening session focused on plans for "organization and future action." The organizers estimated the average of wages of Boston's 40,000 women with full-time, weekly employment at about three dollars per week, "out of which they had to board, clothe, and lodge themselves," and often support "dependent children." About half of these women worked in the needle trades, where wages varied greatly. While skilled women with steady positions in custom shops, like Jennie Collins, could make a decent living, women who sewed at home for clothing contractors fared much worse. The meeting included testimony from outworkers, who reported "that they had recently worked on nice shirts at two shillings a piece." The organizers estimated that at least 2,000 needlewomen in Boston earned no more than twenty-five or thirty cents a day.[57]

Collins, Phelps, Daniels, and other women who worked in the garment industry described the increasing subdivision of labor under the "Boston system." As Aurora Phelps recalled, when she was younger, "girls were taught full trades." Their labor had a progression: "They made pants, coats, overcoats, and then they learned to cut." Now, however, "one stitches the seam, another makes the buttonholes, and another puts the buttons on." Collins accused employers of preventing women from learning skilled trades. When work for these "half-skilled" women slacked, they tramped from shop to shop, often waiting for weeks until they could find a new position. Meanwhile, they subsisted "for a week on a 5–cent loaf of bread." At times, Phelps admitted, she herself had been so poor she was unable to afford the soap and fuel necessary to wash her clothes. In these conditions, she remarked, working women would be "less than human" if they did not "feel the difference between their condition and that of the rich, well-dressed ladies who pass them."[58]

The meeting concluded with several resolutions. First, the women described the system of "divided labor" and the increasing use of machinery as monotonous and degrading to both the minds and bodies of female workers. However, they admitted that a return to household or artisan forms of production was both "impossible and undesirable." Instead, poor working women should be given Garden Homesteads, land and "houses of which they themselves are mistresses, where they may regain their natural health of soul and body." They acknowledged that not all working women wished to move out of Boston and leave the paid labor force, explaining, "those of us who are skilled workwomen, in the receipt of good wages, and therefore in the enjoyment of a high degree of independence" are "not discontented with our present condition and not desirous of settling on the land." However, they endorsed Garden Homesteads as a good option for women unable to make ends meet in the city, especially those supporting dependents.

Collins had been an ardent abolitionist since childhood, and she and the other leaders of the Working Women's League used metaphors of wage slavery to critique the labor conditions of northern white working women.[59] They identified the plight of "the white women and girls who, today, in Massachusetts give a fair day's work for thirty cents earnings" with that of "the negro slave women of South Carolina" before the Civil War. They used the language of wage slavery to present white working-class women as the "objects of enlightened philanthropic sympathy," just as southern slave women had been.[60] Given the success of abolition, identifying working women with southern slaves may have seemed like a good strategy. Virginia Penny recommended that the abolitionist motto "Am I not a woman and a sister?" be applied to working-class women.[61] In her 1871 novel *Work*, Louisa May Alcott described the new movement on behalf of women's labor reform as offering "the chance" to "help lay the foundation of a new emancipation."[62] This identification of wage workers with slaves stretched back to the 1830s, when American and British labor leaders charged the "lords of the loom" and the "lords of the lash" with enriching themselves by stealing the value that their workers produced. The power of the idea of wage slavery lay in its seemingly self-evident contradictions: northern white women should not be slaves, especially in a nation that had just waged a bloody war to abolish the "peculiar institution."[63] Although they opened their new organization to all self-supporting women, the Boston Working Women's League's language of wage slavery identified their movement as white.

The New England Women's Club also investigated the conditions of the city's needlewomen. Drawing from city records and from personal interviews, the group's privately printed report was a landmark in social investigation. Like the Boston Working Women's League, they noted the increasing subdivision of labor, low wages, high prices for board, and dangers of prostitution. Their solutions to these problems reflected their own class position. They called urgently for something to be "done to dignify domestic service," bemoaning that so many women "have been slaves to the unproductive needle all their lives, because they never had any opportunity to learn the work for which they were best fitted by nature!"[64] Ironically, this group of elite women devoted to social progress and determined to forge lives that reached beyond the domestic sphere prescribed domestic service as the best solution to working women's poverty. While the working-class women who proposed Garden Homesteads hoped to turn pieceworkers into independent proprietors organized within a collective, the elite women of the NEWC hoped to turn these predominantly native-born women into servants. United in their mutual concern for the conditions of Boston's poorest wage-earning women, they proposed dramatically different solutions, although Lucy Stone, a radical member of the NEWC, offered her support for Garden Homesteads.

The idea of Garden Homesteads gained enough public attention to be granted an immediate hearing before the state legislative committee on the hours of labor. About a hundred women attended, half working women "in the technical sense of the phrase" and half "ladies of culture and wealth with a liberal representation from the New England Women's Club." The hearing opened with Aurora Phelps presenting her petition. She noted that many of the women who signed it "were deterred from coming by threat of employers; some were persuaded to keep away by increase of pay; many who came were too timid to take a part." Phelps discussed women's limited options for earning a living, noting the declining value of skill and the low rates paid for piecework. To make matters worse, outworkers could not find steady employment, but paid weekly for their board. During slack periods, those without families to fall back on turned to "soup-houses." Phelps saw charity as negative, warning that women who depended on it "feel degraded, lose self-respect, and, by and by go *down*." Phelps presented Garden Homesteads as providing women with the chance to become economically independent. She recommended tracts of land just outside the city, in Medford, Dorchester, and Swampscott, as good places to try the experiment, estimating that "five thousand women would avail themselves of this plan at once, if it could be inaugurated."

The legislators asked Phelps why poor women did not try housework. She explained that women who entered domestic service were "treated as strangers and aliens," adding that she knew of cases "where the very food was grudged to them and hunger was kept off by buying outside, and this in aristocratic circles." She knew what she was talking about, having "tried it herself, both as domestic and as nurse." She might have added that domestic jobs were available only to women without children or other dependent relatives to care for, while her scheme allowed working-class women room for families of their own. Imagine the class tensions in the room as Phelps revealed the conditions of working women in Boston, not just in the needle trades but also in the households of the elite statesmen and clubwomen who attended the hearing; a "hushed and muffled silence brooded over the room."[65]

The Boston Working Women's League embraced a broad agenda. As Elizabeth Daniels wrote in a letter to the *Revolution*: "The organization . . . will accept for woman nothing less than the ballot, and the right to hold any office."[66] While members of the group worked to build alliances with suffragists like Stanton, Anthony, and Stone, they also asserted their own authority on the problems of working women. At an early meeting held at the house of Mrs. Daniels, the women described themselves as "the natural counselors of their less skillful sisters, to the almost utter exclusion of men, and to the absolute exclusion of ladies of refined leisure." Given the interest expressed in working women by the NEWC, this statement can be read as a polite, but firm suggestion that affluent female reformers concerned with the conditions of working women mind their own business. Indeed, this declaration of class difference and organizational independence denied the possibility of class bridging so important to the self-conceptions of Boston's female reformers.[67]

Even Louisa May Alcott, who attended NEWC meetings with her aunt, Abby May, saw female reformers' attempt to connect with working women as awkward. In *Work,* Alcott's protagonist, Christy, watches as erudite reformers recite European statistics, tell stories of women in antiquity, and describe an "Ideal Republic." Meanwhile, "anxious seamstresses, type-setters, and shop-girls" whisper together, wondering how any of these "pretty" ideas will increase their wages.[68] Clearly, good intentions could not bridge the gulf of class that separated these women, especially since so many working-class women had worked as servants.

Members of the Boston Working Women's League hoped to intervene in the market for women's labor by establishing their own employment agency. They criticized existing agencies, run for profit, as preying on women who needed work and misleading both employers and employees. Their nonprofit bureau, run by the women themselves, would "be established on entirely new principles," seeking to match potential employers and employees. Again, they warned of the interference of middle-class and wealthy women in this enterprise; elite women were liable to create an agency "dangerous to the independence of the women who earn their daily bread by the daily labor of their own hands, since it could easily be transformed into an institution (professedly philanthropic) where the working women would be put off, without substantial or efficient aid, with the empty forms of condescending charity." Significantly, the employment bureau they envisioned would place women in "all legitimate industrial avocations, other than that of household service."[69]

Although they had appealed to the language of white slavery at their opening convention, the women made no distinctions of race, ethnicity, or skill in membership. "Any working-woman of Boston, dependent upon the daily labor of her own hands for her daily bread" was invited to join, and there was no admission fee. While committed, above all, to independence, these women were nonetheless dependent on contributions from citizens of "wealth and standing," since working-class women were too poor to pay dues. The organization established an advisory board that included the mayor of Boston and received a significant contribution from Post Fifteen of the Grand Army of the Republic: free use of a building at 815 Washington Street. Collins was well known for her work among soldiers and veterans, and the building may have been given to her fledgling organization out of appreciation. Possession of free space enabled the organization to envision a program of public meeting and debates two or three evenings a week, which employers and "ladies of all classes" would be invited to attend.[70] Middle-class women would not be excluded, but they would be put in the position of students rather than teachers regarding the problems of women's work.

In addition to her leadership of the Boston Working Women's League, Collins advanced the cause of working women around the state as a speaker for the New England Labor Reform League. In July 1869 she was invited to address the first convention of the Daughters of Saint Crispin, a new organization of women who worked in shoe manufacturing. Collins praised the women for their independence and their success in organizing.[71]

In the fall of 1869 Collins traveled to Dover, New Hampshire, where the 800 employees of the Cocheco Cotton Manufacturing Company struck to protest a 12 percent wage cut.[72] The operatives Collins met in Dover resented the company's decision to boost its profits by increasing the number of looms a woman tended from two to six and by raising the prices workers paid the company boardinghouse from $2.25 to $6.00 a week. The ground for this struggle may have been laid by the Ladies Female Reform Association, which had a branch in Dover in the 1840s.[73] Collins built support for the strike in Lowell, where she "rallied the factory women and girls" who "gathered by the thousands in Huntington Hall, one of the largest in New England, to listen to Jennie's appeal for her sisters in Dover."[74]

In the course of the strike, Jennie Collins articulated a new consciousness of female wage workers as consumers. The Cocheco Company manufactured calico, inexpensive printed cloth that factory operatives and farm women made into dresses. Collins felt certain that once women around the country "understood the facts, [they] would allow the Cocheco goods to rot on the shelves before they would purchase them."[75] She embraced the use of the boycott, which became a significant technique for the Knights of Labor in the 1880s and for middle-class women who formed consumers' leagues in the 1890s. The striking women at Dover held out for several months, but were ultimately defeated by the company, which warned the women to return to work or be blacklisted. In a letter to the *Revolution* reflecting on the strike, Collins admitted defeat "for the noble but oppressed women" who took part in the strike, but predicted an eventual victory, declaring: "We working women will wear fig-leaf dresses before we will patronize the Cocheco Company."[76]

Collins's leadership in Dover and her correspondence with the *Revolution* brought her into contact with leaders of the women's suffrage movement, who invited her to address the National Woman Suffrage Association at its annual meeting in Washington, D.C. Leaders of the movement described Collins in sentimental terms, claiming that her speech describing working women's exploitation at the hands of factory owners moved delegates to tears.[77] Paulina Davis described Collins as slight of build, "all brain and soul." Davis noted that Collins told "her touching stories with such a tender, natural pathos that few eyes are dry during her speeches."[78] The earliest historians of the women's rights movement tended to reduce working women to stock characters, rather than acknowledge them as formulators of political ideas. At the Union League, Collins held the audience in her sway "for two full hours." Her success earned her "a purse, and the offer of a free passage to California and back," with the understanding that she would lecture on the conditions of working women along the way.[79]

Collins accepted the offer, and she seemed poised to take her place on the national lecture circuit. However, she felt the need to find more concrete ways to address the problems her speeches described. She transformed the Working Women's Hall at 815 Washington Street into "Boffin's Bower," a new center for working women named after a location in Charles Dickens's novel, *Our Mutual Friend*. In addition to providing a free employment agency, an industrial training program, and free lunches, Boffin's Bower offered working women a parlor for relaxation, complete with carpet, potted plants, a piano, and two canaries. One visitor noted a reading room with "all the Boston Dailies on file, besides quite a good collection of books and pamphlets." Collins managed to acquire a library of "four hundred volumes of well-selected reading matter."[80] The Bower sponsored a full program of music and lectures. A reporter from the Belfast, Maine, *Republican,* described Collins as "a democratic little body, with more nervous energy in her make-up than a dozen women ought to have . . . she talks and walks quickly, plans constantly, and executes as rapidly."[81] Collins subsequently added temporary lodgings for working women and moved the center to 1031 Washington Street, a few blocks away from the original location.[82]

Collins continued to earn money by lecturing, and in 1871 she published a book titled *Nature's Aristocracy,* whose proceeds she contributed to Boffin's Bower. As a speaker, Collins was known for her wit, her common sense, and her use of anecdote.[83] Her book displayed all these qualities, using individual stories of working women's hardscrabble lives to advocate the agenda of the New England Labor Reform League: an eight-hour day, the establishment of workers' cooperatives, and full political rights for women. Collins framed her project as the restoration of American democracy, a system that seemed to be going awry due to the dangerous growth of monopolies of "railroad, land, ship, and telegraph companies" that "threaten to overturn our whole system of government." Like William Sylvis, the recently deceased leader of the National Labor Union, she believed that workers had to organize to gain greater political power. After all, workers were in the majority, and in a democracy, "the *majority will rule.*" As her book's title suggested, Collins saw democracy not as a leveling of all distinctions, but as the removal of the artificial barriers against individuals exercising their full range of talents. She called for restoration of the people's political power, better public education, and a broader field of employment for women.[84] Women's rights advocates such as Susan B. Anthony and Elizabeth Cady Stanton also called for the admission of women to all trades and professions, reflecting their recognition of women's limited choices of occupation as a central element of women's inequality with men.[85]

While Collins advocated women's rights, she did so from a distinctively working-class perspective. Unlike elite and middle-class advocates of women's rights, who embraced a universal vision of "woman" to be freed from the fetters of unjust laws and outdated conventions, Collins saw her sex as sharply divided by class, arguing that there could be no single conception of "woman's rights" since "there are not certain wrongs that apply to the whole sex." In her opinion, working-class women, who generally lacked male protection, felt "the power of the law" most strongly and needed political rights most urgently. For example, Civil War widows who struggled to make a living and pay their taxes had no voice in influencing how their children were to be educated: "In short, they were obliged to do a man's work, and all of a mother's; under the double disadvantage of being physically weak

and of possessing no political influence that would entitle them to respect."
As a result of their political powerlessness, they were often unfairly denied
pensions, or taken advantage of in business. Meanwhile, younger women,
pushed into factories due to the failure of male support, gained "contact with
the world and . . . experience in affairs of business," which gave them "an
independence of character and a knowledge of [their] rights, which under
present circumstances, serves only to aggravate [their] discontent." Given
rights to vote and hold office, working women could push for a government
more responsive to their needs, including an eight-hour day and equal pay
for equal work.[86]

Collins made working women's struggles for independence a major theme
of her book. While Aurora Phelps had pursued independence in terms of
proprietorship, Jennie Collins envisioned working women gaining independence through skilled, respected, fairly compensated wage labor. Sur-
veying the narrow and poorly paid field of women's employment, Collins
admitted that while women who worked in "the store, the tailor's shop,
the printing-office, and binderies" might be "very far indeed from being
independent," they enjoyed "a far greater degree of latitude in mental and
physical action than" women who worked in "the kitchen or chambers of a
modern mansion." While Collins doubted that any woman under the present
economic and political system could be "wholly independent," she urged
her female readers to "adopt the next best course, and be as independent
as they can."[87]

Collins took a dim view of charity, warning in *Nature's Aristocracy* that it
led to dependence in its recipients and a false sense of superiority in its dis-
pensers. Drawing, perhaps, on her experiences as a servant in the household of
John Lowell, she painted the following scenario: "It often happens that while
the mistress of a house is visiting the poor or attending the board meetings of
some charitable institution, there are servant-girls at her home washing the
clothes and ceilings, taking up the carpets, or cooking the dinner, with whom
she has had a long and exciting debate over the twenty-five cents per week
which the servant wished to have added to her wages." Most likely, Collins
continued, the mistress had refused her servant, while donating ten dollars
to a fund to aid former servant-girls, "who would not have been the wrecks
she saw had they received decent compensation for their work." Likewise,
the textile magnate who cut wages could be counted on to contribute money
to aid fallen women, failing to appreciate that women's low wages forced
them to turn to prostitution "to avoid more acute suffering."[88]

Collins continued to comment on the state of women's labor through a
series of annual reports she issued from Boffin's Bower, which mixed anec-

dotes from her work at the center with observations gathered from visits to "work-shops, boarding-houses, lodging-houses, dancing-halls, prayer meetings, the markets, Saturday nights, theatres, libraries, reading-rooms, the tombs in station-houses, the pawnbrokers, and other places including the various public charity and reformatory institutions."[89] Her determination to seek out knowledge of poverty reflected a transatlantic interest in gathering labor statistics in order to pressure the state to take greater responsibility for the conditions of the working class.[90] The Labor Commissioner of the Imperial Council of Berlin requested copies of her reports, as did the U.S. Department of State. Like other members of the New England Labor Reform League, Collins advocated the creation of a state bureau of labor statistics and applauded its establishment in 1869. Benjamin Sanborn, a newspaper editor and a founder of the American Social Science Association, described Collins as "a detective and registrar of charity" who had "more curious and exact knowledge about one class of the Boston poor than I ever found in any other person."[91]

Collins's knowledge of poverty proved especially useful in hard times. The great fire in Boston in 1872 threw large numbers of shop girls and sewing women out of work; Collins assisted the women in getting relief and securing the back wages they were owed.[92] The severe economic depression that began in 1873 reversed the gains made by organized labor after the Civil War and increased the burden of Collins's work in providing aid for the needy. In 1874 Massachusetts passed a law limiting hours in factories to ten hours per day. However, the law applied exclusively to women and children, separating their struggles from those of working men and implying that women, like children, were especially imperiled by industrial labor.[93]

In 1875 Azel Ames, a thirty-year-old sanitary engineer who gathered labor statistics for the commonwealth of Massachusetts, took this argument a step further. His popular book, *Sex in Industry,* condemned women who took jobs outside of domestic service for imperiling their health and threatening the future of the race.[94] Collins countered these allegations with facts: more than three-quarters of the 9,119 women treated at the Boston City Hospital during the past nine years worked as servants, cooks, or housekeepers, while just 7.5 percent of the hospital's female patients worked as seamstresses and 3 percent as shop girls.[95] Despite his lack of proof, Ames's argument continued to hold common-sense appeal. By the mid-1870s a backlash against working women's claims for independence developed as part of a broader cultural shift toward invoking the "natural" differences of gender, race, and class that had come under attack during Reconstruction.[96]

As the postwar movement for labor reform crumbled, Collins became something of a lone crusader for the rights of working women. While strident in her defense of the poor, she became less pointed in her attacks on the privileged. When depression returned during the harsh winter of 1877–78, she provided over 8,000 free dinners, saving many women from starvation. As the director of a charitable institution—even one far more egalitarian than others in the city—she relied on merchants, manufacturers, and wealthy individuals whom she could not afford to alienate. Major donors included her former employer, Macular, Parker & Williams; the labor reformer Wendell Phillips; and the suffragist Mary Livermore, who served as a conduit for donations from women around the country.[97] A profile in the *Chicago Tribune* celebrated Collins's new moderation, noting that many moderates found the theories Collins advanced in *Nature's Aristocracy* "a little bit 'cracked,'" but that she now focused her energies on helping the poor rather than advancing questionable social theories.[98] The speed and distance she traveled may be measured by her 1873 proposal to open a training school for domestic servants, representing a capitulation to popular ideas about women's proper place in the labor market, which she had earlier rejected in no uncertain terms.[99] Collins's trajectory from a militant labor organizer to the director of a charitable institution suggests how quickly hopes for radical social reconstruction faded after the Civil War and how intractable the problem of working-class women's limited occupations and low wages remained.[100]

Collins's friend Aurora Phelps continued to work for Garden Homesteads, celebrating the tenth anniversary of the Women's Homestead League in 1874. Collins, who attended the celebration, endorsed Garden Homesteads "as a means of practical relief to many friendless, but worthy and industrious women."[101] Although the legislature had refused the Boston working women's petition for free land in 1869, two years later they incorporated the "Women's Garden Homestead League" with Aurora Phelps as the director. With the support of a thousand subscribers, Phelps purchased a 60–acre tract of wooded land in Woburn, Massachusetts, adjacent to the Boston & Lowell railroad. She drew up plans for a female community, which she named after herself. In "Aurora," she hoped to realize her vision for Garden Homesteads and to provide residents with an additional source of income by establishing a cooperative laundry. She may have gotten the idea from a cooperative laundry established a few years earlier by unionized female workers in Troy, New York. Like most workers' cooperatives, both ventures would be short-lived.[102]

In October 1873 Phelps held a ceremony to dedicate the Bethesda Laundry. Despite a storm, "a large number of ladies and gentlemen from the surrounding villages" attended, along with several labor reformers. Evidently not a supporter of temperance despite her Baptist faith, Phelps christened the building by throwing a bottle of whiskey at the wood frame. She missed, but the celebration continued with speeches and songs. Reporters who attended noted that several women had already begun digging the cellars for their houses. Despite this optimistic beginning, the plan failed. Three years later, Phelps died destitute in Woburn, possessing little more than "a dilapidated bedstead, ragged bedclothes, two or three rickety chairs, and a few books." Her estate was too small to cover her funeral expenses, leaving them to be borne by the town.[103] Unlike Collins, who was remembered after her death in 1887 with glowing obituaries in the daily papers of Boston, New York, and Chicago, and in women's and labor periodicals, Phelps's demise received barely any public notice. By the end of her life, mainstream publications such as the *New York Times* and the *Saturday Evening Post* had dismissed her as a utopian reformer, and the radical movement she had once been part of had crumbled.

While it is tempting to dismiss Phelps's plan for Garden Homesteads as a quaint protest against the inevitable course of industrialization, the support the idea received among working women should alert us to their strong desires for independence during the 1860s and the 1870s. Ideally, Garden Homesteads would have established working-class women as the heads of their own households and allowed them to gain a fair return on their labor by farming, or working in the cooperative laundry. The plan would have given women a degree of economic independence rarely achieved in families, where men continued to hold most rights to property, or in the labor market, where women continued to earn only half of what men did. The plan reveals women's continued linkage of economic independence with political rights. In Aurora, women would have voted and held office, making it a bold experiment in women's self-governance. Its failure revealed the strength of the very limitations it sought to transcend.

In the turbulent decades that followed the Civil War a small, but significant group of women in Boston came together to claim a new social identity as "working women" who depended "upon the daily labor of our own hands for our daily bread."[104] Their self-definition posed a working-class alternative to the middle-class norm of dependent women, who confined their labor to the unpaid work of caring for their own families.

These working women used their self-support, eked out through long hours at menial jobs in the garment industry or in domestic service, to make new claims as productive citizens. Like former slaves who demanded "forty acres and a mule," these women believed that they had yet to receive fair compensation for their labor. They hoped to enlist the state government in a variety of measures designed to increase their independence, from granting them land for farming, to guaranteeing an eight-hour day, to supporting cooperatives that would offer them a just compensation for their labor. Determined to represent themselves politically, they demanded rights to vote and hold office, recognizing that their political incapacity hindered their ability to make the government respond to their needs. Conservatives denied women's need for individual rights, arguing that women were protected and represented by their fathers and husbands. Women's growing presence as wage workers revealed the fallacy of this assumption. In the breakdown of family support that followed the Civil War, these women seized on a new possibility: independence. Their ability to make good on this claim would be challenged not just by employers but also by their erstwhile allies: working men eager to define women, like children, as properly dependent upon men; and reform-minded middle-class women concerned with their difficulty finding "good help" and determined to put their stamp on social policy by claiming to represent the best interests of working-class women.

CHAPTER 2

Working Girls and White Slaves

Working men and women participated in an unprecedented number of strikes, boycotts, and rallies from the 1870s through the 1890s, pushing the labor question to the top of the nation's political agenda. While industrial unrest dominated the headlines, white working women's movement out of domestic service revealed class conflict to be equally endemic in household labor relations. White working-class women asserted their desires for independence through their labor activism, their departure from domestic service, and their response to social investigators (who framed the labor question for a concerned public). Despite working women's insistence that the problems of long hours, low wages, poor treatment, and sexual harassment spanned the entire field of women's paid employment, middle-class investigators continued to assume that women who needed to earn money would be better off working as domestic servants than as industrial or retail workers. Gilded age investigations of "working girls" laid the foundation for a twentieth century welfare state offering "protection" to female industrial workers, while ignoring equal or greater numbers of women employed as domestic servants.

This chapter examines the work of four investigators who shaped public perceptions of women's place in the labor question during this turbulent period: Carroll D. Wright, the director of the Massachusetts Bureau of Labor Statistics; Leonora Barry, the national investigator of women's work for the Knights of Labor; Helen Campbell, a New York City social reformer and founder of the consumers' movement; and Nell Cusack, an undercover journalist writing for the *Chicago Times*. These investigators looked out on a rapidly changing landscape of women's employment. From 1870 to 1890, the number of women working for wages outside of agriculture doubled, totaling more than 3 million. Across the country, women made up about one-sixth of the paid labor force. In large cities such as Boston, New York, and Chicago, where these investigators focused their attention, nearly one in four women worked for wages. During this same period, the proportion of gainfully employed women working as domestic servants dropped from 61 percent to 40 percent.[1]

As historians have argued, Victorian social investigators constructed the problems they discovered, and articulated their own gender and class identities in relation to the impoverished urban residents they studied.[2] In the United States, as in Great Britain, social science remained a loosely defined field populated by self-taught experts and social reformers. Before 1890, when professional and academic boundaries were constructed around economics and sociology, educated women remained the leading creators of social knowledge about working-class women, with men making inroads largely as directors of new state bureaus of labor statistics.[3]

Gender, class, and political orientation shaped the viewpoints of the four investigators discussed here. Wright, a state-employed statisitician, defined "working girls" as young women employed full-time in industrial, retail, or service jobs. He defended their right to work for wages as essential to family support, but cast them as temporary workers, who would revert to their essentially domestic position by marrying and becoming housewives. Barry, a national organizer for the Knights of Labor, believed that women could exert collective power as workers and consumers. She drew public attention to sexual harassment and noted that many women who married would be pushed back into the labor force due to the failure of male support. Examining the lives of female garment workers in New York City, Campbell urged educated women like herself to consider the welfare of the women who made their clothing and to become ethical consumers. Yet her call for gender solidarity was interrupted by her indignation over white women's growing refusal to work as domestic servants. Writing as "Nell Nelson," Cusack staged a dramatic undercover investigation for the *Chicago Times,* describing girls and women employed in the city's workshops and department stores as "wage slaves" who were incapable of protecting themselves from capitalist exploitation. Yet in the course of these investigations a counter-narrative developed: women used their wage work to gain more power within their families; they claimed a right to equal pay for equal work; and they rejected domestic service as an intolerable compromise of their freedom and independence.

The Working Girls of Boston

Workers who organized into trade unions, eight-hour leagues, and the Knights of Labor demanded that state governments study the labor question, insisting on the need for wider knowledge of wages, hours, unemployment, immigration, and the growing presence of women and children in the labor force. Legislatures agreed to these demands, but their choice of directors for these new bureaus depended on the political power of labor relative to other interests.[4] In Massachusetts, the appointment of Carroll D. Wright to replace Henry K. Oliver represented a setback for the labor movement. Oliver supported shorter hours and better education for workers, but Wright turned the bureau in a less activist direction. Following the advice of his friend Francis Amasa Walker, who oversaw the federal census, Wright sought to make the labor bureau an impartial party in the battle between capital and labor. By casting the bureau's work as furnishing the facts necessary to discuss industrial problems, rather than as solving any particular problem, Wright earned the support of the legislature and the business class.

Wright brought progressive convictions to his new position, along with experience as an attorney, state senator, and colonel in the Union army. Like many men who had fought on the winning side of the Civil War, he saw northern victory as evidence that history followed a divine plan and that good would eventually triumph over evil.[5] In keeping with prevailing laissez-faire economic theory, Wright believed that the laws of supply and demand governed wages. This notion weighed against any state intervention in labor relations and did little to illuminate certain troubling questions, such as the simultaneous growth of prosperity and unemployment, or the sharp differentials in pay between men and women.[6] As a senator, Wright had voted against the state law limiting the hours of female industrial workers to ten per day, encouraging mill owners to adopt the standard voluntarily rather than face state regulation.[7]

Wright became an important arbiter of the identity and position of "working girls" by issuing the first full-length, state-sponsored investigation of their conditions, "The Working Girls of Boston" (1884). As Helen Campbell, a subsequent investigator and a founder of the consumers' movement, noted, Wright's report established the categories adopted by others who studied the problem.[8] Wright defined "working girls" through a series of exclusions. They were not domestic servants. They were not prostitutes. Nor were they housewives, or married women who earned extra money by taking in outwork or keeping boarders. Rather, they were the 20,000 women in the Boston area employed full time "in occupations other than domestic service." This definition excluded nearly half of the 38,881 women in Boston counted by the Tenth Census of 1880 as gainfully employed.[9]

By leaving the city's 16,000 full-time domestic workers out of his investigation, Wright acted on the conservative assumption that domestic labor was women's natural and proper sphere of activity. His decision reveals a reluctance to disturb the privacy of the bourgeois home. Wright refused to consider middle-class or elite households as places of employment, or to acknowledge the class tensions between domestic workers and their employers. This approach also excluded African American women from his study, since few of them were able to find jobs outside of domestic service.[10] Manufacturers refused to hire African Americans to work as factory operatives; merchants refused to hire them as salesclerks; and the City of Boston excluded them from clerical positions.[11] Wright's failure to discuss the status of black female wage earners may have also reflected their small numbers; less than 2 percent of Boston's 362,839 residents were black.[12] While more than half of all African American women worked as servants, they made up less than 5 percent of all domestic servants in the city. White servants were almost equally divided between native-born women and immigrants, with the Irish forming the largest ethnic group. However, Wright made little mention of ethnicity.

In identifying "working girls" as the subject of his investigation, Wright relied on, but sought to reshape, notions of the urban working girl formulated in popular novels, daily newspapers, and critiques of capitalism. In conducting interviews, Wright found working-class women more willing to speak to female than male agents, so he employed college-educated women to gather information. He supplemented these interviews with evidence from public hearings, mailed questionnaires, and inquiries with charity workers.[13] Wright's use of female agents generated some controversy, as it threatened the respectability of the women he hired by exposing them to the "dangerous classes." Wright defended his practice as "entirely appropriate."[14] Indeed, it would have seemed inappropriate at this time for men to inquire too closely into the circumstances of young women's lives. College-educated women used these rules of propriety to justify their entry into the new field of social work.[15]

Wright's report on Boston's working women can be read as a rejoinder both to trade unionists and labor reformers who depicted capitalists as a rapacious class and to social conservatives who frowned on women's entry into the labor market as compromising their virtue. In order to defend the reputation of Boston's working girls, Wright solicited opinions about their moral conduct, including the testimony of a Boston police captain, who assured the public that women employed full time in factories were unlikely to walk the streets as prostitutes. Wright removed prostitutes from his sample, separating the "dregs" of the female working class from the virtuous majority. He projected middle-class standards of morality onto his subjects, ignoring the reality that working-class women who lacked employment or faced a family emergency might barter or sell sex to supplement their income.[16]

Wright celebrated the fact that many of the female agents he sent to interview women after work found these working girls at home sewing, rather than spending their wages going out on the town. In reporting that 880 out of the 1,032 interviewed did their own housework and sewing, he opined, "No stronger evidence of the 'home' character of the lives of working girls could be adduced."[17] While Jennie Collins, the Boston working woman who had become a social reformer, applauded Wright's defense of working women's morality, others found it offensive.[18] Leonora Barry, an investigator for the Knights of Labor, suggested that Wright and his fellow state investigators focus instead on the economic imperatives that drove women to "immorality" and on the men who seduced vulnerable working girls, "who now feel that they cover up their part in the matter while their unhappy victims are left to bear it all."[19]

Within the parameters he defined, Wright painted a portrait of Boston's average working girl. She was young (just under twenty-five), white, single, and likely to live with her parents.[20] She went out to work shortly before turning seventeen to help support her family. The death or disability of one or both of her parents increased the likelihood that she would work for wages. Her sojourn in the paid labor force lasted for eight years, until she married. She generally worked in one or two occupations.[21] After marriage, she stayed home unless her husband was disabled or died, and she had no children old enough to support her. She may have continued to earn money after marriage by taking in laundry, sewing, or boarders, but Wright, like other official investigators, overlooked this economic contribution.[22] She herself may have been born in Massachusetts, but her parents were likely to be foreign-born; three-quarters of Boston's full-time, female industrial workers were either immigrants or their children.[23]

Wright inquired about working women's health, yet he ignored the substance of their complaints. While elaborate statistical tables classified working women's health as "good," firsthand testimony gathered by female agents told a different story.[24] Women described their workplaces as crowded, dirty, and poorly ventilated. Forbidden from using freight elevators, they arrived at work winded from climbing long flights of stairs. Lunch seldom exceeded a half-hour. Toilet facilities were often so dirty and lacking in privacy that women avoided using them. Many women's wages were so low that they could not afford carfare; long walks home in the evening extended their workday. One sewing woman reported "she has only ridden *once* in a horse-car for 14 years." Women also complained of "being obliged to stand all day," a practice popularly regarded as causing reproductive damage.[25] In combination, these factors led to exhaustion and frequent illness.

In addition to the shared stresses of most industrial workplaces, each occupation had its own perils. Feather and cotton sorters suffered from eye and lung irritation because of constant exposure to dust. Printers, sewers, bookkeepers, and button makers strained their eyes. Waitresses were worn out from spending long hours on their feet and from not having enough time to sit down and eat their own meals. Department store salesclerks were forbidden from sitting down at all. Button makers and paper box makers often lost fingers to machinery that lacked safety guards. Work in canneries involved constant exposure to caustic substances, leading to asthma, bronchitis, and skin disease. Workers in type foundries suffered from lead poisoning; straw workers were poisoned by the dyes they used. Between 35 percent and 50 percent of all female industrial workers were paid by the piece (as opposed to 11 percent of men) forcing women to work as rapidly as possible at their repetitive tasks.[26] Wright's agents described many women's health as so poor that it necessitated long, unpaid leaves from their jobs. Yet Wright assured his readers that negative testimony was "that of the few, the great majority being in good health and in good surroundings."[27]

Boston women's detailed testimony about their health problems led some critical readers to doubt Wright's conclusions. Thomas Wentworth Higginson, a strong supporter of women's education, discerned a lack of balance between the report's evidence and its conclusions.[28] Alice Rhine, a socialist advocate of women's rights, remarked that the report, "arranged in the formidable manner of the expert statistician, needed no careful scrutiny of its figures to establish the truth of Disraeli's proposition that 'nothing is so unreliable as facts, unless it is figures.'" She dismissed the entire report as "so biased in favor of the law-making, shop-keeping, manufacturing class as to prove valueless as an investigation into the condition of women dependent upon wages for their living."[29] Ida Van Etten, a journalist who worked to organize working-class women in New York, characterized Wright's descriptions of the conditions of wage-earning women as "a most remarkable perversion of the facts and compiled in the interest of the employing class."[30] Despite these criticisms, the report stood as authoritative.

By focusing his investigation on white women working full-time in factories, stores, or restaurants, Wright recorded the experiences of working-class women who earned the most, but even these women complained of low and declining wages. Women earned an average of $6.01 a week for six days' work. These wages reflected an unwritten pay scale stratified by sex, race, and skill.[31] Skilled workers, who were almost all white men, earned nearly twice the wages of unskilled workers.[32] White men generally earned at least twice as much as white women.[33] In the Northeast, black men remained concentrated in menial occupations. Jobs as servants, laborers, porters, waiters, and whitewashers were not only poorly paid, but also often unsteady.[34] African American women helped compensate for this problem by continuing to work after marriage in greater numbers than white women.[35]

The wages women earned barely covered the costs of individual subsistence, but they were essential for family survival. Once employers made deductions for illness and for time off during the "slack season"—which still affected most industries and might be extended by depression or business failure—the average Boston working girl made only $269.07 a year. After spending an average of $261.30 a year on necessities such as rent, food, clothes, and transportation, she was left with a very narrow margin of $7.77 per year "for everything outside of the absolute necessaries of life."[36] The average annual family income in Boston was around $763, with average expenditures at $738 and savings of $25.[37] A working girl's wages might contribute to this sum, but taken on its own, her pay was meager at best. Still, in many cases, a daughter's wages of four to six dollars a week constituted "the chief, and sometimes the entire support of the family," especially in cases where the father was absent or unable to work regularly because of disability or lack of steady work. Boston working girls reported "supporting invalid mothers, sisters, brothers, or other relatives, in whole or in common with one or more sisters or brothers; in some cases, doing the housework besides." Revealing their suspicions that working men who could not support their families were lazy and likely to be intemperate, agents speculated that these girls' fathers might be disinclined "to work while there is revenue from any other source."[38]

Many Boston working girls thought "their work [was] worth more than they receive[d] for it." A paper box maker earning eight dollars a week complained, "girls work harder than the men and are paid much less—unjustly, she thinks." Women who set type complained of earning less than men in their offices who did the same work. More frequently, women worked in jobs segregated by gender. Employers tended to hire women and men for separate parts of the production process and to pay them according to different wage scales.[39]

After laying out the facts, Wright concluded: "with the progress of the modern industrial system there seems to be no limit to the industrial opportunities of women." He concluded that women's access to jobs had expanded as technological innovations allowed employers to substitute women and children for adult men in "light occupations"—a categorization that ignored the stresses of repetitive, fast-paced work.[40] Echoing Alexander Hamilton, Wright argued that these new opportunities benefited women, "for they are now earning something where previously they could earn nothing."[41] A less optimistic 1897 survey by the U.S. Bureau of Labor Statistics shed light on employers' self-interested reasons for hiring women. In comparison to men, women seemed "better adapted" to factory work since they were cheaper, more reliable, and easier to control. Employers also preferred women because they were regarded as less likely to strike.[42] Given these stereotypes, it is not surprising that many men working in industry feared competition from female labor, a problem that organized labor would attempt to combat by demanding that men and women be paid at equal rates.

While acknowledging women's low wages as problematic, Wright insisted that this problem would adjust itself. Wright opposed any action to raise women's wages by the legislature, labor unions, or by "persons charitably and benevolently disposed."[43] Instead, working women "must depend upon industrial and economic conditions" and on the goodwill of their employers, who should be educated to treat their female help with greater consideration. Like his friend Azel Ames, the author of *Sex in Industry,* Wright rebuffed the efforts of labor reformers to politicize the problems of women's wage work. Writing in the lull between the labor activism of the early 1870s and the rise of the Knights of Labor in 1886, Wright dismissed working people's attempts to exercise more control over their wages and conditions through organization.

Wright's report, combined with widespread anxiety about the place of women in the emerging industrial order, spurred investigations of wage-earning women by new state bureaus of labor statistics in New York, Maine, California, Colorado, Iowa, and Minnesota. With lower levels of funding, these reports were seldom as systematic or extensive as Wright's.[44] As in Massachusetts, women surveyed tended to be in the middle ranks of the female labor market; professionals as well as domestic servants generally fell outside the scope of investigation.[45] The reliance on mailed circulars, given the lack of personnel to conduct interviews, limited the pool to those who were literate and comfortable reading and writing in English. Although investigations in Massachusetts were conducted entirely in English, personal interviews may have included some workers who lacked the literacy or the motivation to fill out written questionnaires. The skeptical attitude of some working women may be gleaned from the California labor commissioner's complaint that many working women "would not fill out the 'forms' left in their hands," and that others "tried to display tawdry wit in burlesque replies to the questions asked." Doubting the impartiality of the state in the

battle between capital and labor, the women's assembly of the Knights of
Labor refused to cooperate.[46]

Keeping in mind these limitations, reports from Colorado and California suggest that the patterns of young, single women working in industry
observed by Wright extended to the West, previously envisioned as a place
of greater opportunity. In Colorado, women complained about low wages,
long hours, and unpleasant working conditions; they expressed a desire for
equal pay, a shorter day, and paid vacations.[47] Investigation in California
reinforced Wright's picture of working girls as first-generation Americans
who tended to live with their families and turn over most of their wages
to their mothers. Contrary to the hopes of some eastern labor reformers,
investigators found wages to be similar in the East and the West. Women
seldom earned more than a dollar a day.[48]

As Alice Kessler-Harris has argued, throughout the late nineteenth century
and into the twentieth, men were paid as individuals who supported families,
while women were paid as supplementary workers supported by men. The
lower wages paid to women reflected and reinforced the popular idea that
women would be better off at home doing domestic work for their families.
An increasing number of families did not conform to this ideal. However,
women consistently earned about half of men's wages.[49] The difference between women who supported themselves and those who pooled their wages
with other family members and enjoyed a larger household income created
tensions within the female labor force. As Wright reported, the "lone working girl who is entirely dependent on her own resources" worried constantly
about her wages being undercut by "girls living 'at home,'" with little or no
board to pay.[50]

The categories of investigation invented by early researchers like Wright
contributed to popular understandings of social problems at least as much
as the data they accumulated.[51] Rather than discovering knowledge, social
investigators create it through the questions they ask. The most lasting effect
of Wright's landmark investigation was to define "working girls" in ways
that separated domestic service from the labor question, while champion-
ing the moral value of women's unpaid domestic labor for their families.
Wright continued the long-standing tendency of male political economists
to naturalize domestic work for women and to deny its status as productive
labor.[52] Although women who worked as domestic servants and women's
labor reformers would dispute Wright's characterization of working girls as
non-domestic workers, his idea became hegemonic. In 1883 he organized
the Convention of Chiefs and Commissioners of Labor Statistics; two years
later President Chester Arthur appointed him as the first director of the U.S.
Bureau of Labor Statistics.[53]

Leonora Barry and the Knights of Labor

In 1887, just three years after he released his report on the working girls of Boston, Wright marveled at the meteoric rise of the Knights of Labor. He estimated membership to have reached nearly 1 million, although most historians give a more conservative estimate of 800,000 members. At least 65,000 women joined the Knights of Labor. Leonora Barry, a former teacher and mill hand who rose to a position of national leadership, did her best to represent these women and improve their position in the labor market through a combination of investigation, organization, and advocacy.

The Knights presented themselves as offering the nation a chance to save its republican form of government from the depredations of monopoly, political corruption, and labor exploitation. Departing from the trade union model, the Knights admitted all workers who could be classified as producers, regardless of whether they were male or female, or would be regarded as skilled or unskilled.[54] The Knights organized workers into a variety of trade and "mixed" assemblies that included workers of different occupations. They also welcomed African Americans; some formed "colored" assemblies, while others joined assemblies that included white workers. They did not, however, extend membership to Chinese workers, whom they saw as threatening "American" standards of labor, and they supported Chinese exclusion.[55]

The Knights advocated equal pay for equal work, just as the National Labor Union had done twenty years earlier.[56] This principle fit within the Knights' egalitarian ethos. However, it also reflected working men's concern that women's low wages would undercut men's wages or lead to their loss of jobs.[57] Terence Powderly, the head of the Knights, publicly welcomed women into the organization, but he and other male leaders never quite shook their conviction that women's growing presence in the labor force was evidence of capitalist exploitation. The Knights idealized women's place in the home in their speeches, literature, and newspapers. As the sole woman in a position of national leadership, Leonora Barry found herself isolated and vulnerable to cuts in funding for her work as an investigator and organizer.[58]

The Knights advocated state investigation of the labor question, but members were not entirely satisfied with the results. In 1885, just a year after the Massachusetts Bureau of Statistics of Labor released Wright's report on "The Working Girls of Boston," female delegates to the national convention of the Knights of Labor initiated their own investigation of women's wage work. While we have no records of their conversation, a large proportion of female Knights resided in Massachusetts and worked in the shoe industry; they may have been dissatisfied with Wright's claims that most working girls were in good health and that no particular action needed to be taken to raise women's wages. The three delegates, who included one salesclerk and two shoe workers, composed a questionnaire to send out to women's and mixed local assemblies. Tabulating their results during the following months, they found an average working day of ten hours and wages of about five dollars a week, except in the shoe industry where women earned more.[59]

The women continued their drive for investigation the following year. At the 1886 national convention, the sixteen female delegates (out of a total of 660) formed a Committee on Women's Work and elected Leonora Barry, a mill hand from Amsterdam, New York, as General Investigator of Women's Work. For the next three years, Barry crisscrossed the country, meeting with female members of the Knights of Labor and reporting on their conditions. Besides adding to the general knowledge of women's compromised position within the labor market, Barry campaigned for equal pay for equal work, drew attention to the problem of sexual harassment, and urged members "to create a demand" for goods made by fairly treated workers by buying labeled goods whenever possible.[60] At this point, local chapters of the Knights put their label on everything from cigars and gloves to canned goods. Consumer organization proved to be an effective tactic, and the Knights used boycotts at least as often as strikes in local labor conflicts.[61]

In her role as General Investigator, Leonora Barry became the most visible and significant female leader of the Knights of Labor. She shared many life experiences with the women she sought to organize. Born in Ireland in 1849, she immigrated with her family to upstate New York at age three. After her mother's death, Barry studied to become a teacher, supplementing her public schooling with private tutoring. She had more education than many members of the working class, but she did not belong to the small elite who attended a female seminary or graduated from college.[62] Barry taught school from age sixteen until her marriage at age twenty-two to William Barry, an Irish immigrant who worked as a painter and musician. Ten years later, William died of lung disease, leaving Leonora with three children to support, one of whom died shortly after his father.

As a widow with young children, Barry was unlikely to be rehired as a teacher. Like many women in her position, she tried to make a living by taking in sewing. Eyestrain forced her to quit. So she left her two children in the care of a neighbor and went out to work in a large hosiery mill in Amsterdam, New York. The first week, she earned sixty-five cents. Rebelling against low pay, she joined a rapidly growing female assembly of the Knights of Labor that soon included 1,500 women. Barry quickly rose to a position of leadership, first in her own local, all-female assembly, then in the mixed district assembly, which included nearly 10,000 men and women.[63]

Embarking on her work as General Investigator, Barry found herself hindered by her lack of legal authority. Factory owners had no reason to grant her access; one Knight who took Barry on a tour of her silk mill was fired as a result. In contrast, state bureaus of labor statistics could demand that factory owners grant them access to inspect their premises and permission to interview their workers. In theory, these state agencies had greater capacity for gathering and interpreting quantitative data, which gave reports by official investigators like Carroll Wright an objective gloss. However, in the 1880s most state bureaus were underfunded and understaffed. Social-scientific methodologies, such as taking representative samples, had yet to be established. Despite its open advocacy, Barry's work was taken seriously; the New Jersey Bureau of Labor Statistics reprinted her 1887 report for the Knights of Labor as an authoritative statement on the conditions of female wage earners.[64]

Barry interviewed workers outside of their places of employment, gathering information from the men and women who came to meetings of the Knights of Labor in the many towns she visited. This practice limited her sample to workers who either belonged to the Knights or were interested in joining. However, the organization had a broad appeal, reaching female wage earners and women who considered themselves "producers" but did not work for wages. Local, all-female assemblies included tailoresses in Milwaukee, cloak makers in Boston, white goods makers in San Francisco, stocking knitters in St. Louis, and shoe workers in Massachusetts. African American laundresses in Pensacola, Florida, joined, as did laundresses, cooks, and housekeepers in Virginia.[65] Together, housewives, servants, and other domestic workers, both paid and unpaid, made up a quarter of all female members.[66]

Despite this diversity, Barry's classification and investigation of working women followed Carroll Wright's example by focusing on female factory workers. Taking in a more diverse group of female workers than Wright, in rural and small-town settings as well as cities, Barry found even lower average wages: only $2.50 to $3.00 a week, compared to $6.00 a week reported by Wright. Most working women Barry met suffered from long hours of labor, stringent work rules, and a lack of effective organization.[67]

Barry urged male members of the Knights of Labor to take action to redress the inequities she discovered. She presented her findings at the General Assembly of 1887, where she warned the mostly male audience that the current industrial system was making their mothers, wives, and sisters slaves to poverty. Sounding the familiar labor reform theme of unbridled capitalism reducing working-class women to prostitution, she described the Committee on Women's Work as seeking "to free from the remorseless grasp of tyranny and greed the thousands of underpaid women and girls in our large cities" who "yield and fall into the yawning chasm of immorality."[68] Barry used this sensational language to advance concrete goals. She urged male Knights to help make the principle of equal pay for equal work a reality. Remarkably, she initiated discussion of sexual harassment, calling on every district assembly to set up a subcommittee of "three active intelligent women" ready to investigate "any abuse existing which a female Local would be delicate in mentioning to the General Executive Board."[69]

Even as she appealed to male members to take a more proactive stance on the issue of equal pay for equal work, Barry pursued alliances with powerful middle-class women. In January 1889 Barry joined Florence Kelley in lobbying the Pennsylvania legislature to enact a bill to regulate the employment of women and children in manufacturing establishments and to appoint female factory inspectors. Kelley continued to pursue these issues after she moved to Chicago, where she joined Hull House, the social settlement run by Jane Addams. Barry also addressed women's clubs, which had proliferated during the 1880s, explaining the need for equal pay and for workers' organization. Like many members of the Knights of Labor, Barry supported temperance, and she accepted several invitations from Frances Willard to address the Women's Christian Temperance Union, the largest organization of women in the United States.[70]

Barry's broad vision, however, could not compensate for the growing weakness of the Knights of Labor. The Haymarket Affair of May 1886 fed middle-class fears of radicalism, clouding the Knights' vision of a broad class of "producers" working together to reform the American political economy. The explosion of a bomb at a labor rally in Chicago set off a melee in which eight policemen were killed and numerous bystanders were wounded. Despite flimsy evidence, eight anarchists, seven of them German immigrants, were arrested and found guilty of conspiracy. Four were sentenced to death. Terence Powderly distanced himself from the anarchists, but many members of the Knights viewed them as martyrs.[71] Internal conflicts left the organization ill equipped to respond to increasing opposition from employers, who turned to the courts to protect themselves from boycotts and to the police to crush strikes. By 1890 membership had declined to 100,000. While locals in particular towns and cities stayed strong and laid the groundwork for future reform movements, the Knights lost steam as a national movement.[72]

At the 1889 General Assembly, when Barry offered her final report, she reflected on her experiences as a worker and an organizer, and demanded full political rights as a precondition for women's economic equality. "When I became one of the bread-winners of the land," she recalled, "I recognized how much the workingwomen needed enlightenment and assistance to maintain the dignity which by our form of government we are entitled to, and protection from the indignities and injustices heaped upon us, in many instances because of our voiceless, helpless condition." Even as she argued for suffrage, she expressed nostalgia for an imagined past, when women could stay home and attend to domestic duties, and only men needed work for wages. If they ever existed, however, those days were gone. Given present conditions, when increasing numbers of women had to work for wages in order to live, "women should have every opportunity to become proficient in whatever vocation they choose or find themselves best fitted for," Barry insisted.[73] Here she gave a working-class emphasis to a point made by middle-class women's rights advocates, who argued that women, like men, should be able to develop to their full capacity and should be given full political rights.

Barry identified several reasons for the Knights' limited success in organizing women. While industrial jobs for men spanned a range of skill levels, most women were unskilled workers, so they suffered from greater competition and lower wages than men. Gendered definitions of skill reinforced a division of labor in which most trades organized into craft unions excluded women from their apprenticeship programs and from membership in their organizations. Discrimination and exclusion left most women who wanted industrial jobs to find positions where labor had been subdivided into discrete tasks that were relatively easy to learn, such as cutting out sleeves, attaching buttons, or gilding picture frames, making female workers who complained, or attempted to organize, easy to replace. Furthermore, it seemed to Barry as though women's "natural pride and timidity," coupled with "the restrictions of social customs," deterred them "from making the struggle that can be made by men." Many women saw themselves as temporary workers, counting on marriage to "lift them out of industrial life to the quiet and comfort of a home." Drawing on her own experience, Barry warned that, unfortunately, marriage did not always offer an escape from wage labor. Women who had looked forward to opting out of dead-end jobs by finding husbands discovered several years later "that their struggle has only begun when they have to go back to the shop and work for two instead of one."

In this final report, Barry again addressed the issue of sexual harassment. From female members, she had learned of many cases "in which men use the power which their position as employers, superintendents or foremen give them to debauch girls in their employ whose employment is dependent on their good will." As a remedy, Barry encouraged the Knights to support legislation making it a crime for "a man holding any position which gives him power over women to make . . . improper advances to them." Like her advocacy of a law mandating equal pay for equal work, Barry's stance on sexual harassment suggested a broad conception of protection. Barry tried to place the demise of her department in a positive light, arguing, "the time when we could separate the interests of the toiling masses is past." However, her report attested to powerful differences between men and women's experiences of work and organization.[74] The American Federation of Labor, the next national labor organization to gain ascendancy, largely served the "labor aristocracy" of skilled white men who continued to control craft production, ignoring the women Barry had worked to organize.[75] Perhaps sensing the limitations of trade union organization for women, Barry continued to advocate organization at the point of consumption. Invoking the evils of the sweatshop system, she urged her audience to buy goods only if their labels indicated that they had been made by fairly paid labor.[76]

In 1890 Barry married Obadiah Lake, a printer. Terence Powderly used Barry's marriage to explain her resignation, but in fact Barry fell victim to factionalism, declining membership, and hostility to her work as a female organizer.[77] After she left the Knights, Barry did not retire to private life as Powderly claimed, but remained active in campaigns for social reform, shifting her energies to Catholic charities, temperance, and woman suffrage.[78]

Barry used her nuanced understanding of the problems facing working women to advance several important ideas for change on their behalf: organization of women as workers and consumers, equal pay for equal work, and protection from sexual harassment. Although she focused on women employed in industry, she considered the experiences of women of different ages, races, and occupations. Her understanding of women's place within the labor question came from her own experiences as a widowed, working mother and as an organizer who had come into contact with thousands of other working women. She fostered alliances with middle-class women reformers. As the Knights of Labor petered out, however, the major vehicle for accomplishing the changes she envisioned vanished.

Recognizing that the vast majority of women worked out of necessity rather than choice and exercised little power as individuals, Barry embraced collective action as offering women a much-needed set of protections against "the indignities and humiliations" they too often suffered.[79] The Knights left a legacy of ideas and organizational experience to be built upon in the 1890s and early 1900s by new organizations, such as the Working Women's Society, the Consumers' League, and the Women's Trade Union League.[80] Barry focused on women in factories. Like the labor organizations that followed her, she had little to say about domestic servants.

Prisoners of Poverty

Helen Campbell sparked the consumers' movement by adapting the consumer consciousness pioneered by the Knights of Labor to a new constituency: educated, affluent women seeking a more harmonious social order. By advocating a broad range of social reforms to improve the urban environment, these women sought to quell class conflict and to assimilate the millions of immigrants pouring into large cities. Some, like Jane Addams, established settlement houses, seeking an alternative to the "family claim" on their own lives and a chance to improve the lives of their city's most impoverished residents. Others formed clubs, associations, and organizations devoted to improving housing codes, ending child labor, and curbing political corruption. Like earlier groups of women concerned with social problems, they turned to social science to illuminate the problem of poverty and light the way toward social progress.[81]

Helen Campbell, a novelist, journalist, and self-taught economist, focused her efforts on the status of female wage earners within the emerging industrial order. *Prisoners of Poverty,* her 1886 investigation into the lives and labors of wage-earning women in New York City, shed new light on the ways in which America's seemingly inexorable march toward "Progress and Poverty" affected women.[82] As an educated woman who made her living as a writer and belonged to Sorosis, New York's elite club for professional women, Campbell saw herself in the vanguard of female progress. However, she questioned, "how far certain special advance[s] for women [like herself] touched the general, whether the breaking of mental and spiritual bonds for the better class had meant enlightenment for the one below."[83] Following ideas developed by the Knights of Labor and by contemporary British and American advocates of socialism, Campbell concluded that women would not be liberated en masse until a "cooperative commonwealth" freed them from having to slave for wages in order to eat.[84] Until the arrival of this utopian moment, which Campbell, like most American socialists, believed would come through the ballot box rather than revolution, Campbell encouraged middle class women to improve the conditions of working women by becoming ethical consumers.

Like other members of a small but influential female professional class of journalists, lawyers, physicians, and ministers, Helen Campbell gained a sense of independence through her own work. Born in 1839, she grew up in New York City, where she attended both public and private schools. At age twenty-one she married a medical student, but the relationship dissolved during the Civil War, when her husband left for several years to serve the Union army as a surgeon. Campbell then became a writer and began publishing children's stories and adult novels. Signaling her distance from her husband and her commitment to a woman-centered view of the world, she dropped her husband's last name and adopted her mother's maiden name. In addition to writing, from which she made her living, Campbell volunteered at a New York City waterfront mission, an experience she reflected on in her 1882 book, *The Problem of the Poor*. That book and her subsequent novel, *Mrs. Herndon's Income* (1886), stressed women's difficulty living decently on their low wages.[85]

In *Prisoners of Poverty*, Campbell relied on vivid narratives rather than statistical tables to impart information. She gathered information primarily from women she met coming from and going to work, including women who worked in factories and retail stores, and those who trudged back and forth to subcontractors with bundles of clothing sewn at home. In New York City, as in Boston, the African American population remained small, numbering less than 20,000 in a city of over 1.2 million in 1880; most black women worked as laundresses or servants. Like Wright, Campbell made no special effort to seek out African American women, and her investigation made no mention of race.[86] Within these limitations, Campbell interviewed a slightly broader group of women than Wright, including outworkers, whom he had ignored. Although at first glance Campbell's approach to gathering information may seem less scientific than Wright's, in fact her sample was no less representative. Claims to objectivity seem strained in all of these investigations, since the investigators, whether officially employed or acting on their own, made arbitrary decisions about whom to include and exclude. Like Wright, Campbell believed that her work was both scientific and truthful.[87] In fact, independent investigators like Campbell may have elicited more frank answers than state investigators who interviewed women at work, often within earshot of their employers.

Campbell took it as her mission to rebut defenders of the status quo like Wright, who framed any kind of paid employment for women as "opportunity" and used statistics as proof that the working class was doing well enough.[88] Campbell also criticized middle-class and elite members of women's clubs such as Sorosis for naively assuming that the universal emancipation of women was "well under way" now that they could buy their way out of household labor, purchasing ready-made goods instead of sewing themselves. She urged her middle-class readers to think about the anonymous women who made the underwear and children's clothes they now purchased so cheaply, warning that "emancipation on the one side had meant no corresponding emancipation" on the other.[89]

Campbell was one of the first thinkers of her generation to analyze systematically the effects of America's breakneck capitalist development on women. The growing availability of mass-produced household goods, such as food, clothing, and soap, combined with the provision of public utilities, such as plumbing, gas, and electricity, dramatically changed the material conditions of middle-class urban households. Middle-class housewives reoriented themselves from producing goods at home, either on their own or with the help of servants, to buying them on the market, spending less time getting their hands dirty and more time shopping. For women who could afford to hire servants to cook and clean, these changes resulted in increased free time, which could be used to entertain, take more interest in the children, embellish the household's furnishings, or pursue volunteer activities. However, this reorientation from production to consumption required purchasing power that not all women possessed. Working-class women still did much provisioning on their own. In more than half the working-class families surveyed by the U.S. Bureau of Labor Statistics from 1889 to 1892, women made their own bread rather than buying it at the store.[90] Cities did a better job in providing public services in wealthier neighborhoods, leaving the poor to live in hastily constructed tenement buildings with cold water and shared privies. Taking a broad view of the economic transformations under way, Campbell saw improvement in the quality of life for middle- and upper-class women, while the material conditions of working-class women seemed to be deteriorating.

Campbell sought to illuminate these links between progress and poverty by focusing on the production of clothing, which freed women with money to stop sewing but enslaved women without money in an endless round of labor that never generated enough income to make ends meet. By focusing on the clothing industry, which employed more women than any other trade in New York save domestic service, Campbell illuminated the connections between women of different classes.[91] Following a fashionable cloak from the shop window where potential buyers admired it back through the subcontracting system that produced it, Campbell demystified commodity production.[92] She urged her readers to educate themselves about the labor processes that produced their clothing and to take responsibility for the women driven by need into low-paid jobs in the needle trades. As historian Eileen Boris has argued, this dichotomy between "women who work" and "women who spend" obscured both the consumption patterns of working-class women and the unpaid labor of upper middle-class house-wives.[93] However, Campbell's formulation made a political point: women of different classes were more connected than they might realize; and through knowledge and action, elite women might begin to use their economic power in socially beneficial ways.

Campbell estimated that one-third of the city's needlewomen, its lowest paid industrial workers, were mothers with young children who labored "night and day" to prevent their offspring from being scattered "into asylums." Women could be widowed either actually or effectively by their husband's industrial accidents, illness, or unemployment. Campbell vividly portrayed working-class families' insecurity through individual stories. A young mother worked fourteen to sixteen hours a day at home, making underwear. She earned eighty-five cents a day. Her husband, a former "boss painter," suffered from lead poisoning and heart disease, illnesses that left him barely well enough to look after the children while his wife sewed.[94] This situation violated all sense of social order, as the mother was unable to care for her own children, the father was incapable of working to support his family, and ceaseless labor yielded only poverty. Stories like this suggested that the "lone working girl" who struggled to feed herself had an even more exploited and vulnerable counterpart: the working mother attempting to feed a family on wages that barely supported one person.

Taking a socialist view of the situation, Campbell regarded appeals to individual employers to treat their workers better as futile. Here, too, she disputed Wright, who advocated no stronger action than encouraging employers to treat their female employees with greater consideration. Capitalism forced employers to get the most labor out of their employees for the least amount of money just to stay afloat. Technical innovations such as steam power made it difficult for small firms to remain competitive, and subcontracting and slashing wages were their only hope of keeping costs down. "Master and servant," Campbell explained, "are in the same bonds, and the employer is driven as mercilessly as he drives."[95]

Although she recognized the dire poverty of many wage-earning women, Campbell celebrated the expansion of their opportunities for employment. Like Wright, she commented favorably on the fact that women were beginning to move beyond the needle trades, taking new jobs in manufacturing, printing, and retail stores.[96] New York City's 200,000 working women had "open to them nearly one hundred trades as against a fifth that number a generation ago," which seemed a sign of progress.[97] However, Campbell found a negative side to this development: white, native-born women's large-scale abandonment of domestic service.[98] Like members of the New England Women's Club, who were shocked to discover that some working-class women preferred prostitution to domestic service, Campbell found working girls' "conviction that private employ of any nature whatever is inevitably a despotism filled with unknown horrors . . . inscrutable."[99] While she drew connections between bourgeois women's increasing freedom from having to make their family's clothes and working-class women's increasing exploitation as needle workers, she remained blind to similar relationships entailed in domestic service. Significantly, this lack of recognition was due to Campbell's own position as an employer of domestic labor. Many people regarded having at least one domestic servant as the measure of middle-class status, and the privilege was shared among a small, but significant group, with approximately 188 servants for every 1,000 families in New York City in 1880.[100]

Working women explained their decision to leave domestic service in terms of their desire for freedom and independence. As Margaret M., a twenty-three-year-old American-born woman who worked in a paper box factory, told Campbell: "It's freedom we want when the day's work is done . . . women care just as much for freedom as men do." Reflecting the popular movement among workers for an eight-hour day, Margaret M. defined freedom as time off from work. In contrast to an earlier generation of workers who had hoped to gain freedom by acquiring land or establishing their own workshops, the current generation sought to make the best bargain they could within a wage system they expected to remain within throughout their lives. Many women experienced domestic work as demeaning. As an Irish American woman, whose mother had been a cook, explained: "We came to this country to better ourselves, and it's not bettering to have anybody ordering you around." One woman currently working as a teacher had left her job as a nursemaid when her employer had demanded that she wear "the nurse's cap and apron." Although she loved the child, she found this badge of subservience intolerable. Given the necessity of working full time, women preferred not to live and labor in another woman's household. While a foreman or supervisor might order female employees around during the day, once they left work, their time was their own, or at least subject to negotiation among family members rather than dictated by employers. Furthermore, nondomestic work gave women the benefit of working alongside other women who were their social equals. This camaraderie opened the possibility of collective resistance to mistreatment, either formally, as when they formed labor organizations, or informally, when they threatened to walk out if wages were cut.[101]

In particular, these women rebelled against the sense of degradation that domestic work entailed. As the Irish American woman whose mother had been a cook explained: "You can do things at home for them as belongs to you that somehow it seems different to do for strangers." A young woman working for a stationer described her year spent in household service as "awful lonesomeness" that "got to feel sort of crushing at last." Another woman left domestic service because her mistress required her servants to entertain their friends in the kitchen; as she explained to Campbell, "I was thirty years old and as well born and well educated as she, and it didn't seem right." Like Jennie Collins, many servants doubted their employers' qualifications to boss them around, which rested solely upon the fact that the employing family had more money. In New York in the 1880s, as in Boston in the 1860s, aversion to working as a servant seemed to be shared throughout the working-class community, with many women complaining that working men took no interest in courting women who worked as servants.[102] While the reasons for this preference remain unarticulated, potential suitors may have been put off by the rules housewives set for their domestic employees, including visits in the kitchen, and only one or two nights off per week.

Despite this testimony, Campbell regarded native-born white women's increasing preference for nondomestic work as irrational, failing to appreciate that working-class women weighed respect, dignity, and leisure time as well as wages in deciding which jobs to take. Native-born women still formed a significant proportion of household servants: according to the 1880 census, approximately 20,000 of the servants in New York City were native-born, while 24,000 were born in Ireland. Most of these native-born women had migrated to the city and needed a place to live. The next largest group of servants, nearly 7,000, came from Germany, but excited no comment since they were unlikely to work outside the German American community because of their limited English.[103] In a prejudiced and myopic analysis of the problem, Campbell accused working-class American women of leaving bourgeois women like herself at the mercy of the "tenement house Irish" who lacked both "modesty" and "decency."[104] Ironically, the widespread migration of Irish women to the United States to work as servants prompted a parallel sense of crisis in Ireland, where social commentators worried about the exodus of young women, who preferred to "slave and scrub and stifle in American cities" rather than work as servants in their home country.[105] The "servant crisis" complained of by Campbell and numerous other bourgeois social commentators must be recognized primarily as anxiety about incorporating workers from different ethnic, racial, and religious backgrounds into their households. Campbell concluded with proposals for making domestic service more like other kinds of wage work, with clearly defined responsibilities and limited hours, in the hopes that this would draw American-born women back to the occupation.[106]

Campbell ended her book with an appeal to educated women to work for change, promising that a combination of socialism and consumer organization would restore "beauty, order, and law" to a nation riven by class conflict.[107] By asserting elite women's responsibility to practice ethical consumption, Campbell translated female labor reformers' sense of responsibility for protecting exploited women into the beginnings of a new movement for social reform. Alice Rhine, a contemporary of Campbell's, described the impact of *Prisoners of Poverty*: the book had "caused a great wave of indignation to sweep over society," as the reading public realized the tremendous human toll taken by mass production and began to see working-class women as some of the chief victims of industrialization.[108] This sentiment sparked the beginning of the middle-class consumers' movement in New York City. Campbell would help lead this movement by working to establish the New York Consumer's League in 1890.

City Slave Girls

Despite their biases, Carroll Wright, Leonora Barry, and Helen Campbell all strove for objectivity. Nell Cusack, a young Chicago journalist, embraced subjectivity. Writing as "Nell Nelson," she launched a month-long undercover investigation into working-class women's wages and conditions. The *Chicago Times* printed her stories in August 1888 under the sensational title, "City Slave Girls." Cusack's stories sold papers by promising readers a glimpse of working-class women in compromised positions. Yet the series, read avidly in Chicago and across the country, inadvertently revealed the ways that working-class girls and women were using their wage work to become more independent.

"City Slave Girls" surveyed an unusually wide range of female workers, from girls of ten pulled out of school to help make ends meet to middle-aged widows trying to get paid for shirts they had finished at home. This broad sample revealed how women's ideas of independence and their chances of achieving it varied according to age and family circumstances. Girls of twelve or thirteen became less subservient to their parents once they began earning, but they were particularly vulnerable to exploitation by their employers. As girls who worked in stores or factories reached their teens or early twenties, they often used their wages to bargain with female relatives for reduced domestic responsibilities. Some delayed marriage, or chose to live in boardinghouses with other women rather than settle down to lives as housewives. Most left full-time employment once they married. However, they often reappeared in the labor force as widowed mothers. While daughters' wages made a significant contribution to family support, women with children who lacked male support found themselves in an almost impossible position. The sole story of prostitution in "City Slave Girls" related the tale of Kitty Kelly, a young widowed mother who had tried making overalls, but could earn only four dollars a week. Picked up for streetwalking and brought before a judge, she asked, "Must I lose my baby because a woman cannot earn more than enough in Chicago to give herself black bread and a garret?"[109] Her question reminds us of the sheer impossibility of family support on a "woman's wage."

"Nell Nelson" portrayed herself as a latter-day abolitionist, writing to expose the inhumane conditions endured by the city's working girls and women, who imperiled their health and endured humiliation to help make ends meet. Her investigation fit within a new journalistic genre: the undercover female reporter who assumed a fictious identity to find the truth. Just months earlier in Minneapolis, Eva McDonald had gone undercover as "Eva Gay" to investigate women's wages and working conditions. These exposés drew the attention of labor leaders and social reformers. Cusack and McDonald may have both been inspired by "Nellie Bly" (Elizabeth Jane Cochrane), the daring female reporter whose undercover assignments for the New York World included a stint in a sweatshop as well as time in a city mental institution.[110] Narratives of cross-class impersonation recognized the difficulties of gaining knowledge of the experiences of members of a different social group. Undercover journalists like Cusack sought to collapse the distinction between subject and object through their performance as narrators. However, the very need for disguise and discovery affirmed the more privileged social class of the investigator and the instability of class boundaries.[111]

The jobs Cusack tried included binding sleeves, sewing coats, pressing neckties, sorting feathers, and selling gloves. Accustomed to mental rather than physical exertion, she found the work rules intolerable, the employers insulting, and the conditions uncomfortable. She seldom stayed longer than a day in each of the positions she tried, and she often quit before the work day ended. Usually she left after a dramatic confrontation with her employer. Cusack's outrage, her discomfort with manual labor, and her lack of dexterity reflected a life of relative privilege, although her need to earn a living suggested a possible failure of family support. While we know few biographical details about Nell Cusack, she belonged to the small elite of female journalists, doctors, and lawyers who earned a good living and found a sense of social purpose through their work. The *Journalist,* a trade periodical based in New York, described Cusack as "clever, bright, witty"; it characterized her work on "City Slave Girls" as "phenomenal in its journalistic excellence." The series ended when Joseph Pulitzer recruited Cusack to become a reporter for the New York *World.*[112]

In her articles for the *Times,* Cusack used the idiom of wage slavery to describe her experiences as a working girl. A typical story began, "I did not realize the ignominious position of respectable poverty till I went to Ellington's cloak factory . . . where labor is bondage, the laborer a slave, and flesh and blood cheaper than needles and thread."[113] Cusack's stories prompted an immediate and intense public response. James J. West and Finley Peter Dunne, who supported labor reform and had recently replaced the paper's conservative founding editor, Wilbur Story, boasted that nothing the paper had ever printed had "provoked more comment or attracted more widespread attention."[114] Daily circulation soared to 40,000 within Chicago, and the *Times* outsold its closest competitor, the *Tribune.* Thousands more read "City Slave Girls" in miniature editions of the *Times* distributed throughout small midwestern towns. Readers multiplied as newspapers across the country picked up Cusack's stories in national syndication.[115] Hundreds of these readers wrote letters to the editor. By mid-August, the *Times* was printing letters from working women, trade unionists, manufacturers, housewives, and farmers alongside Cusack's stories of her fictitious experience as a working girl. Regardless of their veracity, Cusack's stories helped generate a forum in which working-class women could draw on their own experiences of wage labor to enter into public debate about their conditions.

The title, "City Slave Girls," suggested regression from America's imagined march toward freedom, which northerners believed had triumphed during the Civil War with the emancipation of southern slaves.[116] The metaphor of wage slavery suggested that this victory had been hollow. As one woman with a hand "cramped with twenty-five years' sewing" wrote, "We are indeed slaves, worse slaves than those my brother died to free."[117] In Gilded Age Chicago, as in antebellum Lowell or Liverpool, metaphors of wage slavery mingled sympathy for enslaved African Americans with a racist insistence that whiteness ensured entitlement to better treatment.[118] In Chicago in the 1880s, as in Boston in the 1860s, workers' understanding of slavery came largely from fictional sources. In a discussion of "City Slave Girls" at the Ethical Society, a meeting place for labor leaders and middle-class reformers, Thomas J. Morgan, the leader of the Central Labor Union, described the series as exposing "slave life as related in 'Uncle Tom's Cabin' to have been a holiday pastime." While southern slave masters exercised control through the whip, Chicago employers turned to the "vast and constantly growing army of the unemployed" who stood "ready to fill the places of the dissatisfied worker who asks for more pay."[119]

While the trope of "City Slave Girls" invoked southern slavery as a negation of the freedom supposedly guaranteed to all Americans by the Civil War, the paper made nearly no mention of the conditions of African American girls and women currently living and working in Chicago. The black population in Chicago remained small: less than 15,000 in a city of nearly 1.2 million. African Americans would not begin moving to Chicago in significant numbers until the Great Migration, which began in the 1890s.[120] As in other cities, most black women who needed to earn a living were limited to jobs related to cooking or cleaning, and Cusack did not investigate domestic labor. Cusack did mention an African American woman who sold meals to department store employees, but focused on the fact that few of the white female salesclerks could afford to pay twenty cents for lunch.[121] The rhetoric of white slavery combined with the absence of African American women and the biases of the investigator to make "City Slave Girls" an exposé of capitalist labor relations that applied to whites only. These patterns of exclusion reflected widely held assumptions that black women should work outside of their own homes and that white women deserved special protection from verbal insults and physical harm.

In affirming the difference between white and black working women, "City Slave Girls" rhetorically erased the differences in ethnicity that divided the city's industrial labor force, 90 percent of whom were either immigrants or their children.[122] By referring to immigrants from Ireland, Germany, Sweden, Poland, and Russia and their American-born daughters as "slave girls" and depicting them as victims with whom the public should sympathize, the series "whitened" and Americanized an alien workforce that had fallen under suspicion after the events at Haymarket. The writer herself probably shared in this process of ethnic bleaching. Nell Nelson's real name, Nell Cusack, suggests Irish origins. By defining an ethnically diverse group of women as "white," the series helped construct a white working class worthy of middle-class sympathy, even as it marginalized African American women from public concern.

Despite its obvious limitations, the literary understanding of slavery articulated in "City Slave Girls" created space for discussion of sexual harassment. Female abolitionists and African American authors, such as Harriet Jacobs, had told harrowing stories of enslaved women's vulnerability to sexual coercion. Some working-class women who wrote in to the *Times* also used veiled language to complain of abuse. As Mary, a "typewriter" earning three dollars a week working for "a millionaire" wrote in: "Could I but declare myself and make known the indignities to which I have been subjected the earth might better for them open and swallow up the accursed."[123] Stories of harassment at work could draw attention to the dangers of the sexual double standard, which impugned the morality of the women who were insulted and assaulted while leaving the male perpetrators unscathed.[124] Just as often, however, male readers interpreted these stories as evidence that women, like children, did not belong in the labor force since they were unable to protect themselves.[125]

It had taken the Civil War to eradicate southern slavery. The metaphor of white slavery suggested the need for similarly dramatic action on behalf of working women. The *Milwaukee Review,* one of the many papers around the country reprinting Nelson's stories, described the inevitable demise of white slavery as "the triumph of our American democracy [just] as the emancipation of the black slavery is the boast of our republic."[126] In a similar vein, "Byron" wrote to the *Times* urging "those who strenuously advocated the abolition of African slavery in the south" to make abolition of "girl-slavery" in Chicago their next battle: "Here is a favorable opportunity to accomplish much in favor of those who can not talk and act for themselves."[127]

By comparing Chicago's girls and women to slaves, the paper portrayed them as helpless victims and objects of sympathy, rather than as members of the "dangerous classes." The editors seemed touched by amnesia as they ignored the fact that hundreds of working women had participated in the strikes and marches for the eight-hour day that had preceded the Haymarket Affair just two years before.[128]

While some working girls and women embraced the metaphor of wage slavery as offering an opportunity to compare their capitalist employers to southern slave masters, others dismissed the idea as overblown and insulting.[129] Mary McGary, an elderly woman who had spent her life sewing, described herself as "a poor white slave." She noted that her fellow workers "didn't like to be called factory slaves but that's just what we are," citing wages as low as four dollars a week and rules preventing workers from speaking to one another.[130] However, sixty-five workers from Phelps, Dodge & Palmer, a boot factory, wrote in to dispute Nelson's depiction of them as "hollow eyed, stoop shouldered, and miserably clad." True, they did not wear new clothes to work; but "out of the shop," they asserted proudly, "we are dressed as well and comfortably as any girls in the city." Participation in the consumer economy was a point of pride for these wage-earning women, and they invited Nelson to call on them in their homes "and see if she finds us in the hovels described."[131] When Mary Kenney, a founder of the Women's

Trade Union League, arrived in Chicago from a small town in Missouri, she found the women she worked with at a book bindery barely willing to speak to her until they were certain she was not the "lady reporter" from the *Times*.[132] Many women who took pride in their identities as workers did not relish being turned into fodder for sensational news stories.

In particular, working women objected to the implication that they could not live honorably on their wages, which impugned their sexual morality. A cloak maker who identified herself as a "breadwinner" thanked Nelson for drawing attention to the conditions of Chicago's working girls and women, but protested against the reporter's tendency to exaggerate. When she began, her wages were as low as two dollars a week, but now that she knew the trade, she earned from "$7 to $10 per week," and more in the busy season. Like many of the girls in her shop, she lived with her parents and did not have to support herself solely on her wages. By implying that working women were "unable to earn honest living wages," the cloak maker complained, Nelson was guilty of "loading the name of 'factory girl' with a still greater stigma" of prostitution.[133]

Despite the objections of many working women, the metaphor of slavery remained attractive to people interested in defining women's wage work as a social problem. Publishers eager to sell papers and boost revenue through advertising found the public hungry for sensational stories promising to describe white girls and women reduced to slavery. Corinne Brown and Elizabeth Morgan, leaders of the recently chartered Ladies Federal Labor Union, used threats of white slavery and prostitution to get the attention of men in the Chicago Trades and Labor Assembly and encourage them to include women within their organizations and support equal pay for equal work. Brown also appealed to "Chicago ladies" of means and education to support organization among working girls and to share the experience they had gained through membership in their own organizations, such as the Women's Christian Temperance Union.[134] Nelson's series inspired Brown and Morgan to form the Illinois Women's Alliance, which brought together women workers and middle-class club women to fight for better enforcement of the city's workplace inspection and compulsory education laws.[135] However, depicting working women as slaves cast them as the victims of industrialization, rather than as potential agents of their own emancipation.

Yet, in the course of the series, a counter-narrative developed. Rather than weakening and enslaving girls, paid labor made them dangerously individualistic. One mother, whose two daughters had begun working at age thirteen, confided to Nelson, "The minute a girl goes to work and becomes her own boss nobody can prevent her from doing as she wants."[136] Abraham Bisno, a

Russian Jewish cloak maker living in Chicago at the time, recalled that even though most young women turned over the money they made to their parents, "quite a significant minority" held on to their earnings, paying board to their own families and either saving or spending what was left. Girls' new positions as wage earners "gave them standing and authority in their families." To Bisno, this change seemed revolutionary: girls and women who worked for wages, whether single or married, "acquired the right to a personality which they had not ever before possessed in the old country."[137]

Women's new sense of individual identity disrupted family hierarchies, weakening the control of both parents and husbands. A male physician interviewed by Cusack blamed former factory girls for the breakdown of working-class marriages, charging that years spent in factories left women unprepared to be economical or obedient wives.[138] Men's belief that women were best fitted for domestic work cut across class lines. Like many men who wrote letters to the *Times,* "Pater Familias" insisted that women who needed to earn money should find jobs doing housework, thus confining their labor to "a sphere particularly their own for which nature seems to have created them."[139] D. R., a male cloak maker, agreed. He faulted the women entering his trade for undercutting men's wages and ruining their own health. He pleaded for women to return to domestic service, the work they were "born" to do, instead of taking "men's" jobs, a decision they made so that they could have "their evenings to gad about." However, other working-class men supported their daughters' right to take industrial jobs as a family necessity.[140]

"A Working Woman" characterized the idea that "all girls" should do housework as "absurd." "Why," she asked, "in this free county have not women the right to choose their own vocations? . . . Are women to be more slaves than men?"[141] As the historian Kathy Peiss has argued, urban working-class women in the late nineteenth century used their new-found income and leisure time to express a sense of independence missing from monotonous, regimented workplaces, where they were treated as interchangeable parts of the production process. Parks, dance halls, and theaters all became places where young, single women and men met, pursuing "cheap amusements" outside of parental control.[142] Women who chose industrial jobs over domestic work joined men in shifting the popular definition of freedom toward having time off from work and money to participate in the expanding consumer economy.[143]

Affirming a trend observed by Helen Campbell, nearly all the working women whose letters the *Times* reprinted regarded domestic service as their last choice for employment. Women who had worked as servants concurred in describing the work as difficult, disrespected, and poorly compensated. "I have done housework and can do it good, but as one compelled to do either give me the shop every time," wrote one "shop girl."[144] M.H.S., who had worked as a servant, teacher, dressmaker, and nurse, advised young women reading the *Times* that they would have a hard time earning a living at any occupation, but that housework was the hardest; it was "drudgery in every sense of the word."[145] Mrs. A. C. W., who had gone to work as a domestic servant after being widowed, agreed: "I have tried both being a hired girl and keeping a hired girl, and although some domestics are very annoying the annoyance I have had to put up with from my hired help was nothing to compare to the annoyance I had to endure as a hired girl."[146] Her comment reminded readers of women's class insecurity and suggested that women who hire servants treat them fairly lest they become servants themselves one day.

Chicago's "City Slave Girls" were equally adamant in rejecting suggestions that they liberate themselves by moving to rural areas, where they could find jobs doing housework for two or three dollars a week.[147] Numerous women wrote to the *Times* to describe the "beauties" of working in the country, as one of them sarcastically put it. Cast on her own resources at the age of sixteen, Mrs. J. S. R. had left the city for work "in the kitchen of a country farm-house." Her employers offered her "board and clothes" and "time to study" in return for her labor. "The 'time to study' was never found," she recalled, "and at the end of a few months I had worn out my clothes and had seen no new ones." At a farm down the road, "the master of the house made himself obnoxious to me and I could not stay after that."[148] A Chicago schoolteacher agreed that she "should prefer to starve in the city" rather than work in the country, where farmers treated the help like animals. "Look around you," she concluded, "and you will find the poor slave on the farm, in the kitchen, everywhere."[149]

Several readers wrote to urge "Nell Nelson" to expand her investigation beyond slop-shops, factories, and dry goods stores. "I think if Miss Nelson would investigate these 'pleasant homes' and 'bright firesides' she would find a field as great or greater than the one she is now working in," commented one woman.[150] While the *Times* reveled in the controversy over women taking new jobs, it was unwilling to expand the investigation to include household workers. Like Carroll Wright, the newspaper editors refused to violate the sanctity of elite homes by interviewing domestic workers. Like Helen Campbell, they questioned working-class women about their preferences and remained mystified by their answers.

Working-class women not only rejected suggestions that they return to domestic work, but they appropriated the metaphor of slavery to issue a withering critique of domestic service. It was one thing to compare the lords of the loom with the lords of the lash, as labor reformers had done for at least fifty years, and quite another to compare the "pater familias" to Simon Legree, the sadistic slave master in *Uncle Tom's Cabin*, and yet that is exactly what some working-class women did. L. M. H. explained: "Sensitive girls born with some natural independence can not endure the constant slavery that 'going out to service' means." While she admitted that sewing girls might be "slaves" until the workday ended, they were better off than servants, who were "'slaves' during the whole twenty-four hours."[151] S. P. Porter, a domestic servant in Indianapolis, described the job as "a slave's life—long hours, late and early seven days in the week, bossed and ordered around as niggers before the war." Her insulting language associated blackness with demeaning work and excluded African American women from the entitlement to fair treatment she claimed for white women. Porter praised "American girls" for refusing to tolerate such "degradation." She linked these women's rejection of domestic service with wider struggles for freedom, warning that domestic service, like slavery, was destined for extinction.[152]

Porter's letter gave voice to a racial undercurrent that ran through the entire series. Ignoring the substance of working women's complaints about domestic service, the *Times* ran an unsigned editorial bemoaning the unfortunate association of servitude with slavery and "the ownership by one of the superior races of one of the inferior races." Unfortunately, the paper admitted, the term *servant* did seem "revolting to our conception of independence, which is especially dear to the heart of every American." Perhaps this offensive nomenclature explained why, in turn, "American, English, Irish, German, and Scandinavian girls have shown a disinclination to engage in domestic service." The author warned: "Unless some change is made the prospect is that the only persons who will accept situations for domestic housework will soon be blacks and natives of the south of Europe."[153] The editorial revealed the fears of the employing class that they would soon have to share their homes with African American or immigrant women whom they considered different, inferior, and more difficult to manage than native-born white women had been.

Although the *Times* recoiled from acknowledging or investigating working-class women's allegations about domestic service, the paper championed the power of exposure. The editors promised that their work would continue until "public opinion shall demand in imperative terms that the factory hell-holes be transformed into decent work-shops; that the slave-drivers shall be transformed into considerate employers, and the working girl or the working woman shall be paid all that she earns, regardless of her weakness or her sex."[154] While the *Times* anticipated a wave of reform, labor organizers hoped that the stories would awaken female workers to their need for organization. The national Knights of Labor applauded Cusack's stories, proclaiming: "Now is the time to start the ball in motion in Chicago, and keep it rolling until the workingwomen of America shall have been thoroughly awakened to the necessity for organization to secure their rights as citizens, to protect their virtue as women."[155] Unfortunately, the weakness of the organization made this outcome unlikely.

"City Slave Girls" created a unique public forum for Chicago's working women to describe their experiences and voice their opinions about the social meaning of their employment. Some seized on the metaphor of slavery to complain about sexual harassment. Others rejected the label, making a point of calling themselves "breadwinners" or "self-supporting working women." Working-class women who wrote in to the paper affirmed the dignity of their labor and claimed the right to choose occupations beyond domestic service. Furthermore, they rejected the distinction that Cusack and other middle-class commentators drew between industrial and domestic workplaces. To the degree that these women had freedom, they exercised it by leaving domestic service in favor of jobs in stores or factories. Rather than existing in an absolute state of freedom or slavery, women chose work offering them the greatest degree of independence.

Taken together, these four investigations reveal the contested construction of the "working girl" as a new social category in the 1880s. Middle-class investigators sought to contain the labor problem to capitalist workplaces. However, working-class women consistently challenged those limits. Reading between the lines of these investigations, we can discern the ideas and actions of working-class women themselves, who asserted the dignity of their labor and refused to be cast as the passive victims of industrialization. We can appreciate native-born white women's departure from service as motivated by their desires for independence. By taking jobs outside of domestic service, they affirmed their freedom to choose their own occupation, increase their personal autonomy, and secure their leisure time. They also affirmed their desire to continue to live with their own families, or at least live apart from their employers.

Yet the investigators who authored these reports shaped social knowledge in ways that encouraged or precluded particular kinds of action. Carroll Wright took a laissez-faire approach to the obvious inequities of women's position in the labor force, promising gradual progress as market forces corrected themselves. Leonora Barry cast working women's low wages and vulnerability to sexual harassment as part of a larger system of wage slavery, to be corrected through workers' organization and conscientious consumption. Helen Campbell urged educated women to become "ethical consumers," careful to purchase clothing made only by workers who had been fairly paid. Nell Cusack and her editors at the *Chicago Times* characterized the city's working girls and women as wage slaves in order to endorse liberal reform, insisting that the state must take action to protect those unable to protect themselves. Yet in arguing for protection, these well-meaning reformers missed the value that working-class women themselves placed on independence and failed to see their departure from domestic service as a meaningful step toward that ideal.

CHAPTER 3

GENDER, CLASS, AND CONSUMPTION

Leonora O'Reilly fit the profile sketched by Carroll D. Wright in "The Working Girls of Boston" in 1884. Born in 1870, she lived in New York City and worked ten-hour days in a shirtwaist factory to support herself and her widowed mother. Like Wright, she believed in social progress. Unlike Wright, however, she doubted that market forces would "naturally" correct women's economic inequality. In the 1880s and 1890s O'Reilly joined new groups of workers and reformers seeking solutions to the problems identified by social investigators: low pay, long hours, and poor conditions. She supported the organization of both workers and consumers, and campaigned to extend state labor laws to department stores, an expanding sector of employment for women in large cities. Her experiences during the 1880s and 1890s illuminate the meanings of independence to a young, working-class woman and demonstrate how the "working girl" continued to take shape as a social category molded by reformers, politicians, and working-class women themselves.

O'Reilly and the young women of the East Side with whom she associated proudly identified themselves as "breadwinners." Yet, as unskilled workers in the city's dispersed garment industry and as clerks in the grand department stores rising along Fifth and Sixth Avenues, they were easily replaceable. These young women found themselves buffeted by the changing tides of labor activism in New York City. In the mid-1880s, the Central Labor Union (CLU) and the Knights of Labor supported their organization into both trade-based and mixed assemblies of workers. After 1890, however, the CLU fractured and the Knights declined. The American Federation of Labor (AFL), composed primarily of men in the trades, showed little interest in organizing women or other "unskilled" workers, requiring O'Reilly and other female workers to search for new allies. They found them in middle-class women's labor reformers, such as Josephine Shaw Lowell, who established the New York Consumers' League (NYCL). However, these bourgeois women redefined the struggle, presenting themselves as the protectors of working women and of public health. Working-class women's possibilities for organizing shifted from a class-based alliance to a gender-based alliance. While women's cross-class coalitions garnered publicity and helped get legislation passed, they did not meet the broader objectives of attaining independence through collective organization articulated by working-class women themselves.

In New York City, the Knights and the CLU made frequent and successful use of boycotts to demand union recognition, protest wage cuts, and ensure safety standards. By the spring of 1886, however, the courts in New York state cracked down on boycotters as part of a nationwide backlash against radicalism. The NYCL reclaimed the technique as an American tradition, harking back to the abolitionists' refusal to buy goods made by slave labor before the Civil War. Reversing the "black list," these reformers created a "white list" of retail stores that treated their female help fairly. Appropriating another union technique, the NYCL created its own "white label." While the union label showed that unionized workers had manufactured goods, the white label promised that the goods that bore its imprint had been manufactured under sanitary conditions. Although the white list and the white label empowered bourgeois women as consumers, they cast working-class women as the objects rather than the initiators of social reform.

Leonora O'Reilly's Labor Education

Leonora O'Reilly described her activism as springing from the experiences of three generations of working women.[1] Both her grandmother and her mother had been victims of the economic dislocations of an expanding capitalist economy. Her grandparents had emigrated from Ireland to escape the potato famine, selling their small farm to finance their passage, and her grandfather had died shortly after the family arrived in New York City. Leonora's mother Winifred, the youngest of seven children, went out to work as a nursemaid at the age of eight. She was barely fed or clothed. At eleven, she learned fine sewing as an apprentice to a female dressmaker. Several years later she became a sewing machine operator at Seligman's shirt factory, a major supplier of clothing to the Union Army during the Civil War. In 1867 she married John O'Reilly, an Irish immigrant who worked as a printer in a union shop.[2] The couple plowed their savings into a grocery store near their apartment on Second Avenue and First Street, but it failed.

Four years later, John O'Reilly died, leaving Winifred to support their year-old daughter, Leonora.[3]

"Mother O'Reilly," as Leonora's friends later called Winifred, employed a variety of strategies to keep food on the table. To save money, she moved farther downtown, renting three rooms on Division Street.[4] She briefly tried living out as a cook, but found the arrangement incompatible with taking care of her daughter. Like many mothers of young children, she rented her spare room to a boarder and took in sewing, but her earnings were inadequate. So she went back to work full time at Seligman's, first bringing Leonora to work with her in a basket and then placing her in a neighbor's care.[5] She earned extra cash by making dresses and trimming hats for the neighbors after she got home from work and saved money by sewing Leonora's clothes and her own.[6] Having received little formal schooling herself, she desperately wanted to educate her daughter. But in 1881, when Leonora was eleven, Winifred took her out of public school and sent her to work in a collar factory.[7] Many widowed mothers in Winifred's position had to give up their children, who were placed out in farm families, or sent to live in Catholic institutions.[8] The pittance Leonora earned provided the margin mother and daughter needed to stay together.

The young Leonora O'Reilly entered a labor force segmented by age, gender, race, ethnicity, and skill. In New York City, native-born white girls of her age commonly worked as finishers in garment factories or as cash girls in department stores. Immigrant girls often joined other family members doing outwork at home. Given her own difficult experiences as a nursemaid, Winifred chose to send her daughter to a factory so she could continue to live at home and be assured of decent care. By this time, girls and women in New York who could support themselves outside of domestic service did so, leaving the occupation to older, native-born white women who had difficulty securing positions in stores and factories; recent immigrants from Ireland or Germany; and the small, but increasing population of African American migrants from the South.[9] As Jacob Riis, the popular author and investigator of poverty in New York City noted, by the 1880s the "American-born girl" generally refused to work as a servant, "though poverty be the price of her independence."[10] In her teens, O'Reilly moved from the collar factory to an uptown shirtwaist factory, which occupied a single room crowded with about twenty sewing machine operatives.[11] Despite technological innovations, production in New York City remained decentralized; few firms that produced men's or women's clothing employed more than twenty or thirty people.[12] Around the same time, Leonora and Winifred O'Reilly left the Lower East Side for Yorkville, where they lived in a succession of top-floor tenement house apartments near the northern terminus of the Second Avenue Elevated Railroad.[13]

O'Reilly later recalled meeting three types of working girls: shop girls with a common school education and a slight sense of superiority; factory girls from broken homes; and sweatshop workers who had recently immigrated from Poland, Hungary, and Italy.[14] While O'Reilly associated with and soon sought to organize women who worked in manufacturing, the garment industry, and retail occupations, she viewed outworkers with a mixture of pity and fear. She also resented Catholic orphanages, which supported themselves by taking in outwork making gloves, shoes, shirts, and chairs, undercutting the prices paid to regular workers. Meeting many former inmates of these orphanages at work, she complained that their subjection to legions of rules and regulations left them submissive and unprepared for "independent action."[15] In contrast, O'Reilly grew up in a freethinking household, without formal ties to the Catholic Church.[16] Her mother encouraged her to think for herself and look out for her coworkers.

O'Reilly's father, John, had been a trade unionist and a socialist, and mother and daughter continued his commitment to both movements. They also shared a strong desire for education. After dinner, as one washed the dishes, the other would read aloud.[17] They hosted reading groups in their home, studying everything from Edward Bellamy's *Looking Backward* to Lester Frank Ward's *Dynamic Sociology*.[18] From her childhood on, Leonora accompanied Winifred to Cooper Union. After they moved uptown, they took the elevated railway back down to Astor Place to attend labor meetings or hear visiting speakers.[19]

New York City was a hotbed of labor activism during the 1880s, and Leonora O'Reilly's political outlook formed within this milieu. She consulted her godfather, Jean-Baptiste Hubert, about joining the Knights of Labor in March 1886, when a strike of horse car drivers on Grand Street had led to a neighborhood riot and citywide boycotts of streetcar lines. Hubert, a survivor of the Paris commune who worked as a machinist and a brass finisher, was a leader of the city's radical French workers. In a letter responding to O'Reilly's inquiry, Hubert described himself as touched by her youthful appreciation that "working-people [were] crushed by the existing state of society" and by her sympathy with their "struggles & Victory." He promised to propose her for membership in the Knights if Mother O'Reilly granted her permission.[20] Winifred not only allowed Leonora to join, she signed up herself.[21] By this point, nearly 70,000 workers in New York belonged to the Knights, which consisted of 415 locals, most of them mixed assemblies of workers from different trades.[22]

Recognizing Leonora's potential as an organizer, Hubert asked his friends Joseph Banes and Victor Drury to look after her and to help her advance within the labor movement. "They will take good care of you," Hubert promised; "you may trust them like brothers or Fathers."[23] Victor Drury, a veteran of the Paris Commune who led District 49, the largest and most powerful group within the Knights in New York, became an especially important mentor to O'Reilly. Inspired by Charles Fourier and Ferdinand LaSalle, the sixty-one year-old anarchist endorsed cooperation as an alternative to capitalism and rejected trade unions as regressive and exclusionary. He successfully pushed for mixed assemblies in the Knights in New York, viewing them as vehicles for building the broadest possible working-class consciousness.[24] While this strategy antagonized trade unionists, it made room for women. However, as Hubert admitted and O'Reilly no doubt experienced, the women who joined these mixed assemblies were in the minority and seldom spoke during meetings.[25]

Around the same time she joined the Knights, O'Reilly began attending meetings at the Central Labor Union, a diverse federation of workers from a variety of trade unions and labor organizations. Membership in the Knights and the CLU overlapped considerably. Both groups included a small minority of women within a broadly organized movement of native-born and immigrant workers demanding equal pay for equal work, an eight-hour day, and an end to child labor. Both leaned toward socialism, while seeking power in the capitalist labor market by sponsoring strikes, organizing boycotts, and supporting candidates for political office, such as the radical land reformer Henry George, who ran for mayor in the fall of 1886. While the culture of the Knights in New York City revolved around secret meetings open only to members who had been initiated and taught "the secret password," the CLU invited all the city's workers to picnics, concerts, lectures, and steamship excursions. Edward King, a leader of the CLU who worked as a type rubber, helped organize a Free Labor Reading Room, filled with reform-oriented books and newspapers.[26] King and O'Reilly soon became good friends.

Drury and King both supported O'Reilly's entry into the labor movement, where she undoubtedly joined forces with other female members. Yet no strong female leaders emerged within either the Knights or the CLU in New York City. In both organizations, men ran the meetings, and the small number of women who attended seemed intimidated. This limited degree of representation led O'Reilly and several other women she met there to establish the Working Women's Society (WWS). Reflecting the prevailing mood of the labor movement in New York City, the new organization included women employed in a variety of trades, including sewing, box making, and feather work, and clerks in retail stores.[27] The Knights of Labor would have categorized all these women as producers, and they may have felt linked by their common experience as wage-earning women within a labor movement dominated by men.

The Working Women's Society

Although the Working Women's Society has been cast as little more than a prelude to other, more enduring organizations, such as the New York Consumers' League, it had its own identity and agenda. Lack of organizational records make the history of the WWS difficult, if not impossible, to fully reconstruct, but letters saved by O'Reilly, along with scattered references in daily papers, offer evidence of working women's collective efforts to demand rights and respect at work and in the polity.

The WWS began by borrowing space from the CLU, but soon rented rooms at 27 Clinton Place on the Lower East Side and began holding weekly meetings early in 1886. O'Reilly joined a group of women who discussed their work conditions and considered strategies for improving them.[28] They identified women's organization into trade and labor unions as the best way to shorten hours and improve their wages. They also sought to enforce "existing laws relating to the protection of women and children in shops and factories." Determined to set their own agenda and to avoid becoming a sensationalist cause, they excluded men and reporters from their evening meetings.[29] O'Reilly joined a committee that reported weekly to the CLU. Fragmentary evidence suggests that the WWS expanded beyond the Lower East Side, helping to organize a strike of female thread workers in Newark, New Jersey, and appealing to women not to buy thread from the company until the conflict was resolved.[30]

By calling themselves "working women" instead of "girls," O'Reilly and her fellow workers staked out new ground, asserting their identity as self-respecting, independent adults organized to address the problems they faced as workers. Clubs for working girls already existed under the direction of the young philanthropist Grace Dodge.[31] These groups focused on self-improvement, offering classes in subjects such as cooking and hat trimming, and sponsoring "practical" talks focused on girls' family responsibilities. Before the 1890s, the uptown ladies who sponsored the clubs worked to instill "the three Ps" in their working-class protégés: Purity, Perseverance, and Pleasantness.[32] But O'Reilly and her friends—many of whom were, in fact, only sixteen or seventeen—had different objectives. By forming their own labor organization, they sought the same goals being won by organized men, including higher wages, an eight-hour day, and greater control over their working conditions. While working girls' clubs focused on affirming the respectability of their members, the Working Women's Society sought to win greater power for female workers.[33]

The young wage-earning women who joined the WWS sought social adulthood through collective organization. However, they struggled to find their way in a rapidly changing political climate. After Henry George's defeat in his campaign for mayor, the CLU fractured in a series of disputes over socialism, dual unionism, and participation in politics. In New York City and around the country, the Knights lost ground because of factionalism and the political repression that followed the Haymarket Affair.[34] The WWS gained new allies among the city's progressive clergymen. O'Reilly sought out Father James Otis Sargent Huntington, whom she knew as a member of the Knights of Labor and a supporter of District 49.[35] In the fall of 1886 the Harvard-educated priest, who directed an Episcopalian monastery on Seventh Street and Avenue C, drew headlines by campaigning from drays and carts on the Lower East Side on behalf of Henry George. Huntington believed in using the power of the church to crusade against poverty and social injustice. He supported George's proposal for a "single tax" on land as a means of redressing economic inequality. In May 1887 Huntington brought New York City clergymen concerned with social issues into the Church Association for the Advancement of the Interests of Labor (CAAIL), which offered advice and organizational support to the Working Women's Society.[36]

O'Reilly established a close working relationship with Huntington. During the summer of 1888, he invited O'Reilly to his family home, "Forty Acres," in Hadley, Massachusetts. It was her first trip out of the city. Huntington's sister, Ruth Sessions, a writer and social reformer, recalled O'Reilly as "pure Irish," tall, thin, attractive, charismatic, and devoted to the ideals of truth and justice. Sessions was shocked when O'Reilly identified herself as an "anarchist" who believed in "having no government." However, O'Reilly explained her belief that people could live harmoniously without government coercion if they followed "Christian law." She did not endorse violence, but believed that the government should be gradually abolished and replaced by workers' cooperatives. If O'Reilly shared anarchists' hostility to marriage as a coercive institution, she made no mention of it. She never married, but left no evidence of practicing or supporting "free love." Given O'Reilly's lack of formal education, Sessions was surprised by her "astounding familiarity with the great writers, both of history and economics."[37]

O'Reilly was steeped in radical ideas, but she was also pragmatic, and she had a knack for making connections among the city's most important female reformers. She soon became acquainted with Josephine Shaw Low-ell, a prominent philanthropist and leader of the New York State Board of Charities. By inviting Lowell to attend WWS meetings, O'Reilly appealed to "New York's most politically powerful woman."[38] Lowell came from a well-to-do Boston family of radical abolitionists and Civil War heroes: her brother, Robert Gould Shaw, had led the first African American regiment of the Union Army until his death on the battlefield, and her husband, Colonel Charles Russell Lowell, had also been killed in battle, leaving her a preg-nant widow at twenty. Lowell pledged herself to continue their mission of social improvement.[39] Like Father Huntington and other urban reformers from affluent backgrounds, Lowell soon became convinced of the need to understand poverty by witnessing it firsthand.

Meeting with the young members of the WWS, Lowell was impressed by their descriptions of the "moral and physical" dangers they faced at work. She found herself engaged by the women's "honor and generosity" and their "helplessness . . . to cope unorganized with the grave problems confronting them" without the force of public opinion. Lowell and her friend Louise Perkins both joined the group.[40] In addition to political advice, it seems likely that Lowell and Perkins offered help in paying the rent, a constant problem for the young women.[41] These new allies offered their support at the very moment that the Knights and the CLU were losing power in New York City and the American labor movement was shifting toward a more limited vision of the gains to be accomplished through organization. Samuel Gompers, the new president of the AFL, who had cut his teeth as the leader of the Cigar Makers' International Union in New York, rejected the cooperative vision and political aspirations of the earlier labor movement, calling instead for "pure and simple" trade unionism for skilled workers.[42] This shift in focus left little room for women like O'Reilly, who would have been defined as "unskilled," and for heterogeneous organizations like the WWS, which included women from different trades.[43]

Lowell's participation in the WWS marked a turning point in her career and in her understanding of the problem of poverty.[44] In 1889 she resigned from the State Board of Charities. As she explained in a letter to her sister, there was "far more important work to be done for working people." New York City had 200,000 woman and child wage earners, 75,000 of whom labored under "dreadful conditions" and in dire need. After years of charity work, Lowell concluded that criminals and paupers would not exist "if the working people had all they ought to have." She argued: "It is better to save them before they go under, than to spend your life fishing them out when they're half-drowned and taking care of them afterwards!"[45] Clearly, Lowell's encounter with the WWS transformed her understanding of poverty, just as her participation influenced the young women and their organization.

Lowell helped the WWS organize its first mass meeting on 2 February 1888, at Cooper Union.[46] The group used this public forum to announce an agenda that echoed the program Leonora Barry had articulated for the Knights of Labor: fostering organization among women workers, demanding equal pay for equal work, promoting protective labor legislation, and combating sexual harassment.[47] They promised to investigate and curb cases of "cruel and tyrannical treatment on the part of employers and their managers," such as withholding pay, "imposing fines and docking wages on trivial grounds," and using "abusive or insulting language." Any woman could join, "yet the majority of the members" were to be "self-supporting women."[48]

At O'Reilly's invitation, Lowell addressed the women assembled at Cooper Union. Her speech demonstrated her commitment to the cause, while suggesting the different perspective that "allies" brought to the problem of women's labor. Lowell saw great possibilities for the group. For years "the sufferings and wrongs of working women" had "been described and talked about," yet no one had taken any successful action "to remedy them." However, she disagreed with certain elements of the WWS platform. She criticized the precedence the women gave to raising wages over reducing hours and advised them that shorter hours were "the more important object . . . and also the one upon which you can the more easily secure public sympathy." Leisure was more important than wages, she argued, since it allowed workers to improve themselves and the quality of their work. Shorter hours would benefit everyone: employers, employees, and the public.[49]

Although Lowell knew that her audience was composed of working-class women, she addressed them as women, rather than as workers. Like members of the New England Women's Club, Lowell believed in the redemptive value of labor. She presented the women in her audience with a vision of their organization as a middle ground "between the toilers who are underpaid and overworked, and the women who are pining for want of work and are supported in enforced idleness." In Lowell's transcendent view of gender, women, even working women, were meant to be mediators between capital and labor. She worried that the group referred to employers as unjust and "tyrannical," warning her audience that they must be as sympathetic toward employers as they were toward workers. They must approach employers not like "enemies attacking," but like "judges, hearing and weighing evidence." She cautioned them against turning too hastily to strikes, which, "like war," brought "misery." Finally, she gave the women advice on the demeanor necessary for political success. At all costs, they must avoid "scolding" and seek to "conciliate and not antagonize."[50]

At age eighteen, O'Reilly admired Lowell's refinement and appreciated her concern. A decade later, however, she viewed Lowell's advice as condescending and counterproductive. In a speech addressed to women who worked in shops, factories, and domestic service, O'Reilly insisted: "Working for wages . . . should be treated the same for a woman as for a man." She blamed "some of the best intentioned people in the world" for "hinder[ing] the progress of woman in the industrial movement through fear that workingwomen may do something 'unladylike.'" By 1899 O'Reilly was encouraging women to overcome their timidity and organize to gain political rights and demand equal pay for equal work.[51] Her earlier experience with the WWS suggests the awkward position of working women who wanted to organize during the 1880s and 1890s. Although they sought goals similar to those of men in craft unions, they lost these men as allies once the Knights of Labor declined and the labor movement became more limited to the skilled trades. Lack of financial resources and organizational backing pushed them toward alliances with women like Lowell, who were sympathetic but held conservative ideas of proper, "ladylike" behavior. While Lowell's advice may have been calculated to win public sympathy, it left working-class women with a limited range of possibilities for collective action.

Regardless of the value of Lowell's advice, her visibility as a supporter of the WWS undoubtedly aided the group in attracting other powerful women as allies.[52] Helen Campbell, the author of *Prisoners of Poverty*, and Ida Van Etten, an idealistic young journalist, both joined after Lowell's speech at Cooper Union. In the fall of 1888 the group, now composed of equal numbers of wage earners and non–wage earners, supported female ostrich feather workers striking for better wages and improved conditions. Adopting techniques pioneered by the Knights and the CLU, the wealthier members showed their support for the striking workers by refusing to buy feather boas from dealers the workers had identified as unfair.[53] The strike, which began in October 1888 and lasted until March 1889, eventually drew in thousands of workers. Ultimately, the manufacturers agreed to improve conditions, but they did not raise wages or recognize the feather workers' union.[54] Out of this experience, the group moved forward with a dual mission: teaching working women the value of organizing, and teaching female consumers to think about the workers who produced the goods they purchased.[55]

With the help of its allies, the WWS began taking steps to gain publicity in order to increase public support. At a meeting held for the press and for leaders of women's clubs, Ida Van Etten "made an eloquent plea for help and sympathy from the wealthy and educated women of New York for their toiling and downtrodden sisters." At this and other meetings, the WWS took the unorthodox step of introducing working women to speak on their own behalf. Leonora O'Reilly, then working in a shirtwaist factory, joined two veterans of the recent feather strike in making "short addresses, telling the character of and remuneration for their work." Father Huntington then addressed the audience, urging the fifty ladies in attendance "to feel it their personal duty . . . to correct the social evil that permits their unfortunate sisters to be so frightfully overworked and badly paid." Affected by the presentation, many of the ladies, including the syndicated journalist and club leader Jane (Jennie June) Croly, "left their names and addresses, and expressed a willingness to answer any call upon them for the working girls' cause."[56]

From 1889 to 1890, the "ladies" who had joined the WWS began to take a more active role in setting the agenda. The group's activities shifted from encouraging organization and supporting striking women toward goals the original group had viewed as secondary: investigating labor conditions and advocating legislation. It is not clear from the surviving records whether working-class members contested this new emphasis, or deferred to these better educated, more influential women. Under the direction of Ida Van Etten, members of the WWS drafted a bill introduced in the New York state legislature "providing for women factory inspectors, including mercantile establishments, and limiting [women's hours] to sixty per week." Female factory inspectors were a means of addressing the problems of sexual abuse and the harassment of female workers.[57] The CLU supported the bill.[58] The legislature approved female inspectors for factories, but rejected inspection of department stores and limitations on women's hours.[59] If given a choice, most working women would have preferred higher wages to shorter hours, but state laws setting a minimum wage for women would not become politically tenable until the 1910s, when reformers used arguments about women's role as future mothers to carve out an exception to freedom of contract. Even then, minimum wages for women would be set at paltry levels and were vulnerable to constitutional challenge.[60]

The WWS turned to investigation to build public support for new legislation limiting women's working hours and subjecting department stores to inspection. By using investigation as a tool for advocacy, the group followed patterns established by female members of the Knights of Labor and by Helen Campbell, who had written a powerful exposé of the conditions of New York City's female needleworkers several years earlier. Alice Woodbridge, a leader of the WWS who had worked as a retail clerk and had at least a common school education, led the effort. Woodbridge and her colleagues interviewed numerous saleswomen, questioning them about their wages, hours, and working conditions. Lowell helped Woodbridge organize her report and encouraged her to present it to Dr. Mary Putnam Jacobi, a nationally known expert on women's health and a supporter of reform causes.[61] Lowell and Jacobi then called a small group of women to meet at the downtown offices of the WWS to discuss the report.[62]

Maud Nathan, a member of one of New York City's oldest and most elite Sephardic Jewish families, vividly recalled the meeting. Her own life had consisted of genteel charity work and socializing in the upper strata of New York and Saratoga society. The image of Alice Woodbridge "with her fawn-like eyes, her halo of golden-red hair" reading her report to "the group of strange, aloof women" had a galvanizing effect on Nathan and the other women from uptown. Woodbridge's revelations of retail workers' long hours, low wages, physical exhaustion, and arbitrary treatment "proved startling." Shocked by these disclosures, the genteel audience was aroused "to sympathetic indignation," a central component of the progressive impulse toward social reform.[63] Woodbridge presented her findings in subsequent meetings "held in the drawing rooms of Mrs. Josephine Shaw Lowell and other ladies."[64] Her appearances stimulated support for the legislation favored by the WWS, although the road to passing that legislation would be longer and more difficult than advocates anticipated and its results would prove disappointing. More immediately, the report prepared by the WWS inspired the women of the "better classes" moved by Woodbridge's presentations to form their own organization.

The New York Consumers' League

As a garment worker, Leonora O'Reilly had no place in the New York Consumers' League. The new organization excluded both employers and employees from joining, and it focused exclusively on retail workers. The membership of the WWS was initially working-class and had become cross-class, but the NYCL was composed exclusively of affluent women willing and able to shop ethically. This new brand of consumer activism departed from the practices pioneered by the Gilded Age labor movement, which sought to instill in workers a dual understanding of themselves as producers and consumers, and included men as well as women.

Across the country, women's growing presence as workers in mass production signaled broader economic shifts in the manufacture, distribution, and sale of consumer goods. In large cities, palatial department stores stocked with mass-produced goods proliferated, and women gained new visibility as salesclerks. From 1880 to 1890 the number of female retail clerks increased from fewer than 8,000 to more than 58,000. As historian Susan

Porter Benson explains, by 1890 "selling was well established as a women's occupation." Like factory work, retail sales work was segregated by sex, race, and nationality. Since department stores relied on appearances to sell goods, managers sought to match salesclerks to their desired clientele, hiring native-born white women with neat appearances, clear diction, and good manners. They excluded African American women and recently arrived immigrants as undesirable. However, merchants and managers also tried to maintain class distinctions between their employees and their customers by requiring saleswomen to dress in dark colors and to treat their customers deferentially.[65] Working-class women who once would have worked as servants in private households were now recast as service workers, and middle-class and elite women assumed new identities as consumers.

Theodore Dreiser's popular novel *Sister Carrie* capitalized on public anxiety about female virtue in an increasingly commercialized society. Newly arrived in Chicago and in search of a job, Carrie visits a department store, where she is overcome by "desire" for the "remarkable displays of trinkets, dress goods, shoes, stationery, [and] jewelry" laid out before her in "dazzling" array. From here, it is but a few short steps to seduction by a man who takes her shopping for new clothes. Despite their "independent air," sales girls often struggled to afford the clothes they needed for work.[66] Many people assumed that this situation left them vulnerable to prostitution, especially since they were required to wait on any man who entered the store.[67]

In May 1890, the WWS called a "mass meeting" at Chickering Hall, in the heart of the retail district, to discuss the labor conditions in department stores.[68] The event was designed to publicize Woodbridge's report and create public recognition of the need for a new consumers' organization to combat the problems Woodbridge and the WWS had identified.[69] The report and the meeting that followed sought to expand the definition of working women, typically imagined as industrial workers, to include employees of retail stores. Contesting merchants' claims, the WWS and the NYCL depicted modern retail stores as more akin to factories than to households, and thus rightly subject to state inspection and regulation. Although it recast department stores from leisure spaces for a shopping public to workplaces for thousands of girls and women, this definition continued to exclude domestic spaces from investigation or regulation. Domestic workplaces and household labor conditions receded into the background, as public attention shifted toward the growing number of highly visible women who worked in department stores.

Jacob Riis used the "great public meeting" called by the WWS at Chickering Hall as a touchstone for a dawning public consciousness of the desperate poverty endured by many women who worked full time.[70] As the *New York Times* reported the next day, the meeting, held at eight in the evening on Tuesday, 6 May 1890, attracted a large crowd, composed of many "more shop girls than consumers." The shop girls came after work, dressed in "gorgeous light costumes," to hear their conditions discussed.[71] We do not know whether Leonora O'Reilly attended after work, but if she did, she may have felt out of place in her plain white shirtwaist and dark skirt. The evening hour made it unlikely that middle-class women would attend; "respectable" women might shop during they day, but did not go out at night without a chaperone. Women from the propertied class who identified themselves as reformers claimed a wider range of motion in order to address the problems of urban poverty.[72] At least one reporter found the absence of women on the program "curious" and disappointing, given the excitement still attached to women speaking in public.[73] Members of the WWS may have been advised by Josephine Shaw Lowell not to take the podium. Speaking in the evening before a mixed audience of men and women was still regarded as violating the rules of propriety. Individual working-class women could not afford this risk to their reputations, while a public exhibition of young women might have raised questions about the respectability of the entire undertaking. Instead, Everett P. Wheeler, a prominent attorney, settlement house worker, and advocate of civil service reform, presided.[74]

Drawing on the popular labor reform language of wage slavery, Wheeler introduced the meeting "as an attempt to create public sentiment in regard to the horrors of the white slavery in the retail dry goods stores of this city."[75] The lack of African American or even immigrant employees in department stores made this language particularly fitting, even as it affirmed rather than critiqued the city's pervasive patterns of occupational segregation, which relegated most African American women to domestic work and most new immigrants to sweatshops. Of all the city's wage-earning women, shop girls were undoubtedly the "whitest." As Wheeler recognized, the status of department store clerks as clean, attractive, native-born white women made them victims with whom the public could sympathize, rather than the dirty, threatening agents of anarchy associated with the labor movement since the Haymarket Affair.[76]

Archibald Sessions, a Brooklyn lawyer and reformer, presented Alice Woodbridge's "Report on the Condition of Working Women in New York Retail Stores." Sessions, who was married to Ruth Huntington Sessions, must have been introduced to the WWS by his brother-in-law, Father James Otis Huntington. The problems Woodbridge's report identified—long hours, low pay, unfair fines, dirty toilets, and underage workers—were certainly familiar to an audience composed primarily of working women. The crowd's enthusiastic response suggests that these women found it gratifying to hear their grievances expressed publicly. Some members of the audience might have participated in the investigation, which was based on extensive personal interviews.[77] The presence of reporters from all of the city's major daily papers created a secondary audience, the reading public, who were probably surprised to learn that mistreatment of female workers lurked behind the elegant façades of New York's retail palaces.

Although Woodbridge herself had worked as a retail clerk, her investigation appropriated the journalistic convention of exposing "how the other half lives" as a springboard for social critique. In his book of that title published later that year, Jacob Riis relied heavily on Woodbridge's report to describe the conditions of New York's working girls.[78] Like Riis, Woodbridge used vivid descriptions of working women's lives to evoke public sympathy. She related the story of one woman who worked in a Broadway store who took home only three dollars a week after deductions of fines for petty offenses. She paid $1.50 for her room. Her breakfast consisted of a cup of coffee and she went without lunch, eating only a single meal in the evening. A saleswoman simply could not subsist on her salary, Woodbridge explained, "without assistance" from relatives and friends or "without depriving herself of real necessities."[79]

In *Prisoners of Poverty*, Helen Campbell had demystified commodity production. Alice Woodbridge now did the same for labor conditions within department stores. Attractive displays of goods concealed poor sanitary conditions, she warned. Female cashiers worked in unventilated basements, which were breeding grounds for respiratory diseases, such as tuberculosis. The Board of Health ignored "horrible" toilet arrangements, which the audience would have interpreted as an offense to women's modesty and a potential source of disease. Men's and women's toilets were often dirty, lacked privacy, and opened onto the lunchroom. Laws requiring seats for saleswomen, which had been put on the books in 1881 to protect women from the uterine damage believed to result from long hours of standing, "were generally ignored." In one store where seats were provided, saleswomen were fined for using them. Workers were fatigued by long hours with limited breaks. In a workday that began officially at eight and ended at six, saleswomen were given only a half-hour to eat lunch. Moreover, clerks were often required to stay after closing to arrange stock, without compensation. During the three or four weeks before Christmas, they stayed at work until eleven or twelve o'clock at night "without supper or extra pay."

Women who worked in department stores were particularly alarmed by the large numbers of children under the age of fourteen, the legal age of employment, who labored at tasks "far beyond their strength," for wages seldom exceeding $1.50 or $2.00 a week. The girls were especially vulnerable to sexual harassment. Saleswomen reported that salesmen frequently addressed "these little cash girls" in "shocking" language. Board of Education inspections were irregular and ineffective at keeping children under fourteen in school, since their families needed their earnings and employers relied on their inexpensive labor.[80]

In retail occupations, as in manufacturing, wages remained a key complaint. Women found it nearly impossible to live on wages as low as $4.50 or $5.00 a week. Employers pretended that their female employees did not need to support themselves. In fact, Woodbridge insisted, "the majority of women pay board or help support a family." Her report closed by invoking the familiar story of low wages pushing working women into prostitution. Yet Woodbridge revised the dominant narrative, insisting that the "frail, toil-worn woman" who turned to prostitution was not evil, but heroic. Although a working woman might sell her body for bread, her "hands and her heart [were] pure, and her white robe of virtue yet unsullied." In Woodbridge's moral scheme, a working woman's sale of sex for money symbolized her willingness to sacrifice herself to support her family. By blurring the line between virtuous and fallen women, Woodbridge challenged middle-class standards of respectability, and she placed the blame for prostitution on employers who underpaid their female employees.[81] Woodbridge ended with a plea for action on behalf of the underpaid, overworked saleswoman, asking, "Shall we not guard her that her light may glorify the pages of history which we make today?"[82] She insisted on the need to protect women who labored outside the bounds of their own families.

Father Huntington, whom Leonora O'Reilly had cultivated as a supporter of the WWS, now extended his moral prestige to the NYCL. According to one reporter, Huntington's "fine manly speech" captured the high moral tone of the evening. "In this movement," he explained, "we neither wish to be taken for Socialists or Radicals." Like Henry George, Huntington disagreed with state-sponsored socialism, which he viewed as a threat to individual liberty.[83] Like Josephine Shaw Lowell, Huntington imagined working women as a force for transcending class conflict in a divided city. Although he supported workers' right to organize, he believed that female store clerks should look toward socially concerned women of the "better classes" to improve their conditions rather than form a labor union of their own. He described the struggle at hand as "a battle for humanity, for womanhood, for future generations."[84] While claiming that this struggle was moral rather than political, he urged concrete reforms: an eight-hour day, "living wages," pay for overtime, a reduction of fines, and sanitary workplaces.

Without calling it by name, Huntington introduced the NYCL as a force for change. He called on ladies who were "the leaders of society to really become so and assist their poor sisters by refusing their patronage to commercial enterprises" that treated workers unfairly—cleverly shifting the popular meaning of *society* to evoke civic responsibility. To this end, "a commission of ladies should compile a 'white list' of those houses which treat their employés like human beings." The list should be sent "to every woman in the so-called social directory." To gain or retain the patronage of these wealthy, influential women, he assured the audience, stores "would make radical changes in their system of conducting business."[85] These new plans to raise consumer consciousness closely mirrored strategies promoted by Leonora Barry in the Knights of Labor, but they shifted their target from men and women of the working class to women of the bourgeoisie, whose consumer activism confirmed and justified their class position.[86] Women working in retail stores would be the beneficiaries of this activism, not its agents.

After the speeches, a number of resolutions were passed "enthusiastically." These included calls for the Board of Health to correct poor sanitary conditions and for the state legislature to consider a new law limiting saleswomen's hours. Clergymen and editors were asked to use public opinion "to help the salesgirls improve their condition of employment." Saleswomen were urged "to combine for their own protection," although far more time at the meeting had been devoted to encouraging bourgeois women to act as their protectors.[87] This change in direction—from working-class women's own determination to assert their right to dignity and equal pay at work to bourgeois women's view of themselves as responsible for protecting public health—marked the beginning of the NYCL.

Maude Nathan looked toward London, where a recently formed Consumers' League offered a model for upper-class women interested in helping downtrodden shop girls. That organization maintained a register of "fair houses," shops the public could patronize with confidence that female workers received "decent living wages." In New York, Nathan proposed creating a white list of stores that treated their female employees fairly. As the *Washington Post* noted, the white list was "virtually a boycott pronounced by women against men who underpay their sex."[88] Unlike the boycott, however, the white list was a positive means of promoting what Helen Campbell had described as "ethical consumption." The white list also offered a way around recent court rulings construing boycotts of black-listed companies as criminal conspiracies to deprive business owners of their liberty.[89] As Campbell had hoped, bourgeois women now took the helm of the campaign for ethical consumption, rejecting the strident language of class conflict in favor of a call for cross-class cooperation to protect vulnerable "working girls."[90] Lowell, Nathan, Campbell, and Jacobi positioned themselves as civic mothers protecting the city's young white working girls and disciplining its unruly merchant capitalists. Nathan's participation in the league may have stemmed from her desire to revise the popular image of the city's Jews from cutthroat capitalists to principled citizens concerned with social justice.[91]

As it burst onto the public scene, the NYCL campaign to help over-worked shop girls took up most of the public space the press and the city's reformers allocated to consideration of working women and their problems. O'Reilly tried to counteract this exclusive focus on saleswomen by speaking to women's clubs about the wages paid to women who *made* garments, but her appeals had little impact.[92] Ironically, the organization she helped establish ended up marginalizing her and the city's other industrially employed women. To the degree that newspapers reported on working women, they focused on wealthy women's efforts on behalf of poor salesclerks, playing off familiar narratives of the geographic proximity and social distance between the opulence of Fifth Avenue and the squalor of the Lower East Side.[93] As in Nelson's series on "City Slave Girls" or Campbell's stories in *Prisoners of Poverty,* these stories were calculated to stimulate public sentiment in favor of reform. In a further echo of "City Slave Girls," Josephine Shaw Lowell associated the NYCL campaign on behalf of overworked shop girls with earlier boycotts of products made by slave labor.[94] This rhetorical strategy affirmed the idea of female department store clerks as "wage slaves" and distanced the NYCL from the radicalism of the immigrant working class, whose boycotts were perceived as a form of class warfare and were dealt with harshly by the police and the courts.[95]

The WWS had called for female wage earners to direct their own organization, looking toward wealthier women to provide financial support and political connections. As those wealthy allies broke off to form their own organization, the WWS lost important supporters. Ida Van Etten, who was an inspiring public speaker and an effective builder of alliances with wealthy women and with male labor leaders, proved incompetent at managing the group's funds.[96] Financial problems, combined with the loss of the feather workers' strike in the spring of 1889, undermined the strength of the organization. However, Van Etten remained an active and outspoken leader, and the organization retained a public presence into the early 1890s. In 1890, for example, Van Etten met with a representative of the Farmer's Alliance, who had read about the exploitation of New York's sewing women and wanted to work with the WWS to establish a cooperative shop to produce ready-made clothing under fair conditions for purchase by Alliance members. Later that year, Van Etten attended the annual convention of the American Federation of Labor in Detroit, where she spoke on the condition of women workers "under the present industrial system," joining Minneapolis labor journalist Eva McDonald Valesh as one of two women on the program.[97]

Van Etten's speech at the AFL suggested the national and international dimensions of the problems she had tried to address with the WWS. She linked women's growing employment to the development of "so-called labor-saving machinery," such as the sewing machine, which had greatly increased industrial output while bringing "no advantage to the women workers." With one woman now able to do the work formerly done by one hundred, large numbers of women were desperate for employment, no matter how low the wages. These women, many with children to feed, became fodder for clothing subcontractors, who farmed out piecework to tenement house dwellers at starvation rates. Although Van Etten's own experience was limited to New York City, she had learned through discussion and reading that "the same conditions prevail in Philadelphia, Boston, Chicago and Cincinnati." Cities around the country seemed to be "tending in the same direction."

Addressing union men, Van Etten spoke to them of their own concerns: having to accept reductions in their wages when employers threatened to replace them with women, who invariably earned less even if they were doing an equivalent job. Union men could either expand their movement to include women or risk being reduced to similar conditions as low-paid workers with limited control over their conditions of labor.

Van Etten envisioned a positive role for the state in addressing the problem of women's labor exploitation. In this respect, she argued, the United States lagged far behind many European nations, especially Germany, where the "most eminent statesmen and political economists" were giving their "best thought and efforts" to improving the conditions of industrial workers. Laws limiting hours in factories were a start, but in New York state these laws applied only to minors and to women under twenty-one, a fact the WWS had been lobbying to change by presenting legislation limiting the hours of all women employed in retail and industrial occupations to sixty per week.

While Van Etten spoke at some length of the possibilities for labor legislation and made several references to the superiority of socialism to capitalism as a system of producing and distributing wealth, she identified organization of working women as the single most significant factor in changing their conditions. She urged the trade union men assembled before her in Detroit to become more than "passive lookers-on" in wage-earning women's "struggle for existence." Alluding to recent events in her own organization, Van Etten warned that "without the moral and financial support" of organized men, working women "truly become *the victims of charity and philanthropy*." While working men had gained a "sturdy independence" through their organizations, working women who lacked their own organizations were deprived of an equivalent "moral and intellectual independence" and left instead with a "cringing, false respect for money and position." In short, she blamed trade unionists for pushing wage-earning women out of the labor movement and into the arms of bourgeois reformers.

In conclusion, Van Etten contended that women workers "must become organized and receive not only equal pay for equal work, but also equal opportunities for working." If they did not, she warned, they would form "an inferior class," whose presence would drive down wages and extend hours in every trade they entered. Furthermore, if left unorganized, women could be used as strikebreakers. Van Etten urged the men to assist women in forming their own branches of existing trade organizations, "even in the mixed trades, with their own meetings carried on entirely by themselves, with their own presiding officers." Reflecting the history of women's marginalization within the mixed locals of the Knights of Labor, she championed the value of single-sex organizations for working women, even as she pushed for their full integration into trade unions. She warned against expecting women "to become mere addenda to men's organizations," arguing that "neither men nor women will long feel an interest in an organization that is not under their direct management."[98]

Van Etten presented her socialist analysis at the same meeting at which Samuel Gompers, the president of the AFL, rejected socialism as a dangerous distraction from "pure and simple" trade unionism. As Gompers saw it, trade unions should focus on raising wages and shortening hours rather than pursuing broader social and political changes, such as those entertained by the Knights of Labor, which had called for an abolition of the "wages system" and supported candidates for public office.[99] Van Etten and Valesh did persuade Gompers to hire Mary Kenney briefly as the AFL's first female organizer. Ultimately, however, the AFL took no sustained interest in organizing female workers. In New York, this attitude filtered down into the CLU, which was transformed from a diverse and inclusive labor organization in the 1880s into a citywide assembly of trade unions pursuing goals set by the AFL in the 1890s.[100] CAAIL, too, became a more conservative supporter of trade union goals, especially after 1892 when Father Huntington left the Lower East Side and moved the Order of the Holy Cross to rural Maryland.[101]

The WWS continued to take a broad approach to the problems of women's economic inequality. In 1892 the group formed a Tenement House Committee to investigate poor housing conditions in their downtown neighborhood, gaining the support of clergymen in bringing complaints to the city's Health and Building departments. Consulting with Carroll D. Wright, the director of the U.S. Bureau of Labor Statistics, they investigated the conditions of the city's working women, but they adopted a much broader definition than Wright did in his investigations, which focused exclusively on young women employed full time in industrial occupations. The WWS included the unemployed, residents of almshouses, domestic servants, and middle-aged women with chronic difficulty finding work. As a partial solution, the group proposed a state-sponsored system of social insurance, funded by small deductions from women's weekly wages up until age forty-five, creating an annuity whose proceeds would be disbursed as income to women over fifty. Although they acknowledged that some critics would view their plan "as another step toward paternalism," they framed it as a means of securing "independence to those whose days of labor should be over." They asserted "the responsibility of the state" to support and protect "those who devote a lifetime to increasing its industrial and commercial prosperity."[102] Extending the logic of working women's entitlement to rights as well as benefits, they cooperated with the CLU in cosponsoring a bill calling for suffrage for self-supporting women.[103]

Within a few years, however, the character of the WWS and the CLU changed in ways that made further collaboration impossible. The leadership of the CLU aligned itself with the AFL, and it became a conservative and, some charged, corrupt proponent of trade unionism, showing little interest in organizing working women.[104] Ida Van Etten, who had moved to Paris to study European socialism, was found dead of starvation.[105] Her tragic ending came as a blow to Leonora O'Reilly and her old friends in the Working Women's Society and suggested the obstacles Van Etten faced in trying to follow through on her ideals.[106] Alice Woodbridge remained earnest in her support for mercantile inspection, but no longer had a genuine organization of working-class women behind her, but rather one that subsisted on contributions from wealthy women.[107] Leonora O'Reilly left the organization.

The NYCL now became the leading voice in New York City for women's labor reform. Many former allies of the WWS and important formulators of ideas about women and work joined the new organization. Josephine Shaw Lowell became its first president. Helen Campbell and Mary Putnam Jacobi both became vice presidents. Maud Nathan became an enthusiastic supporter, succeeding Lowell as president in 1897. Helen Campbell captured the sense of social responsibility and desire for control that animated the new organization: "As women, we are bound, by every law of justice, to aid all other women in their struggle. We are equally bound to define the nature, the necessities, and the limits of such struggle."[108] For Campbell and other NYCL members, those limits centered on the ability of educated women to decide what was best for working women, an assumption that did little to involve saleswomen in organizing to improve their own conditions. This stance sapped any interest working women might have in the League, and at times led them to resent being portrayed as objects for public sympathy.[109] With Lowell's intervention, the NYCL was able to secure space in the United Charities Building, an impressive new structure on the corner of East 22nd Street and Park Avenue funded by a philanthropist to provide low-cost office space to the Charity Organization Society and the Association for Improving the Condition of the Poor.[110] Although the new headquarters of the NYCL was within walking distance of the headquarters of the WWS, it occupied a very different place in the city's social geography.

The wealthy, progressive women who led the NYCL—Josephine Shaw Lowell, Helen Campbell, Maud Nathan, and Mary Putnam Jacobi—sought to transform the purchasing power of women of their class into political and economic power. Determined to control their own organization, to exude an air of impartiality, and to command public authority, they excluded retail workers as well as employers from membership. They situated themselves as the indirect employers of women and children in retail stores and claimed responsibility for their conditions. Middle-class women dealt with store clerks directly, making the link between workers and consumers more tangible. League leaders emphasized educating and organizing women of their own class to shop ethically.[111] Their activities helped establish middle-class and elite consumers as a self-conscious group. While reluctant to publish stories critical of the department stores whose advertising constituted a major source of revenue for city newspapers, the press proved receptive to stories of New York's wealthiest women helping the city's most downtrodden.[112] Within the parameters of its bourgeois class affiliation and perspective, the NYCL carried out its work zealously. Members pledged, whenever possible, to patronize stores on the white list.[113] The first list, published in 1891, had eight names on it; the following year, it had eleven more.[114] Within a few years, the NYCL had sent the white list to 4,000 women whose names appeared in the social register, distributed it to 7,000 newspapers, and placed it in the Ladies Parlors in twenty of the city's largest hotels.[115]

To be included on the white list, stores were required to follow the provisions for a "fair house" outlined by the NYCL. Following the WWS, the NYCL demanded that stores pay men and women equally when they did the same job. However, there is little evidence that the League pursued complaints of unequal pay. In departments populated exclusively by women, the NYCL set wage rates at six dollars per week for "experienced adult workers." This commonly agreed-upon minimum rate of pay reflected popular assumptions that women's wages needed to cover their individual living costs rather than provide family support.[116] It did represent a substantial raise from the $4.50 to $5.00 a week Woodbridge found some stores paying women. Yet the NYCL set the minimum for cash girls at just two dollars a week. To combat the practice of keeping clerks after work to arrange merchandise, the NYCL demanded that women be excused promptly at six o'clock, or be paid for overtime. However, the NYCL did not demand overtime rates of pay, a standard being won by unionized men in the building trades, who used strikes to establish an eight-hour day and time-and-a-half for overtime.[117] Heeding Lowell's advice, the NYCL focused on limiting hours rather than raising wages as an improvement more likely to be supported by the public and accepted by employers. The white list also required basic public health provisions, such as the separation of toilets from lunch rooms, the use of seats as required by law, and the prohibition of employment of children under fourteen.[118]

Merchants strongly opposed increased public oversight of their operations, whether it came from the NYCL or from the state. They threatened to retaliate against League members by investigating how they treated their own domestic help. Would the bourgeois women who fought so ardently for the saleswomen be willing to answer questions about "how many hours their housemaids worked, or how late at night they were obliged to continue their service, or whether they were given vacations with pay?" According to Maud Nathan, these "arguments cooled the ardour of many members of the Consumers' League." Socially prominent women "were not so eager to have an investigation conducted of conditions" for their domestic workers.[119]

Mary Putnam Jacobi, a popular authority on women's health and an advocate of expanded educational and economic opportunities for women, rebutted the idea that domestic labor relations deserved public investigation. Like her friend Helen Campbell, Jacobi saw labor exploitation as the result of a capitalist search for ever greater profits. Jacobi distinguished between the economics of business and households: businesses made money, while households spent it. Retail workers were rightly considered industrial workers since their work created profit for their employers. Their wages represented their share of this profit. However, she argued, the labor of personal service workers, such as physicians and domestic servants, yielded no profit to those who hired them. These professional and domestic servants worked to increase health and happiness. The personal nature of their relationship to the individual who paid them made public investigation both indelicate and impractical.[120]

Jacobi may have been unique in attempting to provide a logical explanation for the difference between domestic servants and industrial or retail workers, but her assumptions of difference were widely shared. Despite the widespread and visible presence of women wage earners, women were still popularly understood as essentially domestic creatures who belonged, ideally, in homes. For reasons that were seldom articulated, women working as household servants were assumed to be within their proper sphere and not in need of the kinds of protections necessary for those who entered factories and retail stores. The increasing employment of Irish and African American women as servants strengthened these assumptions as many native-born Americans considered women of both "races" particularly well suited for menial labor.[121] Furthermore, middle-class households were considered to be private spaces where no real "work" took place.

Jacobi's own reliance on servants suggests the real reason for her distinction between domestic and industrial or retail workers. Like other members of the NYCL, Jacobi's professional and voluntary activities depended on her ability to hire other women to cook, clean, sew, and watch her children. Jacobi's own loathing for domestic toil once led her to assert that women never "performed any household labor when they could afford to own slaves or pay servants to do it for them."[122] Like Helen Campbell's myopic analysis of domestic service in *Prisoners of Poverty,* Jacobi's view was limited by her class position, which kept her from seeing domestic servants as workers who might need protection as much as women who worked in stores or factories. By the turn of the twentieth century, women's labor reformers such as Charlotte Perkins Gilman suggested solving the "servant problem" by moving work such as cooking and child care outside of individual households, into cooperatives or female-run businesses. The NYCL did not consider these alternative arrangements, insisting instead on a fundamental difference between domestic employees in private households and women employed outside of households in profit-making enterprises such as stores and factories.

League members' class position also came into play when considering the question of labor organization. Most members were not hostile to labor organization, and many supported it, at least in theory.[123] Leaders of the NYCL were proud that the recently formed Retail Clerks Protective Association shared many of their objectives.[124] The new union paid sick benefits and death benefits, and in Chicago it succeeded in winning early closings two nights a week. However, the total number of members was small, and women were an even smaller minority; no more than 2 percent of all saleswomen belonged to unions in the 1890s.[125] Given the weakness of unionism in the retail sector, leaders of the NYCL saw themselves as working toward similar goals by different means.

However, many NYCL members imagined their work as a substitute for workers' organization. They believed that the NYCL could act more effectively for young female retail workers than they could act for themselves.[126] League members, who tended to be older than retail workers, certainly had financial resources, leisure time, organizational experience, and political connections that were impossible for working women to muster. However, their characterization of saleswomen as "timid and unaccustomed to associated action" and as lacking "the wisdom, strength of character, or experience which would enable them to act on their own behalf" may have been self-serving.[127] In a period marked by frequent strikes of working men in New York City and around the nation, and by the strident language of class conflict, bourgeois members of the NYCL may have found it comforting to imagine native-born working-class women as victims they could rescue, rather than as potential insurgents they should fear.

Saleswomen had mixed opinions about the NYCL. Maud Nathan was fond of quoting saleswomen who thanked the League for investigating and improving their conditions. Many working women viewed the NYCL as a more effective agency to appeal to than the Board of Health; women employed in department stores appreciated the cleaner toilets, better lunchrooms, and places to sit that the NYCL had secured. Yet some saleswomen found League members condescending. One newspaper story quoted saleswomen describing NYCL members as "sympathetic cranks," do-gooders who wasted their time by asking them questions.[128] Other working women resented the NYCL for damaging their reputations by exaggerating their problems to the public.[129] Newspapers, the major source of information on working women's opinions, were particularly biased on this issue. Although they had initially celebrated the NYCL and eagerly reported on the activities of New York society women on behalf of their less fortunate sisters, press coverage became more critical in the mid-1890s, when the NYCL began making more forceful demands for mercantile inspection and department stores began organizing to defend themselves against further inspection and regulation.[130] Department stores were major advertisers, and publishers tried to keep the stores happy. Nathan found this conflict of interest a major obstacle in gaining publicity for the movement.[131]

In reality, many saleswomen were not "timid" or "unaccustomed to associated action." When one store owner suddenly lowered wages, a "fourteen year old girl led the others in open rebellion." She and the other workers went to their employer "with their hats and coats on, saying they were going home." He responded by sending them back to work at their old wages.[132] In another incident, five hundred saleswomen from the Siegel-Cooper Department Store gathered outside the ornate building on Sixth Avenue and 18th Street and spontaneously threatened to strike after the management sent out security guards to chase away the men waiting to escort them home after work. Saleswomen leaving work from other department stores "increased the hubub, with offers of sympathy and help."[133] Siegel-Cooper workers also challenged the legality of the company union, to which they were forced to pay monthly dues as a condition of employment.[134] Clearly, female workers could be militant.[135] However, these isolated instances did not lead to lasting or effective workers' organizations, a common problem in nearly all areas of women's employment. In retail work as in manufacturing, most women worked in jobs where they could be easily replaced. Employers often defeated women's attempts to unionize simply by firing the workers who were involved. Few wage-earning women had the free time to attend meetings, since they generally worked long hours and had shopping and housework to do after work. Low pay meant little extra money to spend on dues. Locating space for meetings was always a problem, since working women could not gather in saloons, as working men often did, and going out alone at night after work might be dangerous. Lack of support from male trade unionists only compounded these difficulties, leaving women who were dissatisfied with their conditions few avenues of effective action.[136]

From the Shirtwaist Shop to the Social Reform Club

In the summer of 1892 Leonora O'Reilly continued to work from eight to six at Bellamy's shirt shop. Her spirits slumped as she contemplated the demise of her youthful hopes for social change. The Knights of Labor and the WWS had both faded into obscurity, and the CLU no longer seemed interested in organizing women. Her friend Louise Perkins, who had been an ally of the WWS before moving to Concord, Massachusetts, responded to a sad, tired letter from O'Reilly: "I can imagine that many things have been a keen disappointment to you. Time comes to us all when our bright hopes seem to us dust and ashes, when all the rowing is against the tide. You are young dear and must not yield to such feelings." Although O'Reilly was dispirited, she had not given up hope. Perhaps, like Perkins, she was encouraged that the great strike at Homestead would be a chance "for labour to make its claims really understood" to a "startled" public. That spring, O'Reilly met Mary Kenney, the AFL's first female organizer, who came to New York to survey the conditions of women's labor and to explore the possibility of organizing into trade unions women who made shirts, underwear, and household linens. Kenney hired a hall where she and O'Reilly spoke in favor of organization as a means of ending sweatshop labor and raising women's wages. However, the AFL refused to renew Kenney's appointment, and she returned to Chicago, where she found greater support for her work from the progressive women of Hull House.[137]

During the summer of 1893, the nation slid into a major economic depression. By the winter of 1894 many people in New York City were destitute. The city government provided little public relief, and the mood on the Lower East Side grew restive. A year later, 75,000 workers were unemployed, a quarter of them women. Trade unions set up soup kitchens and organized demonstrations on the Lower East Side and in Union Square demanding relief.[138] In the midst of this general downturn, O'Reilly's own financial situation improved. She was promoted to a position as forewoman, for which she earned twelve dollars a week. By combining their incomes, Leonora and her mother, Winifred, maintained a stable working-class household. Leonora paid her mother six dollars a week for board and spent the rest of her pay on clothes, books, organizational dues, and a bicycle she rode around New York City with friends on the weekends.[139] She and her mother continued to visit Cooper Union, the Brooklyn Academy of Music, and other venues around the city where they heard lectures by Henry George, the author of *Progress and Poverty*; John Altgeld, the progressive governor of Illinois; Mary Elizabeth Lease, the Populist orator; Emma Goldman, an anarchist and an advocate of birth control; and Eugene V. Debs, the head of the American Railway Workers Union.[140]

O'Reilly developed close relationships with many of her female coworkers and maintained a cordial relationship with her boss, Mr. Bellamy. However, she was fundamentally unhappy at her job. She advised a friend against taking a position as a forewoman in another factory, reporting that at times "I wish that I was at the machine, working with no greater responsibility than to do my task well and to see that I got all I could for doing it."[141] She felt caught between the workers and the management, and feared she was distrusted by both. Moreover, the position chafed against her vision of herself as an agent for social change. She resented spending her days "making money for someone else."[142] O'Reilly spent her free time educating herself. She read philosophy, economics, history, and sociology in the "Synthetic Circle," a reading group organized by her friend Edward King, who had helped establish the Central Labor Union and was known as one of the city's best read labor activists.[143] Like many British socialists, King was inspired by the positivist philosophy of August Comte, who believed that society must be organized along more scientific lines in order to progress.[144] Yet King was also a practical man, who encouraged O'Reilly to attend "business training" classes at the Young Women's Christian Association so that she could learn shorthand in order to escape the shirtwaist factory. She took the classes, but did not leave her job, in part because of her sense of responsibility for the young women who worked under her direction.[145]

In 1894, the year of the great railroad strike that began in Pullman, Edward King and Leonora O'Reilly both joined the Social Reform Club (SRC).[146] Organizations like the SRC multiplied in large cities during the 1890s, as industrial depression and class conflict aroused a broad sense of social crisis. O'Reilly added biweekly meetings at the club's headquarters on East Fourth Street to her already crowded schedule.[147] Ruth Huntington Sessions, who was first invited to the club by O'Reilly, vividly recalled its atmosphere. Sessions was living in Brooklyn Heights and working as an organizer for the Brooklyn Consumers' League. Accustomed to addressing parlor meetings of bourgeois matrons, she was struck by the diversity of the crowd, which included "workers, students, and thinkers" seated on hard wooden chairs packed close together into the double parlor of the old house.[148] Sessions viewed the mixed crowd through the Gilded Age lens of social contrast, commenting on the juxtaposition of "swarthy skins besides clean shaven ones." At this point, working-class status had become so closely associated with new immigrants from southern and eastern Europe that Sessions used complexion as a sign of class, reflecting the popular idea that these new European immigrants were not quite white. Despite the "dim" light and the "smoky" air, Sessions discerned "a genuine desire of enlightenment, a mutual distrust of the gradual tightening of restraints and accumulation of power through the capitalist system."

Henry George had faded from the scene, but his economic analysis of "progress and poverty" remained the group's guiding light. Although most members sympathized with socialism, they agreed to bar "all general theories of society" from debate in order to avoid factionalism and to undertake "only such efforts as have a fair hope of early success."[149] The ban on "general theories" prevented debates from bogging down into monotonous restatements of well-known political positions. This practical approach drew an unusually diverse group of members, from Felix Adler, the German Jewish founder of the Ethical Culture Society, to Samuel Gompers, the head of the AFL. Josephine Shaw Lowell and Alice Woodbridge joined, as did Grace Dodge, the philanthropic founder of the city's working girls' clubs. The group required all members "to have a deep, active interest" in the "improvement of the conditions of wage-earners." They supported trade unions, endorsed cheap municipal power, lobbied for tenement house reform, and took a leading role in the campaign for mercantile inspection.[150]

Despite the hours she put into the club's work, O'Reilly found its social atmosphere awkward, viewing it with considerably less romance than Ruth Huntington Sessions, who found its mix of men and women from different social classes thrilling. Although the club aimed to have an equal balance of non–wage earners and wage earners, it attracted twice as many non–wage earners. It also attracted twice as many men as women. Men and women attended meetings together and worked together on committees to study particular social questions or press for specific reforms. However, they socialized separately in the club rooms. Men held smokers; women had teas. Women generally provided entertainment and refreshments for mixed events. They were also expected to do the organization's mailings.[151] Feeling their minority position, the women held their own weekly meetings.[152]

Surprisingly, perhaps, O'Reilly felt more of an affinity for elite, socially engaged women like Josephine Shaw Lowell than she did for the male leaders of New York's Central Labor Union who also belonged to the SRC. Despite their differences in age, class, and strategy, the two women shared a commitment to improving the lives of the city's working-class women.[153] Although the WWS had dissolved, O'Reilly still believed strongly in the necessity of organization. Recognizing the success of working girls' clubs in sustaining and expanding their organization, and after getting to know Grace Dodge at the SRC, O'Reilly began presenting speeches to individual clubs and to the national convention. In one address, titled "How Can Working Girls Clubs Co-operate with Trade Unions?" she encouraged the "ladies" who ran the clubs to stop treating working girls as "consumers" who needed to be taught how "to spend their wages and hours of leisure more profitably" and instead to view working-class women as "producers" who could organize "to get more wages, more hours of leisure, and better conditions of work."[154] While the identity of consumer might empower bourgeois women, O'Reilly worried that it threatened to obscure working-class women's interests and identities as workers.

O'Reilly did not feel entirely comfortable among the women of the SRC. An essay she wrote for a colleague who worked as a teacher and was tutoring her in composition expressed her awkward position. After three years, O'Reilly remained the sole "woman wage earner," an identity she dryly described as "a woman who works at a common trade, and gets about half of what she is worth for her weekly wage." She explained that although "many other women in the club" worked for pay, they did so in professional occupations. As a result, O'Reilly felt pushed into the artificial position of being "the only the real representative working-woman: in other words . . . the only factory girl." It seemed slightly absurd to O'Reilly that she should be called on to give "the working woman's point of view."[155]

In spite of the awkwardness Leonora O'Reilly felt at the Social Reform Club, she joined the committee for mercantile inspection, which included her friends Alice Woodbridge and Josephine Shaw Lowell. As a result of pressure from the committee on mercantile inspection, as well as from the NYCL and settlement house workers, the New York State Assembly appointed its own committee to study the problem in March 1895.

The workings of this committee revealed the shortcomings of state-centered solutions to working women's problems. Chaired by assemblyman Philip W. Reinhard of Manhattan, the Special Committee of the Assembly Appointed to Investigate the Condition of Female Labor in the City of New York received a broad mandate to study women's labor conditions.[156] The Republicans who dominated the committee had no special interest or expertise in the subject. Instead, they were players in party politics: skilled at bringing patronage into their districts, and content to draw out the hearings as long as possible in order to receive free transportation to and from Albany and to advertise their concern with the working class during a period of high unemployment and prolonged depression.[157] During the spring and summer of 1895, the Reinhard committee heard testimony from ninety-five witnesses in New York City. Members of the NYCL and the SRC testified about labor conditions in department stores; merchants were also called in for questioning. Saleswomen themselves were interviewed in closed hearings, which may have been arranged in deference to their respectability, or to protect them from being black-listed if they criticized their employers. However, the privacy of these sessions also served the interests of mercantile firms by shielding them from negative publicity.[158] The saleswomen called to testify before the Reinhard committee seemed intimidated by the proceedings. The women generally limited their responses to "Yes, Sir," or "No, Sir." Young working women questioned by a committee of distinguished gentlemen would be unlikely to respond candidly, and may have doubted that their anonymity would be protected.

A woman who had recently retired from Macy's after thirty years gave extensive and shocking testimony. She recounted several stories about young girls being harassed and sexually molested in the course of their work. She had often "seen the little girls come back" from the shipping department "with their faces red and sometimes crying" as a result of "vulgar" comments—or worse actions she did not venture to name. Despite their pretenses to gentility, middle-class managers were equally menacing. An assistant superintendent was known to make passes at the "little cash girls" who came at night to clean his office. Other managers indulged in similar behavior without fear of discharge. In the experience of this female manager, poor mothers mistakenly sent their children out to work in stores, believing that they were "trusting them to gentlemen" who would treat girls and women with respect, regardless of their social class. Unfortunately, she concluded, "they do not get the protection they have a right to expect."[159]

Having crossed the line from worker to reformer, Alice Woodbridge joined a delegation that testified publicly. Woodbridge urged the state to recognize stores as analogous to industrial workplaces by placing them under the direction of the factory department. The city government was notoriously corrupt, and Woodbridge probably hoped that the state agency would be more difficult to bribe. Merchants routinely violated state law by hiring children under age fourteen, and Woodbridge emphasized children's right to remain in school long enough to learn to read and write. She also reiterated the demand that women's wages be brought up to the level of men's, warning that otherwise employers would fire men and hire women at cheaper rates.[160] Members of the NYCL were also called before the committee. Josephine Shaw Lowell, Mary Putnam Jacobi, and Maud Nathan each made several appearances, describing retail women's working conditions, detailing the public health issues at stake, and voicing their support for state regulation.[161]

Support for or opposition to the legislation did not break down along simple lines. Elbridge T. Gerry, director of the Society for Prevention of Cruelty to Children, opposed the legislation, arguing that children were better off at work than on the streets. Gerry warned that girls under the age of fourteen thrown out of work by the proposed legislation would turn to prostitution.[162] Bloomingdale's, an uptown store that distinguished itself through its progressive management, supported the legislation. Downtown firms opposed it: if they did not stay open after six o'clock, their working-class clientele could not shop after work.[163]

The Reinhard committee concluded its work by proposing legislation that fell short of what advocates in the NYCL and the SRC demanded, and was a far cry from what the WWS had proposed five years earlier.[164] Mercantile firms backed by large donations may have dissuaded committee members from advocating effective regulation of department stores.[165] The new law did not include any provisions regulating wages or requiring paid vacations. Its limitations on hours merely ratified prevailing practices: ten hours per day, six days a week. It waived the ten-hour limitation on Saturday, when stores traditionally stayed open later, and lifted the sixty-hour weekly limit during the Christmas shopping season. Seeking to stay within the courts' recent strictures on abridging workers' "freedom of contract," the law applied only to minors: women under twenty-one and men under eighteen.[166]

In a further defeat for long-time advocates of mercantile inspection, the Reinhard committee assigned the work of inspection to local health departments, even though these agencies had shown themselves incapable of enforcing existing legislation.[167] By refusing to place stores under the jurisdiction of the state factory inspector, the committee depoliticized the issue of women's labor in department stores, defining it as an issue of health and morals rather than labor relations. While the records do not reveal the reasoning behind the committee's decision, the NYCL emphasis on female workers' health may have backfired, formalizing the separation from a broader labor movement determined to secure better wages, shorter hours, and safer working conditions. As a result, the legislation was doomed to the fate of most labor laws during this period: ineffectiveness because of its patchwork nature and weak enforcement, especially at the city level.[168]

To make matters worse, the legislature struck out against female factory inspectors, whom the WWS had worked to get appointed five years earlier. As Kathryn Kish Sklar has explained, campaigns for female inspectors, carried out by cross-class coalitions of women in New York, Pennsylvania, Massachusetts, and Illinois, resulted from an understanding that female workers would be more likely to complain of sexual harassment to female inspectors.[169] In 1890 the CLU had allied with the WWS to support the appointment of female inspectors. Now, hungry for patronage positions, the CLU urged the legislature to get rid of the female inspectors. Claiming the mantle of chivalry by insisting that the work was not "fit for women," the Reinhard committee added a proviso that in the future no more than ten out of the thirty deputy factory inspectors should be women.[170] Clearly, working women had lost their allies in the CLU.

The New York state legislature approved the legislation recommended by the Reinhard committee in the fall of 1896. Annie Ware Winsor, who chaired the SRC committee on mercantile inspection, acknowledged that the law was sure to be "criticized severely" and "could be improved." Repeating the familiar theory that the law could be an entering wedge for future legislation, she argued that consumers would have to push for its enforcement. "Shops, unlike factories, are wide open to the public," Winsor pointed out. Women should limit their patronage to establishments that obeyed the law and complain to local boards of health when it was broken.[171] Members of the NYCL advocated the formation of new groups across New York state. They were encouraged that consumers' leagues had been established in Brooklyn, Philadelphia, and Chicago, and they had received inquiries about forming new leagues from women in Boston, Detroit, and Baltimore.[172] The NYCL insisted on a far tougher set of standards for stores to be put on its white list than New York state did for stores to be within its law. The League inspected stores constantly to ensure compliance. Within a few years the government's intentional neglect had rendered the law a dead letter.[173] This unsatisfying conclusion to the lengthy struggle for mercantile inspection illustrates the obstacles women's labor reformers faced in moving the state to take effective action on behalf of working-class women. It also shows the limitations of arguments on behalf of public health in achieving the results workers and reformers desired.

The state's failure to pass or enforce effective labor legislation left women's labor reformers searching for new ways to improve wage-earning women's conditions. Continuing to emulate working-class strategies of consumer activism, Maud Nathan decided to create a Consumers' League label to appeal to middle-class women concerned with the conditions under which the goods they used in their households were manufactured. The "union label" had been inaugurated in 1874 by the San Francisco cigar makers' union as a way of fighting competition from cheaper cigars made by the Chinese workers whom the white men excluded from their union.[174] From these nativist beginnings, the label spread among trade union locals of both the Knights of Labor and the AFL as an effective tool, along with boycotts and strikes, for workers to support organization and increase their control over production. Labels drew support from class-conscious workers determined to use their purchasing power to keep union shops in business and to foster the broadest possible organization of workers. By the 1880s workers in Brooklyn and New York, like those in other cities with a strong labor movement, used labels to signify union-made boots, shoes, hats, and cigars. Workers' commitment to buying labeled goods remained strong through the 1890s.[175]

The union label enabled working-class women to support the labor movement even if they did not work for wages or belong to labor organizations themselves.[176] Among women who did work for wages, enthusiasm for the label ran high. When Leonora O'Reilly needed a new pair of boots, she spent the morning tramping through Brooklyn looking for some that were union-made. In Chicago, when Mary Kenney's female bookbinders held a fundraising ball, they checked inside the men's hats to be sure they had union labels.[177] By 1897 the SRC reported that in "some towns" concern for workers' patronage had "been sufficient incentive to make every dealer in certain lines sell only 'labeled' goods." As a result "conditions of trade [had] been completely changed as regards clothing, hats, cigars and some other articles of everyday use."[178] Of course, the success of the union label depended on class consciousness and on workers having the time and money to make careful choices about the goods they purchased. While bourgeois advocates of the consumers' movement, such as Helen Campbell, exhorted members of the social register to shop ethically rather than search for bargains, and working women like O'Reilly and Kenney who made a decent wage could search for labeled goods, women in poorer families might simply buy the lowest priced merchandise they could find. Most mothers managing large households lacked the time and the money to leave their neighborhoods in search of labeled goods.

Maud Nathan saw her opportunity to move forward with a Consumers' League label in 1897, when the Ladies' Tailors of New York went on strike. These tailors, who were considered to be the most skilled makers of women's clothing in the city, were exclusively men. The League's involvement with the strike shows how its emphasis on protecting public health could conflict with workers' own desires. In coming to the assistance of the striking tailors, NYCL members discovered that the garments they purchased from master tailors on Fifth Avenue were actually made in workers' homes, often with the assistance of their wives and children. While Nathan supported the tailors' union and backed its demand for fair rates of pay, she emphasized the need for tailors to have "sanitary quarters," explaining that League members did not "want the germ of diseases carried from the tenements" into their own homes. Sanitarians and state boards of health warned that clothing, blankets, toys, furniture, and even household pets could spread diseases such as scarlet fever and diphtheria, which had no cure and took a high toll among children.[179] In pressing for a resolution of the strike, the NYCL went against the tailors' own wishes by insisting on the abolition of home manufacturing, which was an integral although previously unacknowledged part of the tailors' family economies.[180]

By this point, abolition of tenement house manufacturing had become a highly charged political issue in New York, Massachusetts, and Illinois. Depending on their interests, organized male workers might either defend their right to draw on the labor of their wives and children, as the Ladies' Tailors' Union did, or oppose tenement house manufacturing as inhibiting organization and undermining wages, as the United Garment Workers did. Trade and labor unions found small, dispersed shops difficult to organize, and they saw the subcontracting system as undercutting the wages paid to workers in regular factories. Historian Eileen Boris has shown that labor leaders and reformers depicted the women who worked in tenement house manufacturing as "white slaves," powerless to change their own conditions. Union leaders argued that husbands needed to earn higher wages so that their wives and daughters would not have to work under these exploitative conditions. However, this rationale did little to help women without husbands or fathers to rely on and, as Chicago labor leader Lizzie Holmes warned, legislation to protect public health by ending outwork might have the paradoxical effect of depriving many needy women of their jobs.[181] Characteristically, Nathan did not stop to consider these consequences, focusing instead on the imperative of protecting consumers and ignoring the interests of workers themselves.

Nathan presented her proposal for a Consumers' League label at an acrimonious meeting of the SRC in April 1897. The club's trade unionists challenged the League's appropriation of union techniques. Nathan parried by posing the elite consumers as responsible for protecting working women from exploitation and protecting middle-class consumers from goods tainted with disease.[182] Nathan was not alone in her fear of disease spread by goods manufactured in sweatshops. Native-born politicians, journalists, and factory inspectors all characterized the Jewish and Italian immigrant workers who toiled in sweatshops as unhealthy and racially degraded. New city and state laws designed to stamp out sweatshop production were passed in the interest of protecting public health—that is, the health of consumers, not the health of immigrant workers. Again, lack of adequate inspection rendered these new laws ineffective.[183] The Consumers' League label promised consumer protection and better inspection, despite opposition from trade unionists at the SRC, who stressed "the Union Label stands for more than better sanitary conditions."[184]

The NYCL introduced its white label in the spring of 1897. To use the label, manufacturers were required to follow all state factory laws, send none of their goods out to tenement houses for finishing, pay workers extra for overtime, and prohibit child labor. These measures did improve the conditions of the workers who were hired to work in factories, but it impinged on the livelihood of older, married or widowed women with children, who had relied on outwork (however poorly paid) to help make ends meet. Furthermore, the white label left the maintenance of the improvements it did secure for workers in the hands of motivated consumers rather than the workers themselves. Nathan successfully urged the Merchants' Association to carry labeled goods.[185] In May 1898, the NYCL combined with the leagues of other cities to form a National Consumers' League to promote the white label, reflecting the increasingly national production and distribution of goods.[186] By 1906, the League had approved sixty-one manufacturers of ladies' underwear, shirtwaists, corsets, curtains, and pillowcases.[187] Despite past conflicts with merchants, the Consumers' League hewed to its position as an impartial arbiter in the battle between capital and labor, working on behalf of the public good.

The fight for a white label demonstrates the shift in women's labor reform during this period. Rather than trying to change working women's conditions, as the WWS had tried to do, the NYCL fought to ensure that those conditions did not imperil public health. Oddly, the health of workers themselves was often overlooked, except in cases where native-born, white women's reproductive capacity was at issue, as in providing seats for saleswomen. Otherwise, journalists, reformers, and politicians identified promoting public health with protecting the bodies of middle-class consumers. Workers continued to insist on the necessity of their own organization, but women found limited roles for themselves in trade unions.

Leonora O'Reilly's experiences during these years suggest the awkwardness of the new social identity she and her comrades were attempting to claim. By defining themselves as "working women," they demanded to be paid at the same rates and treated with the same respect as male workers. Their exclusion from most trade unions prevented them from achieving the increases in wages and decreases in hours being won by organized men. Progressive, bourgeois women offered help, but often it came at the price of control. While the rhetoric of protecting white working-class women from wage slavery proved to be a powerful political tool, it discounted working-class women's own efforts to protect themselves through collective organization and to establish independent identities as wage earners and as citizens.

CHAPTER 4

SOLVING THE SERVANT PROBLEM

The "servant question" exposed the fault line of class running through the nineteenth-century movement for women's labor reform. Nowhere was this more visible than in Boston, where affluent, socially conscientious women who had joined in the struggle against slavery felt a special responsibility for their less fortunate sisters. Shortly after the Civil War, a group of women who knew one another from the fight against slavery established the New England Women's Club (NEWC). They elected Julia Ward Howe, the author of "The Battle Hymn of the Republic," as their president. Like most members of the club, Howe supported women's suffrage and advocated a wider field of employment for women.[1] Responding to the growing visibility of an impoverished class of female workers, the NEWC investigated the conditions of Boston sewing women in 1869. While some club members supported working-class women in their efforts to organize and to petition for land from the state legislature for Garden Homesteads, most ignored the substance of working-class women's desire for independence, advising them to preserve their health and morals by leaving new jobs running sewing machines and returning to their former positions as cooks, chambermaids, and waitresses.

In 1877 a small group of women broke off from the NEWC to form the Women's Educational and Industrial Union (WEIU). The new group planned to address the problem of women's labor more directly. Led by Harriet Clisby, a British-born physician, the WEIU set out to unify women from different backgrounds based on their common desire "for self-support, for practical advancement, for social, intellectual, and spiritual growth."[2] The WEIU drew from the same social group as the NEWC. However, dues were set at a dollar a year in order to make membership more inclusive, and the group expanded to include professional women and middle-class housewives while retaining a core of "Boston's Best."[3] The WEIU began by establishing an exchange for women's handiwork, a downtown lunchroom for women, and a legal department to assist working women pursuing claims of unpaid wages.[4]

Abby Morton Diaz, who had grown up in an abolitionist household and spent her twenties as a teacher in the utopian community at Brook Farm, became the president of the WEIU in 1881. Diaz supported herself and her two children by writing domestic advice manuals and children's stories. She was well aware of the labor necessary for a middle-class household to function smoothly and of the difficulties middle-class housewives and professional women faced in finding "good help."[5] In 1881 the WEIU set aside a desk at its headquarters where women looking for jobs "as seamstresses, nurses, lady's maids and housekeepers" and members looking for help could be matched up by WEIU staff. Despite its egalitarian name, the WEIU consisted of women who employed servants, not women who worked as servants themselves. As one woman who worked to support herself complained, the WEIU was "composed in the main of women of leisure and wealth," who profited by charging commissions to those they were supposed to be helping. Declined gentlewomen who sold their fine handiwork at the exchange found that the WEIU charged a significant fee for this service, as did the women who used its employment bureau to find jobs.[6]

In 1892 Mary Morton Kimball Kehew took over as president and set the WEIU on a more practical course, emphasizing education, vocational training, and sociological research.[7] Like Diaz, Kehew belonged to one of Boston's first families, and she had been raised as a Unitarian. Forty years younger than Diaz, Kehew came from a generation that turned to progressive reform rather than transcendentalism. Her marriage to a wealthy oil merchant produced no children, leaving her free to devote her time to social causes. She supported labor organization as a solution to some of the problems facing women who worked in industry, and she convinced Mary Kenney O'Sullivan, a labor organizer who had recently moved to Boston from Chicago, to join her in establishing the Union for Industrial Progress. This cross-class group of men and women worked to improve industrial conditions through investigation, organization, and legislation; it became a forerunner to the Women's Trade Union League, which Kehew helped establish.[8]

Like other women of her social class devoted to progressive causes, Mary Morton Kehew recognized domestic service as problematic for both employers and employees. Under her direction, the WEIU worked actively to elevate the occupation so that native-born, white women with other options for employment would continue to work as servants and so that elite households would run more smoothly. Kehew and the WEIU fought a losing battle: native-born, white women continued to leave jobs as servants for positions in factories, stores, and offices. Women who remained in household employment lacked public recognition as workers. The story of the WEIU's failed efforts to reform domestic service reveals the meanings of independence to working-class women and the centrality of domestic work to broader debates about working-class and middle-class women's place in the paid labor force.

By the 1890s social investigators, labor reformers, and working women themselves had drawn public attention to the conditions of young women working in the garment industry and in large department stores. Women's magazines addressed the "servant problem" more frequently than any other topic, but labor investigators avoided peering into labor relations in private bourgeois homes.[9] Most middle-class reformers, even those committed to women's rights, viewed domestic work as "woman's" healthiest and most natural occupation, and agreed that working women would be better off in households than in factories.[10] Most working-class women disagreed, and native-born white women with new options for employment in manufacturing, retail, or clerical positions left the occupation in droves.

In 1897 Lucy Salmon, a historian at Vassar, inaugurated a more systematic approach to problems of domestic labor through her study *Domestic Service,* the first full-length social-scientific investigation of the topic. Salmon, born in 1853, had been raised in Fulton, New York, where her father was a successful businessman and her mother worked as a seminary principal. Even after her mother's death when Lucy was seven, the family continued to place a high value on women's education, and Lucy attended the seminary her mother had directed (reorganized as a coeducational school), before going on to college and graduate school in history at the University of Michigan. She earned an additional graduate degree in American history at Bryn Mawr in 1887 and became Vassar's first history professor the following year.[11] Like the women who formed the WEIU, Salmon came from the employing classes. As an academic, however, she was determined to take a scientific approach to the servant problem.

Salmon used her study to bring intellectual legitimacy to a topic she considered wrongly neglected by economists and by social scientists in previous discussions of the "labor question." While acknowledging that most considered the relationship between mistress and maid a personal one, she insisted on gathering empirical data in order to understand labor relations in households. In formulating her study, she consulted with Carroll D. Wright, whose report on "The Working Girls of Boston" had established the norms for social-scientific investigation of wage-earning women. Although Wright had excluded domestic servants from his study, he was receptive to Salmon's project, perhaps because it promised to shed light on a field of women's employment he had neglected. Like Wright, Salmon gathered information from both employers and employees. However, Salmon relied more heavily on printed forms than on personal interviews. The Massachusetts Bureau of Statistics of Labor supported her work, collating her data during the spring and summer of 1890.

Salmon received 1,025 responses to a questionnaire distributed primarily to Vassar alumnae. Unlike Salmon, who had foregone marriage for a professional career, most of these women had married and were now employing servants to help them keep house. Salmon sent additional forms to women's clubs, statistical associations, and organizations of college graduates. She also distributed questionnaires to servants, receiving 719 responses. While most servants received forms from their employers, some wrote directly to Salmon asking to be included in the study. A few former servants established a correspondence with Salmon. However, many women still employed as servants "seemed hesitant to commit anything to writing" or to sign their names to the forms they submitted. While Salmon attributed this reluctance to ignorance, it seems more likely that servants were silent out of fear that negative responses could jeopardize their jobs. Although the form promised confidentiality, it asked for the name, age, and address of each employer and employee for the purposes of verification and further research. Servants were instructed to return the form to the person who gave it to them, or to send it directly to the Vassar history department.[12] Even if the servant had the time and the postage to send in her form directly, she may have worried that information she revealed would be divulged to her employer.[13] Given these considerations, Salmon received quite a large number of responses from servants, who may have hoped that answering the questions would improve their working conditions.

Despite its bias toward employers, Salmon's study revealed new facts about domestic service, analyzing the servant population by race, region, gender, and nativity. She described service as an urban phenomenon. The nation's fifty largest cities, which had 18 percent of the total population, were home to 32 percent of all domestic servants. She noted a relationship between the degree of industrialization and the number of servants, arguing that less industrialized southern cities had more servants and more industrialized northern cities had fewer, since northern women had other opportunities for employment and industrial workers could not afford to hire servants themselves. Most women went into service because they wanted to save money, needed a place to live, or considered it healthier than industrial work, which tended to be fast-paced and repetitive, especially because women were frequently paid by the piece. Those servants who were foreign-born, who made up about one-third of servants nationally, tended to be from Ireland, Germany, Sweden, Norway, Great Britain, and Canada. More than half of all foreign-born servants were Irish, reflecting well-established networks of single Irish women who migrated to the United States to find work as domestics.[14]

Although Salmon commented on the rising number of immigrants working as servants, she said little about race, since most of her respondents were from northeastern and midwestern cities, where the proportion of servants who were African American or Asian remained low.[15] She considered proposals to solve the "servant problem" in the Northeast and the Midwest by importing African Americans from the South, or Chinese servants from the West "Doubtful Remedies," arguing that southern and western housewives were plagued by their own "perplexities." In the South, a stream of newspaper articles complained of the declining quality of servants as the older generation trained under slavery gave way to a younger generation who displayed "the same tendencies" to demand independence as white servants in the North. In the West, employers complained that the new act restricting Chinese immigration had "made the Chinese very independent"; many of them, aware of the reduced supply of Chinese domestic workers, were now demanding higher wages.[16]

W. E. B. DuBois's path-breaking sociological investigation, *The Philadelphia Negro* (1899), provides insight into the racial formation of the domestic labor market. Sponsored by the University of Pennsylvania, where he had recently taken a position in the sociology department, DuBois conducted his investigation over a fifteen-month period, personally visiting each household in the seventh ward, a historically black neighborhood.[17] Having earned a doctorate in history at Harvard, DuBois interpreted the history of service and race as inextricably intertwined. Enslaved African Americans had served in white households, and after emancipation many continued in the occupation. In the industrialized Northeast, those white people who entered into service were now more likely to be immigrants than native born. "Thus," DuBois concluded, "by long experience the United States has come to associate domestic service with some inferiority in race or training."

According to DuBois, African Americans were no more enthusiastic about domestic service than European immigrants or native-born whites, but they had few other reliable options for employment. Lately, in the fashionable homes bordering Rittenhouse Square, African American men who worked as cooks, butlers, and coachmen, and African American women who worked as nursemaids faced competition from English and Swedish servants. DuBois hoped that African Americans would gain a wider sphere of employment, but in the meantime, he advocated systematic training "in proper cleaning and cooking, and in matters of etiquette and good form"— the type of vocational training more associated with his nemesis, Booker T. Washington.[18] Middle-class black clubwomen, such as Fannie Barrier Williams and Nannie Burroughs, agreed that African American women would profit from any programs that would dignify domestic labor.[19] Josephine St. Pierre Ruffin, an African American editor and journalist who belonged to the NEWC, joined the Domestic Reform League, indicating her commitment to domestic reform.[20]

DuBois considered the subject of domestic service "so important" that he asked Isabel Eaton, a white settlement house worker, to prepare a "Special Report on Negro Domestic Service." An 1888 graduate of Smith College, Eaton had learned the techniques of social investigation at Hull House in Chicago under the direction of Jane Addams. She joined DuBois's investigation as a Fellow from the College Settlement Association. She consulted with Lucy Salmon and DuBois, both of whom acted as mentors, in formulating her study, which became her master's thesis at Columbia. Like DuBois, Eaton focused on the seventh ward, spending nine months living in a settlement house in the neighborhood while she conducted interviews and gathered statistics.[21]

Eaton emphasized the economic significance of service for African Americans. In Pennsylvania, 90 percent of African American women in the labor force worked as servants, as did 60 percent of African American men. Despite some instances of white servants earning more than African Americans, race made little difference in average wages: white and black women who worked as servants in Philadelphia generally earned about the same amount. Eaton speculated that the traditional association of service with African Americans in Philadelphia provided some form of job protection, since in most other positions black women earned less than white women. However, the rule of men earning more than women held fast: male servants, who tended to work as butlers, gardeners, or coachmen in wealthy households, earned, on average, twice as much as female servants. The majority of African American servants—women as well as men—whom Eaton interviewed supported other family members, including aging parents, younger siblings, nieces, nephews, and children. While Salmon characterized service as an occupation of last resort, Eaton found many African Americans working as servants even though they had trained for other occupations. In response to job discrimination, teachers worked as chambermaids and carpenters as coachmen.[22] Ironically, investigators in Boston would discover that discrimination in hiring extended to domestic work, with most employers expressing a strong preference for white household help.[23] This pattern accorded with the city's long history of racial segregation, which was extreme even by contemporary standards.[24]

Salmon's study confirmed a sense of crisis in domestic service, revealing that neither employers nor employees were satisfied. On average, the servants in her sample stayed with their employers for less than a year and a half.[25] In contrast, in Philadelphia, Eaton found the average African American domestic servant worked for the same employer for nearly five years, reflecting either greater loyalty or lack of mobility.[26] Like earlier commentators on domestic subjects, such as Catharine Beecher, Salmon attributed middle-class housewives' difficulties in finding "good help" to servants' overweening desires for independence. As Salmon explained: "That spirit of restlessness, nervous discontent, and craving for excitement which foreigners find characteristic of all who breathe American air is not confined to business men and society women—it permeates the kitchen, the laundry, and every part of the household."[27] If domestic service were to survive into the twentieth century, Salmon argued, it would have to be reformed to give employees the independence they demanded. Salmon warned her readers, who she assumed would be middle-class housewives, that if they were to regain their ability to command a desirable labor force, the "aristocracy of the household" would have to "succumb" to the "universal desire for personal independence on the part of employees."[28]

Taking the contemporary business corporation as her model, Salmon recommended several reforms in household organization. Housewives must begin by acquiring "scientific" knowledge of housekeeping. They needed to learn to treat their domestic employees like modern workers, with limited hours and clearly defined duties.[29] As part of this modernization, Salmon recommended that all "unnecessary" labor be removed from the home. For example, bread should be purchased, and laundry should be sent out.[30] She also suggested a domestic form of "profit sharing" as a means of attracting and retaining reliable employees. Housewives would set a budget, and servants who spent less than the allocated amount would split the difference with their employers, earning a bonus for their economy. While Mary Putnam Jacobi of the New York Consumers' League had described household labor as a means of increasing health and happiness rather than producing profit, Salmon believed that households would run more smoothly if they became more impersonal and more businesslike. In proposing these reforms, she encouraged housewives to emulate corporate managers and create modern workplaces, free (at least in theory) from labor conflict.[31]

Inspired by their own difficulties securing satisfactory household help, members of the WEIU formed a new committee, the Domestic Reform League (DRL), to study domestic service and to improve household labor relations.[32] The DRL remained a branch of the WEIU from its founding in 1897 until its demise in 1910. Almost immediately, the organization invited Lucy Salmon to lecture.[33] Its leaders aligned the group with the new, national movement for home economics, which endorsed better training for servants, associations for housewives, and the opening of nonprofit or government-sponsored domestic employment bureaus.[34] In an early solicitation for membership and financial contributions, Ada M. Child, a founder of the DRL, reminded her audience: "Educational forces do not push from the bottom, they pull from the top." She encouraged the "public-spirited and progressive women of Boston" to aid in this reform, "which touches more or less closely every *home*."[35] The DRL extended a tradition initiated by the NEWC of organized middle-class and elite women using social science to position themselves as mediators of class conflict. In the case of domestic service, however, the conflicts they sought to mediate were in their own households, a fact that strained their claims of objectivity and exposed their class interests as employers.

The new organization met with an enthusiastic response. Mary Morton Kehew, the president of the WEIU, championed the DRL as spearheading a "movement to dignify housework in the eyes of both employer and employee by lifting it to the level of other trades."[36] The DRL's roster of early leaders read like a "Who's Who" of progressive Boston society. Kehew herself directed the DRL, indicating its importance within the WEIU. Abby Morton Diaz lent her expertise on domestic topics and her experience with cooperative living arrangements at Brook Farm. Helen Hamilton Gardener, a sociologist and biologist who argued for men's and women's equal intellectual ability, also joined the group, as did Elizabeth Glendower Evans, a pioneering penal reformer and social worker best known for her later defense of Sacco and Vanzetti.[37]

The DRL began with what seemed the most obvious solution to the domestic service problem: increasing the supply of workers by recruiting women from industrial to household labor. A journalist predicted certain success: after all, it seemed "so palpably true that a girl would be better off in a clean, warm, well-lighted kitchen than in an ill-ventilated and crowded workroom."[38] To oversee this transfer of women from industry, the DRL hired Mary Dewson, a recent graduate of Wellesley, who went on to become a prominent progressive reformer. Dewson distributed cards inviting "women wage-earners, whether experienced or not in housework," to "consult" the WEIU about "the possibility of entering domestic service." The invitations invoked "the unsatisfactory conditions in the industrial world," promising "good conditions and fair wages . . . in exchange for intelligent and faithful service."[39] But the DRL found few takers.[40] The organization's high hopes for solving the problems of domestic service through a simple readjustment of supply and demand were quickly dashed.

The DRL turned to social science to explain the failure of its intuitively logical plan. Mary Dewson shifted from recruitment to investigation. Using statistical forms approved by Carroll D. Wright, now head of the U.S. Bureau of Labor, and Horace G. Wadlin, head of the Massachusetts Bureau of Statistics of Labor, Dewson interviewed one hundred women who worked in stores, one hundred women who worked in factories, and about fifty employers. Cooperation with Wright and Wadlin reflected the WEIU's broader strategy of increasing women's power by collaborating with state government in order to accomplish reform.[41] The resulting report set the agenda for the future work of the DRL.[42]

Women's reasons for preferring industrial to domestic work remained consistent with those expressed a decade earlier by women interviewed by Helen Campbell for *Prisoners of Poverty* and by those who wrote to the *Chicago Times* in response to "City Slave Girls." Domestic work required long hours of hard, tedious labor; it isolated women from their peers; and it forced them to live apart from their families. Women complained that living in someone else's household as a servant compromised their independence, just as they had in 1869 in response to NEWC investigators.[43] Most servants now worked alone, rather than alongside other servants, increasing this sense of isolation. Some women reported that although they preferred doing general housework, they took more specialized jobs as chambermaids or waitresses so that they would not have to work by themselves. They also tried to counter the isolation from coworkers, friends, and family by taking jobs in the central city rather than the suburbs.[44] Even with these adjustments, however, most working-class women interviewed by the DRL agreed with DuBois that the job carried a social stigma and implied a "loss of caste."[45]

Boston remained a center of clothing manufacturing, giving most single young white women options for employment beyond domestic service. The DRL succeeded in convincing industrial workers to try service only under exceptional circumstances. For example, it found the oldest daughter of a large family willing to take up "house-work to escape from the duties imposed on her at home after factory hours." A "tailoress" suffering from eyestrain and a telephone operator who felt nervous prostration coming on both left their jobs to try housework. In general, however, the investigation suggested "no hope" of shop and factory girls rejecting "their present occupation in favor of housework." Elizabeth Glendower Evans, who wrote the report based on Dewson's findings, recommended studying domestic service to find out why so few women wanted to do it and seeking to reform the occupation to make it an attractive alternative to other kinds of employment.[46]

The DRL's next report, "The Hours of Labor in Domestic Service," provided quantitative evidence of the growing divergence between domestic and industrial work, particularly in the hours of labor.[47] According to the calculations of the DRL and the Massachusetts Bureau of Statistics of Labor, the average domestic worked for eighty-five hours a week, while her sister in the shop or factory seldom worked more than sixty. Domestic workers were on call twelve hours a day, meaning that in addition to their regular duties, they might be asked to answer the door, watch the children, run errands, serve lunch, or do any other work their employer requested. Women employed in stores and factories generally worked no more than ten hours per day. Nearly half of the servants interviewed were given no "day out," and even those granted a day off generally worked for about seven and half hours on that day.[48] Industrial workers generally had Sundays off and frequently had a half-holiday on Saturdays, particularly during the summer. The movement for an eight-hour day was gaining ground, and state laws already set a limit of fifty-eight hours per week for women and minors employed in factories.[49] Hours in domestic service remained unregulated and seemingly off the agenda of both labor unions and state agencies.

Not only did domestic servants work for longer hours, their time off was not entirely their own. As the investigators from the DRL explained, "The free time of the domestic employé . . . is often subject to certain restrictions imposed in order to conform to the customs or peculiarities of the family." For example, "employés [were] expected to obtain permission before going out"; they were generally granted no more than three evenings out a week, and many got less. When they did go out, they were expected to return home by ten o'clock. Servants' social life was curtailed by having to entertain their visitors in the kitchen and being unable to serve them food. Many employers forbade visits by men who were not relatives.[50] Women resented this surveillance and lack of autonomy. Although industrial work was demanding and poorly paid, it allowed women to be part of a collective at work and to live with family or friends. Even if women struggled to pay for their room and board, during their time off they were free from their employers' supervision. All of this added up to a greater sense of independence.

Although the DRL was an organization of employers, it did not shrink from exposing employers' responsibility for some of the problems with domestic service. In "The Social Conditions of Domestic Service," a report published by the Massachusetts Bureau of Statistics of Labor, Mary Dewson forcefully presented domestic workers' point of view. After interviewing 231 servants in 181 families, Dewson concluded that the occupation offered "neither the clear recognition of mutual responsibility and reciprocal rights and duties which marked the old relation of mistress and servant, nor the equally well-defined relations which in industrial or mercantile employment exist between employer and employé." Dewson, like most commentators on the subject, harked back to an imagined or long-vanished past when the servant was the neighbor's daughter, who was happy to earn some extra money by learning skills that she would need as a housewife. However, the modern domestic servant, who was likely to be foreign-born and of a different class than her employer, occupied an awkward position: "in the family, but not of it." While her work was essential to her employer, it had little socially recognized worth now that "productive" labor had moved outside the confines of the household. Moreover, domestic servants lacked the "social opportunities" shop and factory workers enjoyed. Nor did they benefit from the "unity of action" that female workers in factories might exercise, even if they lacked formal organization. Domestic workers in Boston seemed isolated and subject to the whims of individual employers.[51]

Interestingly, servants in southern cities, who were almost all African American, may have experienced less isolation and exercised more collective power. In Atlanta, for example, most African American women refused to live with their employers, and many belonged to secret mutual aid societies. In the summer of 1881, Atlanta laundresses staged a large strike, to which whites responded, in part, by threatening to open commercial laundries staffed by Yankee girls. Although the outcome of the strike was inconclusive, it revealed a sense of community cohesion that seemed to be lacking among domestic workers in Boston. However, southern domestic workers resembled white workers in northern cities in their frequent recourse to quitting as a means of exercising control over their labor conditions.[52]

Turnover among all servants in Boston was high, and African Americans, who were concentrated in domestic work and other menial jobs, tended to be transient.[53] Difficulty in finding decent work hindered the establishment of a stable African American community in Boston and the surrounding area. By 1900 only about 4 percent of all domestic servants in Massachusetts were African American.[54] In contrast, African Americans in Philadelphia gained a modicum of economic security from the fact that a significant group of white employers either preferred African American servants, or hired servants based on "individual" qualities rather than race.[55] In 1905 a "colored butler" interviewed by the DRL claimed that he had been unable to find a job after answering no fewer than 200 advertisements for work. Ironically, he commented, "Boston people . . . will have mass meetings and raise money to help Mr. Washington educate 'niggers' down South, but they will let a decent Northerner starve before they will give him a chance to earn an honest living." As a result, he was on his way back to New York City, where he felt he was more likely to find a job.[56] Although the leaders of the WEIU viewed members' preference for white servants as retrogressive, they had little success in breaking down employers' prejudice against African Americans, or countering the pervasiveness of racial segregation, which increased throughout the country at the turn of the twentieth century.[57]

The dissatisfaction of Boston women who did work as servants was measured by Mary Esther Trueblood, a young mathematician and sociologist hired by the WEIU fresh from graduate work at the University of Michigan and at Göttingen.[58] Trueblood interviewed twenty employees each in Lowell textile mills, Lynn and Haverhill shoe factories, Boston stores and restaurants, and Boston households. Household workers were the least content. Only three of the twenty domestic servants Trueblood interviewed reported enjoying their work. The others expressed varying degrees of dissatisfaction. One woman said she was "discouraged because her work is not appreciated." One interviewee confessed to be working "in a private family" only so long as she needed to save money to take a stenography course. Another servant complained that "she hates housework, and has no time to see her friends and relatives." Finally, "an intelligent chambermaid," whose "surroundings" Trueblood described as "unusually good," characterized her job as "slavery." Like Lucy Salmon and Mary Dewson, Trueblood traced domestic servants' dissatisfaction to their lack of independence, which encompassed their subservience in a household that was not their own, long hours of labor, and lack of control over their free time. Significantly, women employed in stores and factories did not object to domestic work itself, but considered it demeaning when performed for someone who was not a member of their own family. Women who worked in restaurants—which were just beginning to become a significant area of female employment—seemed happier than those employed in private households.[59] Restaurant waitresses questioned by Trueblood described their positions as offering "greater freedom" than employment as a private waitress or a maid.[60]

While Domestic Reform League investigators such as Dewson and Trueblood appreciated and publicized problems with hours and conditions from employees' point of view, they remained firmly allied with the employing classes on the issue of wages. The DRL considered domestic workers' wages too high. Because the supply of servants was considerably lower than the demand for them, wages had risen to an average of five dollars a week in cash. Dewson and Trueblood calculated room and board at four dollars, raising real earnings to nine dollars a week. According to these estimates, servants earned more than either textile operatives (about seven dollars a week) or saleswomen (about six dollars a week).[61] However, servants valued the room and board they received at a much lower rate than their employers did; women frequently cited scanty meals and cramped quarters as reasons for leaving the occupation.[62] It seems unlikely that servants would have valued their board and lodging at more than $2.50 per week.[63] Even if we consider servants' weekly earnings to be on par with those of textile and retail workers, their hourly wages were not. Servants worked far longer hours, meaning that they made only eight or nine cents an hour, while employees in stores and factories earned ten to twelve cents an hour.[64] Dewson and Trueblood certainly could have done these calculations themselves, but this information would not have been welcomed by their own employer, the WEIU, whose members complained of the high cost and poor quality of domestic workers.

The DRL advanced its study of domestic service by taking over the registry for servants that the WEIU had been running since 1881. To help fund the organization's work, it increased the fee servants paid to use the service. In its report for 1898, the DRL admitted that many domestic workers were reluctant to register, since they now had to pay two dollars per year in addition to "10% of the first month's wages in every situation secured." Members of the WEIU continued to use the service for free. The DRL assured club members that by charging servants to register and requiring them to provide references from a previous employer, they secured a "better class" of servants.[65] Private agencies charged both employers and employees from fifty cents to a dollar to use their service for several months. The DRL revealed its bias toward employers by making servants bear the cost of running its agency.[66]

The DRL introduced a labor contract as part of the effort to make the occupation more modern and businesslike and to bring employers and employees into a shared understanding of the terms of employment. Seeking to imbue domestic service with new dignity, the DRL presented the contract as a strike against "the haunting traditions of feudal days."[67] DRL members could imagine the past either as the golden age of domestic relations in New England, when the "help" seemed like part of the family, or as a dark relic of medieval society. Despite this dramatic lead-up, the contract was brief, merely stating the names of the two parties and the wages agreed upon. It also included a brief clause explaining that during the first week of employment, an employer could discharge the employee, provided that she pay "the employee the full week's wages." However, if an employee decided to leave, she forfeited her week's wages, as well as "the use of [the DRL] office." After the first week, either party could terminate the contract with a week's notice. The contract attempted to stabilize a mobile labor force made up largely of single migrants to the city, who might desert their posts to seek another position, return to their families, or simply take time off to rest.[68] By promoting a labor contract, the DRL sought to introduce the principles of free labor to household employment, which still had lingering associations with slavery and with binding daughters out to service.

The DRL insisted that employers and employees sign the brief contract.[69] Through its publications, and undoubtedly through its mediation between employers and employees, the DRL advocated a particular understanding of the contract. As interpreted by the DRL, the contract gave employers the right to terminate employment without notice for illness, disobedience, moral misconduct, or habitual negligence. The employee could leave without notice if she was not paid, or if her employer struck her. "Harsh language or fault finding by the employer" were not, however, sufficient grounds for a servant to break her contract.[70] The DRL sent clarification of the contract to all its members as a defense against the "many and romantic versions" heard rumored around the employment office, including inaccurate allegations that it "contained limitations on the hours of labor; that it fixed the time for the meals of the household; that it forbade dictation as to dress; and that it affixed strange penalties for the use of the Christian name of the Employee!" While the DRL *Bulletin* did not specify where these rumors came from, it seems likely that they encompassed the desires of employees for greater control over their conditions of labor and more respect in their workplaces, and the fears of employers, who did not want their household labor relations subject to external regulation, even by their own organization.[71]

Many women who worked as domestic servants were reluctant to use the registry because of its high fees and stringent requirements, but the DRL still attracted thousands of women looking for positions. For the 1898–99 year, 5,890 employees and 3,187 employers signed up with the registry, which successfully placed only about a third of the servants it registered.[72] Many of those who were not placed did not have the experience and impeccable references that the DRL required. In future years, such women were not allowed to register, and the placement rates rose to 80 percent of registered employees by 1903.[73] Soon the DRL was operating the largest domestic employment agency in Boston. To accommodate its operations, it moved its offices from WEIU headquarters at 98 Boylston Street to a new location at 264 Boylston Street. The service produced hundreds of dollars per year in revenue, and the WEIU hired eight workers to run it.[74]

The popularity of the DRL's registry with both domestic workers and employers suggests that it compared favorably to Boston's other domestic employment agencies. As Lucy Salmon had complained, many of these agencies were dishonest and had associations with "vice and crime."[75] Some were known to ensnare women new to the city into prostitution by promising them jobs as servants.[76] The DRL was reputable. It did not cheat its clientele or send them out to work under false pretenses. If an employee could afford to pay the DRL's fees and had the experience necessary to provide the required references, she could be fairly sure of finding a position in a middle-class or well-to-do urban household. Although the contract favored the employer, it did provide some protection against being dismissed without being paid because it provided proof of employment.[77] Servants' most common legal problems were nonpayment of wages, followed by illegal deductions from wages for breakage.[78]

Although meeting its members' daily needs for domestic help was a large part of the DRL's work, the organization hoped to move beyond this model of domestic service. It began by trying to professionalize domestic work through its Boston School of Housekeeping. When this failed, the DRL turned to schemes for outsourcing domestic work. It attempted to meet working-class women's demands for independence by encouraging employers to hire their domestic workers for a set number of hours per day and allow them to live outside their employers' households.

The Boston School of Housekeeping, opened under the auspices of the DRL and the WEIU in October 1897, promised to transform mistresses and maids into "housekeepers" and "houseworkers."[79] Emulating the latest techniques in modern factory management, which sought to reduce reliance on skilled labor by transferring knowledge of the production process from workers to employers, the Boston School promised to give mistresses an upper hand by increasing their "scientific" knowledge of housekeeping, while training domestic workers to become dutiful and efficient employees who followed orders.[80] The school institutionalized this modern separation between management and labor by running parallel courses in a pair of adjoining houses on St. Botolph Street, one for employers and one for employees.

By making housework scientific, the DRL not only attempted to exercise control over household labor relations, but also sought to dignify the unpaid labor performed by upper middle-class women as housekeepers for their families. Housekeeping, school administrators insisted, was a profession, even though it was not paid. Specifically, they sought to appeal to "young college women . . . who wish to fit themselves to manage a household on the best economic and hygienic basis." Evidently, they assumed that marriage would preclude pursuit of paid professional work. Nannie Burroughs, an African American educator and reformer who opened the National Training School for Women and Girls outside of Washington, D.C., in 1909, shared this emphasis on dignifying domestic labor, both as wage work and as a crucial service that black women provided for their families and communities.[81]

The School of Housekeeping run by the DRL offered future employers of domestic labor a series of twelve-week courses in sanitation, food chemistry, household economics, and "principles" of cooking and housework.[82] As Mary Esther Trueblood reported in an article for *Good Housekeeping*, women "taking the employers' course" could be found studying in classrooms and "doing every kind of work connected with housekeeping in order to estimate the time that is necessary for each piece of work."[83] Presumably, practical experience would enable housekeepers to manage the time and allocate the labor of their servants more efficiently, but it also implied a transfer of knowledge from women doing the work to those directing it. Likewise, rather than relying on their cooks to do marketing and meal planning, bourgeois housewives in training learned how to compose nutritious menus and how to control food expenditures by studying the cost of ingredients and by learning to estimate how much time should be spent on meal preparation.[84]

In contrast to the academic approach taken with employers, the five-month course for employees emphasized "practical" skills. During their enrollment, aspiring employees were required to live at the Boston School of Housekeeping, where training went on twenty-four hours a day. Ironically, although the DRL encouraged employers to consider hiring workers by the day, the directors of the school were reluctant to give up complete control over their house workers, closely regulating their diet, clothing, sleeping arrangements, and use of leisure time. Students who enrolled in the school were asked to become live-in servants, not the more modern day workers the DRL promoted. The program was open only to young women between the ages of sixteen and thirty who wished to study housework as a trade. Students were expected to be intelligent, of "good character," and in "good health."[85]

Pupils at the Boston School learned by doing, performing all the domestic labor needed by the school in exchange for their room, board, and tuition. The school also instructed employees in bourgeois standards of privacy and self-presentation. Students slept in individual spaces with fixed partitions. As a prerequisite for entrance, they were required to own plain cotton frocks, collars, cuffs, aprons, and underclothing. Students who successfully completed the five-month employees' course were placed on a three-month probation during which they earned two dollars a week working in the household of a DRL member. If they jumped this hurdle, they would be awarded diplomas and placement by the DRL's domestic service registry. Their pay in these first jobs was to be determined by their grades.[86]

The school envisioned itself as "a bridge" stretching "from the congested field of labor in factory and shop, to a field of labor which ethics, education and science shall have made honorable and attractive."[87] It offered employees no incentives to cross, or even step onto, the bridge, however. Pressure from WEIU members to have a large pool of possible servants at their disposal meant that graduates had no advantage in finding jobs, since the DRL registry remained open to all domestic workers with experience and references. The directors of the school admitted defeat for the employees' program during the winter of 1900, when only five students were enrolled, all in the cook's course, and they were forced to hire servants to perform the school's domestic work.[88] As Lucy Salmon had observed in 1897, training schools for servants were generally unsuccessful since servants had no desire to attend them. She dismissed these schools, which had opened and closed in a few cities, as "the introduction of a caste system utterly at variance with democratic ideas."[89] Likewise, Nannie Burroughs found African American women reluctant to study domestic service once they arrived at the National Training School, with most women preferring to major in business or learn advanced sewing skills so that they could become dressmakers.[90]

In contrast to its failure to attract employees, the course for employers at the Boston School of Housekeeping was popular with recent graduates of Vassar, Wellesley, Radcliffe, and the University of Michigan.[91] But without training for employees, the school could make no pretense of solving the servant problem. Instead, it began offering graduate courses to women who wished to work in "applied sociology" as teachers, civil servants, or managers of institutions.[92] In 1902 the Boston School of Housekeeping became part of the Home Economics Department at the newly opened Simmons College.[93] The institution ended up affirming the role of expertise in social management rather than reforming the day-to-day practices of most households.

With its School of Housekeeping gone, the DRL pursued its dual agenda of supplying WEIU members with "good help" and modernizing housekeeping through different avenues, experimenting with outsourcing and day work. In 1889 the novelist and social theorist Edward Bellamy described servants as "anachronistic in a democratic society."[94] Under Nationalism, Bellamy's conflict-free version of socialism, the servant problem would disappear as domestic work was transferred outside of individual households and women were guaranteed complete economic independence.[95] In *Looking Backward*, Bellamy's enormously popular novel describing life in 2000, servants were unnecessary, except in case of emergency, in which case they were supplied by the state. The introduction of electricity had made the lighting of lamps and fires unnecessary, while washing and cooking were all expertly performed in public laundries and kitchens.[96] Early advertisements for gas and electricity capitalized on this fantasy by promoting new appliances such as lamps, stoves, dishwashers, and washing machines as the ultimate solution to the servant problem.[97]

By 1900 some progressive, college-educated women had become ashamed of their need for domestic help. As members of the Boston Collegiate Alumnae Association explained, they "felt that the solution for the problem of domestic servitude—so embarrassing in democratic communities—lay in the continued transfer of work from dependent producers within the household to independent workers without."[98] Note that by this point, work within households had been classified as dependent whether performed by a servant or a housewife, while work outside of households held out the promise of independence for women across social class.

Charlotte Perkins Gilman linked women's independence with jobs outside the household in her influential book *Women and Economics* (1899). Gilman described "the increasing army of women wage-earners" as changing the world by their "steady advance toward economic independence."[99] Gilman redefined independence along a market axis, arguing that women would become independent individuals once they earned their own income. She viewed housekeeping as constraining for middle-class women because it consigned them to monotonous labor, deprived them of contact with the outside world, and earned them no money. Recognizing that household workers were underpaid and lacked respect, she recommended professionalizing domestic work and transferring as much of it as possible outside the home. Gilman saw the modern household as a site of consumption rather than production. In following this last industry out of the home, Gilman promised, a woman could go from being a "penniless dependent" to a "self-supporting" businesswoman.[100]

The idea of changing the structure of domestic work by reconfiguring the material structure of the household was not new, especially in and around Boston. Members of Brook Farm (1841–46) shared the tasks of laundry, cooking, and child care. In 1868 Melusina Fay Pierce attempted to reorganize household labor to make servants in individual households unnecessary. She drew up plans for a cooperative housekeeping society in Cambridge, where families would subscribe to have their laundry, cooking, and child care done in a central location, but it lasted scarcely a year.[101] In Boston and New York, entrepreneurs and cooperative societies constructed hotels and apartment buildings with a common kitchen to supply meals to all residents.[102] In most places, however, residents reverted to individual kitchens. As Kate Gannett Wells, a health reformer who belonged to the WEIU, remarked, "as long as a man has but one wife he will prefer his individual kitchen and cook."[103] The idea of collectivizing domestic work remained controversial even among the progressive members of the WEIU.

Nineteenth-century domestic reformers mixed cooperative and profit-making approaches. By the early twentieth century, reformers including Lucy Salmon, Charlotte Perkins Gilman, and the members of the DRL all identified domestic progress with making households more businesslike and efficient. They anticipated and welcomed the arrival of a service economy. Would this new economic configuration put an end to the class tensions embodied in the servant problem? In 1887 Gilman's close friend Helen Campbell had observed that the transfer of sewing from a task performed within households to a paid occupation outside the home organized according to profit-making imperatives had emancipated middle- and upper-class housewives from domestic work at the same time that it trapped working-class women in an endless round of toil that never paid enough to put food on the table. Would moving cooking, laundry, and child care out of households truly emancipate women? Or would it just create new categories of low-paid female workers? Members of the DRL did not consider this question. Instead, they viewed transferring domestic work outside of households as a progressive response to servants' disdain for living in and to middle-class housewives' growing embarrassment at having to employ them.

Like previous domestic reformers, the DRL identified cooking as an area ripe for removal from middle-class households. In a widely publicized study, Mary Dewson compared the cost of buying fifty food items ready-made with making them at home. Goods in high demand, such as bread, could be bought almost as cheaply as they could be made. Women "who [did] their own work or who live[d] in small apartments " often patronized "delicatessen shops," which sold prepared food at relatively low prices.[104] In general, however, prepared food cost more than homemade food. A subsequent study by the Boston Collegiate Alumnae Association estimated that a prepared meal cost twenty-five cents; the same meal could be made at home for sixteen cents, including the costs of fuel and domestic labor.[105]

Dewson introduced a new consideration into calculations of domestic economy: the money that an educated woman could be earning by *not* doing domestic work. As she put it: "the time of the housekeeper might be spent in teaching, writing, or otherwise in earning money which would exceed the increased expense of ready cooked food. It would then be economical for her to devote her time to these more remunerative occupations."[106] Educated women would work to earn money so that they could afford to buy domestic goods and services on the market, creating a new form of class differentiation. According to Gilman, this would make women more independent by freeing them from domestic labor and from financial dependence on their husbands. In hindsight, however, we can see that this emancipation was partial, at best. It did not include women who continued to be employed in households, nor did it consider whether the expansion of the wage-earning imperative would ultimately increase women's freedom.

The WEIU and the DRL pursued their vision of outsourcing domestic labor by creating several new organizations. Responding to the conviction that "the time has come when we can so organize the work of our homes as to give the household employee the same definite hours and personal independence that are enjoyed by the worker in other trades," the DRL formed the Household Aid Company in 1903 to provide domestic workers on a daily basis.[107] As an article in the *Woman's Journal* explained, the Household Aid Company sought "to give the housework girl as good social standing as is held by the factory girl or the salesgirl." To this end, she was called an "aid" rather than a "servant." The company established a boarding home for female day workers at 88 Charles Street, where the worker would pay room and board, and be "free to come and go at will when off duty, her cherished 'independence' unquestioned." Like her sister in the factory, the household aid enjoyed companionship, definite hours of labor, and guaranteed pay.[108] Long hours remained a chief complaint of domestic servants. Day workers had more success in controlling their hours than household employees who lived with their employers.[109] In addition to its three-year experiment with the Household Aid Company, the DRL promoted day labor through its own employment registry, which reported a steady increase in orders for day workers, from 580 in 1898 to 3,206 in 1906. Unlike contemporary day workers, who often work for different employers on different days, those sent out by the DRL generally worked full-time for a single employer. To the dismay of the DRL, however, most employers continued to prefer live-in help.[110]

In keeping with the conviction that the servant problem could be solved if properly understood, the DRL turned once again to social-scientific investigation. In 1906 it launched a study published by the Massachusetts Bureau of Statistics of Labor to examine housewives' reluctance to replace live-in domestic help with day workers.[111] The DRL interviewed female members of Boston-area alumnae associations, whose leaders expressed embarrassment at their continuing need for servants. Yet these same women refused to consider employing workers by the day for reasons the authors found "singularly unprogressive." Housewives expected their servants to be available at all times, day and night. They refused to give up control over what their servants ate or their personal hygiene habits. Housewives distrusted servants and worried that those who lived outside of their households were more likely to get away with stealing.[112]

By holding such retrograde attitudes, the DRL warned, housewives were not only destroying the homes they should be preserving, they were subverting democracy. By treating their household employees like "chattel to render personal service," employers were undermining the dignity of housework, which was already threatened by "a social system, which makes the 'doing of one's own housework' the line of demarcation between those who are 'in society' and those who are not." Employers who treated their help without respect could not expect to find or retain satisfactory household employees. The authors of the report cautioned that to solve the domestic problem by simply doing away with the private household by boarding at a hotel, as some married couples were now doing, was "to do away with the home and strike a fatal blow at national, civic, family, and individual welfare."[113] Although experiments in living outside of private households were currently under way in hotels, settlement houses, and workers' cooperatives, the DRL revealed its own conservatism when it came to middle-class family life: it should be carried on privately, in a detached single-family home or a private apartment.

Although shifting to day work was one step toward more modern labor relations between mistress and maid, it did not actually transfer domestic labor outside the household. The Laboratory Kitchen, however, did.[114] The service, incorporated in 1903, and supported by the DRL and the WEIU, provided home delivery of hot dinners. The *Woman's Journal* noted that it was particularly attractive to middle-class dwellers "in modern apartments, where light, heat and hot water [were] on tap." By hiring day workers, buying delivered dinners, and sending out the laundry, the *Journal* reflected, housekeeping could be reduced to its "lowest terms." A light breakfast could be had in the apartment, or skipped altogether. Lunch could be had "near the office or store." In the evening, "a hot six o'clock dinner can be brought in a box, and the cook, as well as the hearthstone is eliminated from that home."[115] The author found this prescient vision of modern life rather cold. It left out the emotional sustenance derived from cooking and eating at home. Moreover, it did not solve the problems of the vast majority of housekeepers, who could not afford these services, nor did it have much relevance to residents of tenement houses, who still lacked electricity and central heat.[116]

The DRL encountered resistance to its proposed innovations from socially conservative men and affluent housewives. At a meeting of the Massachusetts State Federation of Women's Clubs, Harvard professor Edward S. Cummings made headlines by speaking on "The Relation of the Domestic Problem to the Present Industrial Problem." He insisted that social preservation relied on a separation between affairs of the household and those of the commercial world. He faulted modern women for forgetting "that the household remains the institution from which all other institutions devolve."[117] He blamed household problems on women's seemingly universal discontent. "The mistress would leave the word 'obey' out of the marriage contract; the cook, too would [prefer a system of] mutual obligation," Cummings commented. Marriage and domestic service would be on firmer ground, he argued, if both returned to older, more stable ideas of duty and service.[118]

The DRL responded by inviting Professor Cummings to lecture.[119] In his appearance, Cummings remarked, "home life today consists largely in getting ready to go elsewhere, to all kinds of public places." He noted the tendency for "various lines of business" to "assume responsibilities once found in the household." The professor suggested "that a limit to which this process of evolution may be carried might well be considered of some importance." For example, he warned that the work of rearing children should not be lightly given up to outsiders.[120] While no record of DRL members' responses to Cummings's speech exists, they may have tolerated his conservative ideas about marriage and home life because of the social importance that he, like they, accorded to the domestic sphere. While the DRL projected an image of a new, more modern household, most members remained tied to an older style of housekeeping because of their continued reliance on servants and their class position, which kept most of them out of the paid labor force.

Whether out of conviction or convenience, the DRL generally avoided discussing the work of child care, preferring to keep the conversation about domestic labor focused on cooking and cleaning. Transferring child care out of private homes remained controversial, except in cases where mothers had no choice but to go out to work. Many reformers, such as Florence Kelley, who supported day care initiatives for working-class families, believed that women and children would be better off if they received state support, in the form of "mothers' pensions" that would allow them to remain at home.[121] Among upper-class Americans, private nannies, especially those from England, were a mark of status. In the late 1890s private child care became a specialized occupation separate from the more general work of cooking and cleaning.[122]

The DRL predicted a crisis. Most employers refused to consider day workers, and fewer and fewer native-born white women were willing to work as domestic servants. The DRL found limited success in placing African American women who registered at their offices, finding jobs for just half of those who registered. In 1905 it admitted that only "the desperate suburban or country housekeeper [would] consent to try colored help." The WEIU tried to overcome this prejudice (which they preferred to think of as "fashion") by urging "patrons to try colored girls." However, the effects of their efforts were "hardly perceptible." During the previous year, the number of colored women had risen from 1 percent to 2 percent of the total number of employees placed.[123] African Americans in New York or Philadelphia had a much easier time finding employment, despite a vogue for white butlers, coachmen, and nursemaids among the rich.[124]

Admitting the racial prejudice of WEIU members, the DRL set out to discover whether recent European immigrants could be transformed into satisfactory domestic workers.[125] The WEIU supported this research by joining the New York Association for Household Research and the Philadelphia Civic Club and Housekeepers Alliance in forming the Inter-Municipal Committee on Household Research.[126] To oversee their investigations, they hired Frances Kellor, one of the most promising sociologists of her generation.

Kellor had received a doctorate at the University of Chicago. Her thesis advocated an environmental approach to social problems, illustrating the links between criminality and lack of education and opportunities for employment.[127] Despite her high level of education, she had grown up in moderate circumstances. Kellor's mother had worked as a laundress and a domestic. Kellor's father was absent, and as a teenager in Coldwater, Michigan, Frances had to leave high school to work at her mother's side before finding employment as a typesetter and a reporter for the local newspaper. She gained the patronage of a local family who funded her college education at Cornell and her graduate study at Chicago.

In 1902 Kellor moved to New York City on a fellowship from the College Settlement Association to study employment offices in New York, Boston, Philadelphia, and Chicago. Kellor employed eight female agents, many of whom worked undercover, to investigate over 700 employment agencies. Kellor found these unregulated agencies to be exploitative. Many cheated the women who registered, and some served as fronts for prostitution rings.

Men who used the agencies fared no better, often being lured to labor camps where they were underpaid and mistreated. She identified African American and immigrant women as particularly vulnerable to mistreatment.[128] Those women who did find domestic jobs faced long hours, low wages, heavy labor, inadequate food, poor lodging, and unlimited demands from employers. These factors, Kellor concluded, made domestic work less healthful than other occupations, not more healthful, as many assumed. In proposing improvements, she cited the DRL as offering the most "progressive" and "scientific" approach to these problems by providing a contract and by serving as a general clearinghouse for information on domestic service. She hoped the state would follow the example of the DRL and begin regulating domestic employment.[129]

Kellor lived in a Lower East Side settlement house and became friends with the progressive group of women who belonged to the Social Reform Club, the New York Consumers' League, and the Women's Trade Union League, where she met Mary Dreier, who became her life partner. Kellor also got to know Lucy Salmon and Florence Kelley, the director of the National Consumers' League. Kellor's work brought her into contact with President Theodore Roosevelt, who made her the national director of publicity and research for the Progressive Party when he ran for president in 1912.[130]

Kellor's 1906 study for the Inter-Municipal Committee on Household Research set out to discover whether immigrant women could be the answer to the servant problem. Gathering data from Boston, New York, Philadelphia, and Chicago, Kellor classified the immigrant woman as a "transient" domestic worker. As a servant in an American household, the immigrant woman would acquire "knowledge, efficiency, culture, and a democratic spirit." Armed with these new qualities, she would become an American; she would leave domestic service in favor of a better job, offering more regular hours and definite duties, and less isolation and discrimination. Kellor presented domestic service as a kind of way station between the feudalism of the Old World and the freedom of the New. On a practical level, service presented an opportunity for immigrants to learn English and absorb American culture and values.[131] While Kellor considered herself modern, the idea of the mistress as a cultural missionary to the immigrant working classes stretched back to the mid-nineteenth century, when large numbers of Irish women began entering the occupation, and native-born women such as Harriet Beecher Stowe urged their peers to endure the difficult process of "civilizing" their immigrant maids.[132]

In Kellor's view, immigrants benefited from domestic service. Employers were not so lucky. By hiring new immigrants, middle-class housewives performed a civic duty, but they did not assure themselves of long-term, dependable help. Recent trends in immigration exacerbated the problem. The numbers of German, Swedish, English, and Irish arrivals were declining. Kellor considered these "old immigrants" desirable employees compared to "new immigrants" from southern and eastern Europe, forgetting that native-born Americans had once viewed the Irish as undesirable household workers.[133] Like many of her native-born contemporaries, who worried about the distinctive social characteristics and apparent physical inferiority of the new immigrants flocking to the United States, Kellor described arrivals from countries such as Hungary, Poland, and Lithuania as "untried" and "more difficult to assimilate" than their Northern European counterparts. Many were peasants, accustomed to rough conditions, ignorant "of the methods, appliances, or utensils in use in American homes." To make matters worse, they had "crude" ideas about "food and its preparation, housing sanitation and cleanliness."[134] This charge carried particular weight since sanitarians linked household cleanliness with the prevention of infectious diseases, such as cholera, typhus, and tuberculosis.[135] Kellor's analysis resonated with popular concerns that unrestricted immigration threatened America's civic and racial health.[136]

Kellor reported another significant fact: these new immigrants did not want to become domestic workers. Like most immigrants, they came "to America to be free, and especially from all badges of servitude."[137] While immigrants from Ireland, Germany, Scandinavia, Great Britain, and Canada continued to work as domestic servants and made up a significant part of the domestic labor force, immigrants from these new places showed little interest in the occupation.[138] Italians considered domestic work dangerous since it removed unmarried girls from family guardianship. Jewish girls and women were unwilling to live apart from their families, and the community disdained "personal service." Kosher laws prevented Jewish immigrants from working for Christian families or for Jews who were not observant. "Domestic training-schools started for Jewish immigrants failed utterly."[139] Italian and Jewish women in Boston, like those in New York and Chicago, frequently had experience in the needle trades, and they often found work in factories or sweatshops run by other members of their immigrant group.[140] While immigrants who worked in manufacturing were vulnerable to exploitation, they preferred jobs that allowed them to stay within their own communities and to work among family members and friends.[141] In short, immigrant women seemed an unlikely solution to the servant problem as outlined by the WEIU.

While nearly every reform the DRL initiated ran into a brick wall, the registry for domestic servants continued to be remarkably successful. In May

1910 the DRL's dual roles as a provider of servants and an agent of reform came into conflict. The WEIU employed a field agent to work for the DRL recruiting suitable servants to the registry and investigating the practices of other employment agencies. The agent found numerous placement agencies in violation of state law. As a result, the DRL emulated the Consumers' League and began compiling a white list of reputable agencies for would-be employers and employees. This action angered the owners of other domestic agencies, who did not appreciate being investigated by the DRL and accused the organization of luring away their registrants. It also drew the ire of the state excise board, whose competence the DRL had questioned publicly. In retaliation (and perhaps under pressure from the owners of private agencies), the excise board revoked the WEIU's license to run its employment bureau, as the registry for domestic servants was now known.[142]

The leaders of the WEIU, the DRL, and the city's settlement houses characterized the state's actions as politically motivated and unfair. In an article for the *Boston Globe,* Mary Kenney O'Sullivan, who had joined the DRL several years earlier, pointed out that although numerous laws protected female and child wage earners in Massachusetts, household workers were "practically overlooked by law and left with no protection against unscrupulous exploitation." This was a significant problem since one-fourth of all female workers in the state were domestics. More than four-fifths of this group of 80,000 workers were either foreign born or the children of immigrants. Poor, isolated, and lacking "the collective experience and self-confidence that women in shops and factories get by working in large numbers together," domestic workers needed protection from fraudulent employment agencies and unscrupulous employers. Given domestic workers' lack of labor organization or coverage by state labor laws, O'Sullivan saw the DRL as providing an important service. Settlement house leaders blamed the state excise board for their failure to regulate domestic employment agencies effectively and charged the state with shutting down the DRL's employment office to head off an investigation of the state excise board.[143] Although the DRL had successfully allied with the Bureau of Statistics of Labor, it found itself out of step with the excise board, which served the interests of the businessmen who ran regular employment agencies.

The WEIU and the DRL had many sympathizers in this struggle, but they were not without their detractors. One newspaper article complained that the club had become "primarily a commercial venture, plus sociological laboratory where ill-digested ideas are often tried out." It had long ago abandoned its mission to provide a means of social advancement for working women. The DRL had proposed a series of "freakish innovations," yet its "boasted reorganization of domestic service merely established an employment office for servants of the rich." The anonymous author hoped that the state-mandated shutdown, which coincided with the resignation of WEIU president Mary Morton Kehew, would push the organization to abandon its reckless commercial and social experiments and renew its commitment to philanthropy.[144] The closure of the agency, combined with Kehew's departure, served as the death knell for the DRL.

The Women's Educational and Industrial Union and its Domestic Reform League did not succeed in solving the servant problem. Yet the women who ran the two organizations looked more deeply into the conflicts between domestic servants and their employers than any previous investigators. The DRL's programs floundered because they lacked appeal for both employers and employees. Upper middle class housewives proved unwilling to give up their full-time, live-in servants, and working-class women with other options for employment saw little reason to sacrifice their independence by taking domestic jobs. They experienced subservience in another woman's household as demeaning, they resented employers' control of their leisure time, and they preferred to work with other women. As the leaders of the DRL admitted, women employed in stores and factories worked shorter hours, earned higher hourly wages, and gained more positive social recognition for their labor.

The failure of the DRL pointed the way toward the future: the continuing disorganization and lack of regulation of domestic service, and the outsourcing of domestic labor through the growth of commercial enterprises providing goods and services formerly produced in the home. While members of the DRL envisioned the growth of the service industry as freeing housewives from their reliance on servants, they could not foresee how the growth of the service industry would create a new category of low-paid female workers, or how increased need for money to purchase ready-made domestic goods would give most women no choice but to enter the paid labor force.

CHAPTER 5

Democracy Is Only an Aspiration

Early in the spring of 1899 Leonora O'Reilly took the stage at the "People's Home," a radical workers' club on the Lower East Side, to advocate votes for women. Tall, slim, and dressed, like many of the city's laboring women in a white shirtwaist and long dark skirt, O'Reilly addressed women "from the factories, the shops and from the domestic branches," joined by a "sprinkling" of working men. In the decade since she had first gained public notice as an organizer for the Working Women's Society (WWS), O'Reilly had formed alliances with radicals and reformers, established a cooperative shirtwaist shop, lived in a settlement house, and become an instructor in machine sewing at the Manhattan Trade School for Girls. O'Reilly now combined her advocacy of increased economic power for working women with an urgent demand for full political rights.

Having worked in the garment industry since she was eleven years old and joined the labor movement at age sixteen, O'Reilly spoke to her audience from deep personal experience. Aware, perhaps, that the meeting would be covered by the city's daily papers, she drew on a recent report from the National Commissioner of Labor to quantify working women's difficult struggle for self-support. Across the country, the earnings of employed women averaged only $295 a year. Food and lodging cost $286 a year, leaving just $9 for all other expenses. Saleswomen earned as little as four dollars a week, a measly sum upon which they were expected not only to subsist but to appear every day in "good clothes, as a mark of respectability." Immigrant women were even more exploited; those who toiled in sweatshops labored "amid squalor, dirt, and disease," pushing their bodies to the limits of physical endurance. O'Reilly urged the women in her audience to address these problems by joining labor organizations and demanding political rights, concluding: "Women, whether you wish it or not, your first step must be to gain equal political rights with men. The next step after that must be equal pay for equal work."[1]

O'Reilly's speech at the People's Home shows that working-class women did not have to wait for educated, affluent women to explain their need for the ballot. In fact, working-class women in New York City became interested in suffrage before elite women became interested in them.[2] Like Leonora Barry, a leader of the Knights of Labor in the 1880s, O'Reilly linked working women's struggles for equal rights and equal pay. O'Reilly attributed women's lower rates of pay to their political incapacity, challenging the laissez-faire assumption that women earned lower wages than men due to an imbalance in supply and demand. Although "freedom of contract" continued to weigh against state intervention in labor relations, workers in trade, labor, and socialist organizations were receiving a hearing from state and local politicians and, in New York, successfully running for office.[3] For working women's voices to be heard in labor politics, O'Reilly believed, they needed to become voters.

By 1899 Leonora O'Reilly was convinced that male and female workers must organize together and become politically active in order to compel the state to serve the interests of the entire working class. She became a suffragist because she believed that women needed full political rights to participate in class politics and to further their quest for independence. In 1912 these convictions led her to organize the Wage-Earners' Suffrage League (WESL), an organization composed primarily of working-class women. As president of this group, she worked tirelessly for suffrage in New York and nearby states, helping to ensure the eventual victory of a state amendment enfranchising women in 1917. Suffrage, as Leonora O'Reilly conceptualized it, and as thousands of working women who heard her speeches and read her articles would agree, was not just a bourgeois demand for rights, as some European and American socialists contended, but rather a precondition for women's full and equal participation in the labor force and the polity.[4]

Campaigning for suffrage before trade unions, women's clubs, socialist societies, and state legislators, O'Reilly advanced a vision of female independence based on economic equality, collective organization, and political rights. Synthesizing her wide readings in sociology and political economy with her experiences in the labor movement, she argued that women, like all wage workers, should be compensated in relation to the value they produced. Women who were employed and paid on an equal basis with men would be able to support themselves and other family members who depended on them. Organized into trade and labor unions, and possessing full political rights, wage-earning women could press the state for policies that served their interests, such as equal pay for equal work, an eight-hour day, healthy workplaces, and an end to child labor. In their families and communities, working-class women would be recognized as breadwinners as well as bread givers. In industrialized cities and states across the nation, working-class women would no longer be the objects of charity and philanthropy: instead, they would gain stature as "citizen workers" capable of speaking on their own behalf and representing themselves politically.

A close examination of Leonora O'Reilly's suffrage work from 1899 through 1920 demonstrates the powerful links she drew between working women's roles as workers, citizens, and providers for their families. Previous historians have noted O'Reilly's support for suffrage; however, none have fully reconstructed the depth of her political beliefs or the breadth of her organizational work.[5] O'Reilly's suffrage activism illuminates working women's intertwined struggles for economic independence and political equality. Working women's positive response to O'Reilly's ideas and organizational initiatives reveal their aspirations for independence, even if the goals O'Reilly hoped to achieve through women's full citizenship were not entirely realized once women won the vote. This story invites us to rethink the class dynamics of the suffrage movement, and to appreciate working-class women's distinctive reasons for demanding full political rights. Furthermore, the story of the WESL underlines the significance of grassroots organization as a vehicle for working-class women to develop and express their ideas of independence.[6]

Leonora O'Reilly was one of several female labor organizers who joined the campaign for suffrage in New York state. In their speeches, O'Reilly and her coworkers, who included Maggie Hinchey, Clara Lemlich, Rose Schneiderman, and Pauline Newman, emphasized that millions of women across the nation now worked for wages. Between 1900 and 1920, the number of female wage earners in the United States increased from 5 million to 8 million. Across the country, one-quarter of the female population now earned their daily bread, and in cities the proportion rose to one-third.[7] From her base in New York City, O'Reilly traveled to Rochester, Philadelphia, New Haven, Baltimore, Pittsburgh, St. Louis, and industrial communities in Ohio, Maine, Connecticut, and Massachusetts to spread her message. As O'Reilly insisted, and enthusiastic audiences composed largely of female workers agreed, wage-earning women were not just supplemental or temporary workers; they were breadwinners whose labor deserved social recognition and a political voice.

As in previous decades, however, working-class women had difficulty sustaining their own independent organizations. Limited funds and lack of political power led O'Reilly to seek alliances with union men and organized, elite women devoted to social reform. Both groups proved problematic. Although tens of thousands of female workers entered trade unions of garment makers and laundry workers during the strike wave that stretched from 1909 until 1915, the union leadership in New York City, as in the rest of the nation, remained male-dominated and ambivalent about including women. As a 1915 report from the U.S. Commission on Industrial Relations acknowledged, the "labor problems of 6,000,000 women workers lie not merely in their relations with employers, but in their relations with men's unions."[8] Rather than endorse wage-earning women's call for equal pay and economic independence, national leaders such as AFL president Samuel Gompers focused on guaranteeing men a "family wage" so that their wives and children would not have to work outside the home, attempting to shore up the antiquated idea the women, like children, were properly dependent upon and protected by men.[9] As a labor organizer and a suffrage activist, O'Reilly tried to persuade union men to include women in their organizations, support the principle of equal pay for equal work, and join working women's campaign for the vote, but she had limited success.

The progressive, college-educated women who led the campaign for woman suffrage proved more receptive. Influenced by Charlotte Perkins Gilman and by the links between feminism and socialism, many saw the women's movement and the labor movement as the "twin" forces remaking American society. Theoretically, the working woman stood at the crux of both, symbolizing all women's possibilities of living a more independent existence by earning their own living. This idea may have glamorized the lives of working women, most of whom still struggled to make ends meet.[10] However, it represented a new, more positive social meaning for women's wage labor, which had been associated with prostitution and had been seen as compromising women's respectability through the end of the nineteenth century. Despite theoretical affinities, personal relations between women of different classes were often strained. Affluent, college-educated women sometimes treated working-class activists as employees rather coworkers.[11] Some of the "allies" who supported working women's organization into trade unions and entry into the suffrage movement viewed womanhood as a category that transcended class. This assumption ran contrary to the experiences of the young, mostly immigrant working-class women who joined these movements.

Despite these class tensions, women's suffrage organizations in New York City, such as the Woman Suffrage Party (associated with the New York State Women's Suffrage Association), actively recruited working-class women into their campaigns for the vote, sponsoring organizers, providing space for meetings, and facilitating access to the press and audiences with politicians. Much of this cross-class interaction was facilitated by the Women's Trade Union League (WTUL), which O'Reilly helped organize at the 1903 annual convention of the AFL. The small group of socialists, settlement house workers, and women's labor leaders who formed the WTUL sought to improve working-class women's economic circumstances by increasing their representation in the trade unions. Early branches of the WTUL formed in New York, Chicago, Boston, Philadelphia, Cleveland, St. Louis, and Kansas City, and the organization established national offices in Chicago.[12]

Drawing on her experience as a worker and an organizer, O'Reilly became a leader of the New York WTUL, helping to establish or expand local unions of corset makers, jute makers, laundry workers, garment workers, shirtwaist makers, and white goods workers.[13] At the WTUL headquarters in New York, one of the strongest branches, as many as fourteen shop meetings might be held in a single evening.[14] As the historian Eleanor Flexner remarked, "There was hardly a strike of women workers from 1905 on in which the Women's Trade Union League was not be found taking an active part in organizing the strikers, or picketing, raising bail or strike funds, mobilizing public opinion, or running relief kitchens and welfare committees."[15] O'Reilly was on the forefront of many of these struggles; her own background as a "working girl" made her a popular figure among the young women the WTUL sought to organize. At times, however, O'Reilly was frustrated by the unconscious sense of superiority the elite and middle-class "allies" projected by hosting teas, staging dance recitals, and paying for summer vacations for working-class members.[16]

In addition to providing assistance in particular labor struggles, the WTUL contributed to a new climate of self-expression among working-class women. The emergence of young women bold enough to speak in public represented a dramatic change from Victorian conceptions of womanhood, in which those who appeared in public before mixed audiences risked tarnishing their respectability. As late as 1888, even the Working Women's Society bowed to the pressure of public opinion by using clergymen to present their case to the public. By the turn of the twentieth century, young women joined radical men speaking on street corners, and women increasingly participated in strikes, protests, and parades. As Pauline Newman, an immigrant garment worker who became a labor organizer and a suffragist, explained, in the early 1900s radio did not exist, halls were too expensive to rent, "and so the only way to reach numbers of people was to get an American flag and a soapbox, and go from corner to corner."[17]

The WTUL became an important vehicle for women's cross-class activism in support of suffrage and of labor organization. Through the WTUL, Leonora O'Reilly met Harriot Stanton Blatch, who identified wage-earning women as important players in an eventual socialist revolution and in women's struggles for political equality.[18] In 1907 O'Reilly joined Blatch's new cross-class suffrage group, the Equality League of Self-Supporting Women (ELSSW). Blatch, the daughter of suffrage pioneer Elizabeth Cady Stanton, appealed to both working-class and professional women by invoking their shared goal of economic independence. During the next two years, the ELSSW and the WTUL shared goals, membership, and office space.[19] Both groups combined the financial support of wealthy allies with the street smarts of working women to launch ambitious new campaigns to organize and enfranchise women, enlivening the suffrage movement through parades, rallies, street speeches, and the visual display of banners, buttons, and hats.

As a female labor leader, Leonora O'Reilly became an important member of the ELSSW. Welcoming Anne Cobden-Sanderson, a socialist suffragette visiting from England in 1907, to a public meeting at Cooper Union, O'Reilly described the "enfranchisement of women" as "the logical development of democracy." Countering the elitism of some suffrage leaders, who objected to the fact that working-class, immigrant men won the vote before educated women did, O'Reilly presented women's participation in trade unions as a training ground for their participation in politics.[20] That same year, she joined a delegation of working women who traveled to Albany to present their case to the New York State Senate.[21] From 1908 through 1909, O'Reilly made more than thirty speeches to women's clubs, trade unions, alumnae groups, settlement houses, and working girls' clubs in and around New York City, New Jersey, and Massachusetts. In nearly all of her appearances, she advanced a socialist message and she linked labor organization and political rights as necessary to give working women more control over their wages, hours, and conditions at work.[22]

The "Girls' Strike," as newspapers christened the New York City shirtwaist makers' strike that stretched from September 1909 through March 1910, accelerated the politicization of the city's working women. The strike seemed to herald a new era of unionization for women and to symbolize new opportunities for cooperation among trade unionists, socialists, and suffragists. Contradicting popular assumptions that young women were incapable of organization, twenty to thirty thousand garment workers went out on strike, the vast majority of them immigrant women. The WTUL played a leading role in the strike, with Leonora O'Reilly, a former shirtwaist maker herself, at the helm. At the headquarters of the WTUL, she could be found working the phones, speaking to the press and to lawyers who volunteered to defend arrested workers. New women's trade union leaders emerged from the strike, including Clara Lemlich, Pauline Newman, and Rose Schneiderman, all of whom became active and committed suffrage advocates and friends of O'Reilly.[23]

Many of the women who participated in the shirtwaist makers' strike became convinced of their need for political rights by their confrontations with abusive police, biased judges, and indifferent politicians. Six hundred women were arrested during the strike, many on the recommendation of thugs hired by the companies to protect their property. Most were arraigned in night court, where prostitutes were tried and sentenced for streetwalking. Strikers looked on as judges meted out fines, knowing that the women charged with prostitution would have no choice but to continue to ply their trade in order to pay their fines.[24] In a further testament to women's unequal treatment before the law, elderly women were brought in on vagrancy charges and sentenced to spend days on their hands and knees scrubbing floors, providing free labor to the penal system and to city hospitals.[25] When a delegation of strikers appealed to Mayor George B. McClellan to complain about women's mistreatment at the hands of the police and the courts, he refused to see them—hardly a decision he could have afforded if the same delegation had represented thirty thousand voters.[26]

The strike provided O'Reilly with a new platform to draw public attention to working women's need for the vote. In February 1909 she traveled to Albany to attend a hearing on suffrage before the State Senate. Opponents and proponents of suffrage were each given two hours to present their case. In keeping with the sentiments of the majority of the senators, the "antis," as women opposed to suffrage were known, went first. They began by declaring that women did not want the vote. Then, displaying the elitism typical of their political position, they complained that the country was already suffering from "too much suffrage," especially as exercised by ignorant and intemperate working men. Mary Dean Adams, an antisuffragist who worked as an inspector for the New York State Immigration Commission, claimed that women who lived in tenements were not fit to vote and most would "sell their vote for a pound of macaroni," adding a new twist to the charge that immigrant men would sell their vote to whichever candidate offered them a drink. Based on her experiences as a state investigator, but speaking out of her own political convictions, Adams described the "immigrant woman" as "a fickle, impulsive creature, irresponsible, very superstitious, ruled absolutely by emotion, and intensely personal in her point of view." In the course of her work, Adams claimed to have witnessed "a hair pulling match in a tenement that demonstrated to anyone who had seen it [immigrant working-class women's] lack of qualifications" to vote. Other antisuffragist speakers continued this class-based assault, charging that suffrage would alienate "woman from the duties and responsibilities of the home" and warning that enfranchising women would simply add more unqualified voters to the rolls, including prostitutes.[27]

In explaining working women's need for the vote, O'Reilly also had to contend with the elitism of her fellow suffrage advocates. While waiting to speak that day in Albany, she heard testimony from Reverend Anna How- ard Shaw, president of the National American Woman Suffrage Association (NAWSA), who drew on the results of a recent election in Denver, where women had just won the vote, to promise that women of the "slums" were far less likely to vote than those who lived in the city's most prosperous residential districts. While Shaw's argument harked back to the elitism of the suffrage movement in the 1890s, most proponents of woman suffrage speaking before the senate presented democratic arguments: women paid taxes but received no representation; they were subject to the laws, but had no voice in their formulation or enforcement. Many suffragists also argued that women would elevate politics: they were less self-interested than men, and they would put morality above partisanship.[28]

The antisuffrage and prosuffrage forces each took the full two hours allotted to them, much to the annoyance of the senators, assemblymen, and reporters, who found themselves forced to stand or to sit on the floor of the chamber packed with nearly one thousand people.[29] Toward the end of the afternoon, according to Hearst's *America*, Leonora O'Reilly "deliv- ered the one gripping speech of the day." Dressed in her customary white shirtwaist and dark skirt, she stood out among the jewel-toned feathers and silk of the matrons who surrounded her. At thirty-nine, she was still described in the daily papers as a "working girl," reflecting her youthful appearance (evident in photographs) and her unmarried status, as well as the tendency of the press to slight working women by describing them all as "girls." Unlike the other women, O'Reilly used no notes, seeming to speak extemporaneously, despite the careful planning that went into her speeches. Dispensing with the rhetorical flourishes of earlier speakers, she addressed the legislators as "men." Immediately, they "stopped fidgeting and watching the clock" and listened closely to her "direct appeal." She spoke on behalf "of women in the mills and the factories, and she spoke as one of them." She defended the rights of tenement house dwellers to vote, having been born in a tenement house and living in one still. She addressed the fallacy that women did not want the vote, explaining in reference to the strike now occurring on the Lower East Side, "I am here to speak for the thirty thousand women who *do* want it." She ended by invoking working women's status as breadwinners, concluding, "We believe that a wage earner supporting a family by her toil has a right to the ballot!" The unnamed reporter commented, "It was a voice out of the depths and it challenged and held breathless both sides of the great hall. Whatever they might think, there was a woman who was desperately in earnest." O'Reilly's forceful presentation broke through flippant characterizations of her as a "working girl," leading the reporter to acknowledge her as an adult.[30]

A week later O'Reilly discussed her experiences in Albany at a rally in honor of "Woman's Day," a new holiday declared by the Socialist Party on the last day of February to celebrate its support for suffrage. One of the largest of the many rallies held in cities across the United States took place at the Murray Hill Labor Lyceum, on Thirty-fourth Street and Third Avenue, where two thousand people gathered.[31] O'Reilly shared the podium with Anita Block and Meta Stern, two leading female members of the party in New York. She began by responding to Mary Dean Adams, the immigration inspector who had spoken out against suffrage, describing her as a "horrible little mite, who wasn't a grandee herself, but who was hired by the grandees to sell her sisters."[32] O'Reilly warned the men in the audience that the antis wanted to restrict rather than expand the franchise, "and it was up to them to get busy or the same arguments that were being used against women would be applied to them." She addressed the antis' contention that giving votes to women would enfranchise prostitutes, asserting: "We working women aren't afraid of the unfortunates who have been driven by our social conditions to lives of shame and hopelessness." In other words, she viewed prostitutes as the victims of a capitalist system in which women, who earned just half of men's wages, could barely support themselves. She added that she would be "specially glad to see this class of women gain the ballot as a weapon with which to protect themselves." For O'Reilly, this protection would include laws raising women's wages. She concluded to "such a storm of applause" that she was called back up to the high podium, which she mounted two steps at a time, for an encore.[33]

Working women's dramatic public appearance as strikers and as public speakers inspired mainstream suffragists to branch out from parlor meetings and take to the streets themselves. Seeking to reach a wider audience, suffragists from elite backgrounds began holding mass meetings, distributing handbills, and staging parades. In May 1910, ten thousand women marched down Fifth Avenue in the nation's largest prosuffrage demonstration to date. Grouped according to trade, working women made a particularly impressive showing. The parade culminated in a rally at Union Square, where a newspaper reporter observed that Leonora O'Reilly "drew forth the first big demonstration of applause from the street crowd." Characteristically, her speech mixed socialism with suffrage, to the dismay of some of the elite "devotees for the 'Cause'" who shared the platform with her.[34]

Strains in the cross-class coalition supporting the "girls' strike" had already become apparent by then, as some wealthy allies had encouraged the shirtwaist strikers to settle with the manufacturers rather than hold out for recognition of their union, Local 25 of the International Ladies' Garment Workers' Union (ILGWU).[35] While O'Reilly and her colleagues in the WTUL insisted on the importance of union recognition, Harriot Stanton Blatch sided with her wealthy supporters, curtailing her outreach to working women in favor of a new focus on elite opinion-makers and politicians. Blatch changed the name of her organization from the Equality League of Self-Supporting Women to the Women's Political Union (WPU), shifting away from her earlier emphasis on women as wage earners and identifying herself with Emmeline Pankhurst's Women's Social and Political Union in Great Britain.[36] O'Reilly continued to cooperate with Blatch, but their relationship remained cool.[37] Like other working-class suffrage advocates, O'Reilly soon established a closer relationship with the Woman Suffrage Party of the City of New York, which took a more grassroots approach to winning votes for women and included working class men and women in its campaigns. Neither the WPU nor the Women's Suffrage Party emulated the violent tactics adopted by the Women's Social and Political Union, which included throwing stones, smashing shop windows, and starting fires.[38]

The tragic fire at the Triangle Shirtwaist Factory in March 1911 amplified working-class women's sense that they needed political power to protect themselves at work. When the fire broke at the end of the day in an eighth-floor workroom, women found the exits barred, ostensibly to prevent employees from stealing. To the horror of onlookers, 146 workers jumped to their death rather than be engulfed in flames. Sued in court for negligence, the owners were found not guilty. The Industrial Workers of the World, which was initiating an organizing campaign among Lower East Side garment workers, saw the decision as evidence that the state would always act to protect private property.[39] However, O'Reilly and her associates in the WTUL viewed the fire, which had aroused widespread sympathy for the victims and their families, as an opportunity to increase state responsibility for workers' health and safety. She joined the New York State Factory Investigating Committee, which studied the causes of the fire and made extensive recommendations for reform, including a new state labor code mandating minimum wages, limits on hours, and closer regulation of workplace safety.[40]

O'Reilly spelled out the political stakes in winning shorter hours for women in her state legislative testimony supporting a fifty-four-hour bill recommended by the New York State Factory Investigating Committee in May 1911. The door to special legislation limiting women's hours of labor had been opened in 1908 in *Muller v. Oregon*, when the U.S. Supreme Court upheld Oregon's ten-hour law for female industrial workers as necessary to protect the health of future mothers.[41] Like the middle-class reformers in the National Consumers' League who crafted the defense of the Oregon law from constitutional challenge, O'Reilly argued that workers' efficiency declined after eight hours and that "to work them beyond this limit [was] cruel and uneconomic." O'Reilly argued that women's hours should be limited to forty-eight per week, rather than the fifty-four under consideration.[42]

O'Reilly described the exhaustion of a ten-hour day spent at a machine as a "sinking, all-gone feeling" that left working women without "energy enough to even jump over a puddle on their way home." Long, tiring workdays gave working women "no time to think," or to be engaged in civic life—obstacles O'Reilly had surely faced in attempting to organize working women into unions. Responding to a question as to why more working women had not come to Albany to plead for shorter hours, she explained that most did not know that a bill for shorter hours was before the legislature. Those who were aware of the bill and supported its passage could hardly afford to lose a day's wages, risk their jobs, or pay the railroad fare required to travel upstate. Furthermore, even the working women able to overcome these economic obstacles would not feel entitled "to ask for a hearing before such an august body," although as "citizen workers" they had every right to demand that the legislature serve their interests. Implicitly, enfranchisement would help change working women's sense that they had "only duties," while men had all the rights.[43]

The state remained ineffective in protecting laboring women and children from exploitation. The legislators appeared to give O'Reilly and the other advocates of working women sent by the WTUL a sympathetic hearing, but once the women returned to New York City, the legislators quickly caved in to pressure from manufacturers, who warned that voting for the bill would be political suicide.[44] Under pressure from organized labor and the WTUL, a law limiting women's hours of employment was passed the following year, but it included an exemption for canneries, which employed women and children for up to 119 hours a week during the peak season.[45] If women were enfranchised, O'Reilly believed that they would be more effective in their campaigns for labor legislation.

Investigating the causes of the Triangle fire, O'Reilly described working women as wage slaves. As a member of the New York State Factory

Investigating Committee, O'Reilly read hundreds of letters from women working in dangerous conditions, many of them afraid to sign their names for fear of being fired. Speaking to a group of working women in lower Manhattan in the spring of 1911, O'Reilly described those who worked in "firetrap factories" as being in a state "no better than slavery." The metaphor of wage slavery mocked the idea of "free choice" for women who had to remain in jobs they knew were dangerous in order to put food on the table. In her use, it also suggested the inevitability of change. Just as chattel slavery had been abolished in the interests of humanity, so too would wage slavery be ended. Simplifying a complex issue, O'Reilly described the ballot as the "only way out" of wage slavery and exhorted her audience that "the only way to be sure of a good ballot is to cast it yourselves." She urged the women to march in the next suffrage parade, painting the issue as one of life or death.[46] The metaphor of wage slavery continued to resonate with industrial workers, in part because it helped establish a common ground of whiteness among an ethnically diverse workforce, but also because abolition remained a touchstone for the positive use of state power on behalf of exploited workers.

Regardless of the venue, O'Reilly reached her audience through her straightforward but dramatic style of presentation. A middle-class reporter found her voice "rich and sympathetic and stirring," noting that her way of speaking owed more to "socialist mass meetings where melodrama goes" than to the staid style of "Lyceum lectures."[47] As Pauline Newman, who worked with O'Reilly in the WTUL and the New York state campaign for suffrage, recalled, her "voice alone would get you." When O'Reilly spoke, she sounded almost "on the verge of tears" and immediately "caught the attention of the strikers," even in halls that held five or six thousand workers. She was equally effective in reaching middle-class listeners. In a letter to O'Reilly, a member of the Greenwich, Connecticut, Equal Franchise League described herself as "one of those thrilled with your straightforward, stirring presentation of your Cause."[48] Rose Perkins Hale, the wife of a Union College professor, who invited O'Reilly to speak on suffrage before a group of uptown working girls and planned to travel downtown to discuss suffrage with a group of female office workers at General Electric, added, "I do love your way of presenting the matter to these girls."[49] Encouraging O'Reilly to write an article explaining the connection between labor and suffrage to those "suffragists who don't know that there is a labor problem," Florence Woolston, who replaced Mary Ritter Beard as the editor of the *Woman Voter,* advised, "Just imagine that you are talking to a crowd on the street as to what the workers want and what they are getting."[50]

Appreciating the need to dramatize the cause to appeal to a working-class audience, O'Reilly staged a vaudeville show in support of suffrage at Hammerstein's Victoria Theatre. "Suffrage Vaudeville Week" featured street meetings outside the theater and presentations on stage by Harriot Stanton Blatch, the New York Women's Suffrage Association, and Max Eastman, a women's suffrage supporter and editor of the radical magazine, *The Masses*. The speeches were interspersed with vaudeville acts and a comic antisuffrage monologue performed by Jennie Marie Howe, a leader of Heterodoxy, the Greenwich Village club where the term *feminism* was coined.[51] A flier advertising the show was designed to look like a ballot. The Suffrage Party was represented by the Statue of Liberty standing on a platform of Justice, while the Anti-Suffrage Party featured a woman chained to a throne atop a platform of prejudice. The show, promising "Special Effects, novel surprises," and "500 suffragists on the stage," drew hundreds of working men and women, many of whom had never considered the question of woman suffrage before.[52]

Suffrage parades used theatrical techniques to broadcast their message to as many spectators as possible. O'Reilly helped organize the delegations of wage-earning women who marched in New York City in support of suffrage in 1911. The entire event celebrated the unity of labor and suffrage, reflecting the conviction of its organizers that wage-earning women best symbolized all women's pressing need for full political rights. In keeping with early narratives of women's labor history written by suffrage advocates such as Edith Abbott and Helen Sumner, the parade featured floats illustrating women's industrial progress from spinning to modern industry. Garment workers interrupted this optimistic narrative by marching with their crimson banner draped in black, memorializing their coworkers killed in the Triangle fire and casting doubt on whether real progress had been achieved.[53] The domestic labor women continued to perform as housewives and as paid domestic workers had no place in this display. Although women who worked as domestics were offered a place in the parade alongside other working women, they had no banner to march behind. Those who attended found their labor erased rather than celebrated. The press took no notice of them.[54]

Although she continued to collaborate with elite suffrage leaders, by the fall of 1911 O'Reilly felt the need for a new organization devoted to advocating suffrage from working-class women's point of view. Frustrated by constantly having to explain working-class women's need for the ballot to middle-class and elite allies and by Blatch's marginalization of working-class women within the WPU, O'Reilly formed the Wage-Earners' Suffrage League (WESL), a new group made up primarily of working-class women.[55] She was inspired, in part, by the Wage Earners' Suffrage League of San Francisco, which played an important role in campaigning for the passage of a California amendment granting women suffrage in October 1911.

Wage-earning women who supported suffrage in San Francisco faced many of the same class tensions O'Reilly experienced in New York. In September 1908 the San Francisco Equal Suffrage League, a cross-class women's suffrage organization, divided over a streetcar strike, just as the ELSSW split over the shirtwaist makers' strike. Louise LaRue, a leader of the waitresses' union, formed the WESL with the support of Maud Younger, an affluent veteran of the New York Women's Trade Union League, who had returned to her native city of San Francisco after working to organize waitresses in New York. The working-class women of San Francisco who joined the league contrasted their reasons for seeking suffrage with those of their middle-class sisters. Many were waitresses, and they opposed temperance as well as legislation preventing women from working in places that served alcohol, since both measures threatened to compromise their earning ability. However, they supported an eight-hour day for all workers, and they looked toward the vote as a means of making their voices heard within the Union Labor Party, which controlled the city government.[56] In 1909 the national WTUL sponsored Louise LaRue's attendance at the national convention of the WTUL in Chicago, where she and Leonora O'Reilly may have met.[57] O'Reilly borrowed the name from the San Francisco group, although the two organizations operated independently.

In establishing a Wage-Earners' Suffrage League in New York City, O'Reilly found an eager supporter in the historian Mary Ritter Beard, who saw the WESL as a means of following her "dream to develop working women to be a help in the awakening of their class."[58] Beard first became interested in the problems of working women in 1900, during a year she spent living in England with her husband, the historian Charles Beard. The couple had met at DePauw University in Indiana, where both attended college. In 1898 Charles began his graduate studies at Oxford and helped establish Ruskin Hall (later Ruskin College), an adult education school for workers.[59] In 1901 Mary Ritter and Charles Beard moved to Manchester so that Charles could pursue his research and direct a branch of Ruskin Hall.

In Manchester, Mary Ritter Beard, who had come from a comfortable family, witnessed the problems of industrial poverty firsthand. She also learned to think of those problems in socialist terms, influenced by the progressive educators who supported Ruskin Hall and by Emmeline Pankhurst, a neighbor, who became her good friend. Pankhurst would later become famous in Great Britain and in the United States for her leadership of the

WSPU and for her use of violence in protesting on behalf of woman suffrage. She inspired Mary Ritter Beard to join the suffrage movement and to focus her attention on working-class women.[60] While in England, Beard read *Women and Economics* (1898) by Charlotte Perkins Gilman and began writing women's history. Her first article, assessing the status of women in the new century, appeared in *Young Oxford,* the journal associated with Ruskin Hall.[61] She would go on to write extensively on women's history, American citizenship, and the labor movement.

Mary Ritter Beard carved out time to write and pursue her political work amid increasing family responsibilities. A few months after the birth of their daughter, Mary and Charles Beard moved to New York City, where both enrolled in graduate school in political science at Columbia. While Charles completed his degree and joined the faculty, Mary, who had another child in 1907, left Columbia and began volunteering for the WTUL, where she met Leonora O'Reilly. Like O'Reilly, Beard joined the ELSSW and the Woman Suffrage Party (WSP), editing their magazine, the *Woman Voter.* Admiring O'Reilly's intentions to start a new suffrage organization for working-class women, Beard helped O'Reilly get the WESL off the ground by publicizing its activities and helping O'Reilly strengthen her contacts with leaders of the WSP.[62]

According to Beard, about twenty-five working women, "representing the bookbinding, shirtwaist making, gold leaf laying, shirt making, and other trades," showed up for the first meeting of the WESL, held at the WSP headquarters in the Metropolitan Tower. The women who gathered elected O'Reilly as their president and Clara Lemlich, a Jewish immigrant who had been a leader of the shirtwaist strike of 1909, as their vice president.[63] O'Reilly and Lemlich were two of the city's most forceful and articulate advocates for working women. Both were socialists who believed strongly in trade unionism; both viewed political rights as an important symbol of equality and as a tool for demanding city and state laws that would serve working-class women's interests. The WESL's fragmentary records say nothing about the ethnic composition of the membership, but in its choice of leadership and in political appeals that invoked poor conditions in working-class neighborhoods and workplaces, the group sought to reach working-class women across lines of age, ethnicity, occupation, and marital status.[64]

O'Reilly had extensive experience in women's cross-class organizations, from the WWS through the WTUL and the ELSSW. In each of these groups, struggles emerged over who would set the agenda: middle-class allies or working-class women. O'Reilly hoped to avoid these problems by structuring the WESL so that wage-earning women remained clearly in charge of their organization. The group's constitution established two classes of membership, active and associate. Active members included women who belonged to "labor organizations" or who worked in "factories, shops, or other places, where a trade organization might be possible." Associate members would be admitted so long as they were willing to work "under the direction" of the active members and to "contribute service." Only active members had the power to vote, and any associate member who missed two consecutive meetings would be dropped from the organization.[65] These strict requirements discouraged professional or elite women from joining unless they were willing to work under the direction of working-class women. Having watched control of cross-class organizations shift time and again to the allies, who tended to be older and more politically experienced, O'Reilly made sure the membership and leadership of the WESL would remain working-class.

Ideally, a woman who became interested in suffrage would share her enthusiasm with other women working in her "store, factory, mill, or business office."[66] The organization made no mention of women employed in domestic service, nor did it reach out to African American women. However, O'Reilly sympathized with African Americans' long struggle for freedom. She was an early member of the National Association for the Advancement of Colored People, and she addressed "colored working girls" at the Union Baptist Church in San Juan Hill, a predominantly African American neighborhood on the West Side of Manhattan, on the need for suffrage.[67] As a teacher at the Manhattan Trade School for Girls, O'Reilly trained African American women to become dressmakers. Once her students graduated, however, they had difficulty finding jobs in the garment industry due to the prejudices of employers and of white working women.[68] While O'Reilly had no sympathy for race prejudice, she may have felt limited in her ability to address the issue in the WESL. Given her own identity and experiences, O'Reilly spoke primarily for native-born and immigrant women employed in industry.

Despite its declaration of organizational independence, the WESL remained financially dependent on the WSP and the WTUL. With dues set at ten cents a month and a membership that never exceeded a few hundred and sometimes dipped below fifty, it was unlikely to become financially viable. So O'Reilly turned to her wealthier friends in the WSP and the WTUL to provide space, print fliers, and fund bands for rallies and parades.[69] She found the lack of a meeting place particularly trying. In a letter to a young protégée in Rochester, O'Reilly emphasized the need for workers to raise money so that they could have their own space in order to meet and act independently.[70] O'Reilly had difficulty scheduling the evening meetings of the WESL, since the WSP headquarters was often booked with other meetings, or with appearances by visiting suffragists.[71] The WESL raised funds by selling suffrage pamphlets and by holding a large annual meeting, where only working women would speak. A collection taken at that meeting helped fund the group's work for the following year.[72] O'Reilly's services as a speaker on labor and suffrage were in high demand during these years, and her contributions helped keep the group afloat. She made sure that the WESL contributed to the WSP on a regular basis, an act that affirmed its organizational independence.[73] Given the finances of the two groups, however, this contribution was largely symbolic.

Clara Lemlich, a talented public speaker who had been black-listed since the shirtwaist makers' strike, began working full time as an organizer for the WESL, with the WSP paying her salary. A flier she distributed at lunchtime meetings held in front of women's workplaces posed nine questions, beginning with: "Why are you paid less than a man? Why do you work in a fire trap? Why are your hours so long?" The answer to all of them was simple: "Because you are a woman and have no vote." The flier then explained that women who wanted better conditions at work and in their neighborhoods "*must* vote" and urged women to address these problems and work actively for the vote by joining the WESL. Frances Duncan, another organizer, contrasted the WESL's grassroots approach to that of "parlor suffragists who do nothing but dream and talk of the day when we shall have the right to the ballot."[74] Despite elite suffragists' new willingness to march in parades, older ideas about female respectability lingered, and Duncan viewed working-class women as less hindered by concerns about propriety and more willing to take to the streets to voice their demands.

O'Reilly fully appreciated class-based differences, even as she appealed to wealthy female allies to support the WESL. In a letter to her friend Margaret Dreier Robins, the president of the National WTUL, she explained that a working-class women's suffrage organization must be run by working women themselves, since even their best-intentioned middle-class friends "really don't speak our language" and "rub the fur the wrong way." She appealed to Robins to support the new venture, explaining, "We have to build a woman's movement in this land on a Labor Foundation." With the support of the WTUL, the WESL could help the working woman "understand her relation to the vote." The WESL would also take on the task of explaining the importance of suffrage for working women to "women of leisure" and to working men. Robins believed in suffrage, and O'Reilly hoped to win her support for establishing a branch of the WESL in every state where the WTUL existed.[75] Aside from strong local organizations in New York, Chicago, and Boston, however, the WTUL remained shaky. In January 1912 O'Reilly traveled to Kansas City to try to prop up a failing branch; and Robins gave up on a local they had begun in Pittsburgh.[76] WTUL members in Chicago contacted O'Reilly for advice on starting a WESL in Chicago, and by 1914 the WESL of Chicago was holding weekly meetings. Women from the two organizations shared ideas for interesting working-class women in suffrage, but operated within the context of local campaigns.[77]

Margaret Dreier Robins' sister, Mary Dreier, the leader of the New York WTUL, supported O'Reilly's efforts to educate working women about their need for the vote. In March 1912, 250 working women visited the headquarters of the WTUL at 43 East Twenty-second Street to see "The Home Thrust," a suffrage play. Clara Lemlich gave a speech, and the young women broke into small groups to discuss suffrage over refreshments.[78] Theater continued to be an important means of reaching young, working-class women, many of them immigrants, who might not have the time or the English-language skills to read about the movement.

The WESL achieved a new degree of public visibility in April 1912, when it hosted a mass meeting at Cooper Union to counter the "Sentimentality of New York Senators" with the "Common Sense of Working Women." Mary Ritter Beard, who was outraged that state assemblymen and senators had entirely ignored working women in a recent debate over suffrage, urged O'Reilly to orchestrate the meeting, writing: "Do tell me you like this idea for I am thrilled by it." O'Reilly got to work immediately, choosing particularly ridiculous characterizations of women from the senate debate and making a list of female trade unionists affiliated with the WTUL to respond to each one.[79] By claiming "common sense" (the title of a revolutionary pamphlet by Thomas Paine) and charging the senators with sentimentality, the women reversed common gender stereotypes, using humor to catch the attention of the public and the press.[80] They also reversed the polarity of most cross-class interactions among women, which consisted of working-class women serving or being instructed by women who were wealthier and better-educated. At this meeting, members of the Collegiate Equal Suffrage League acted as ushers dressed in their caps and gowns, dramatizing their service to the working-class women of the WESL.

The meeting provided a rare opportunity for working women to take center stage and explain their desire for the vote to the public. The city's daily papers carried news of the meeting, expanding the audience far beyond those who attended. By all accounts, even that of the antisuffrage *New York Times,* the meeting was a smashing success. O'Reilly served as the mistress of ceremonies. "Take it home and dream about it tonight," she instructed her largely working-class audience; "women who have had opportunities and privileges are waking up to their responsibilities to those who have less." She then introduced six female labor organizers, each of whom used a chauvinistic statement from a senator as a jumping-off point to explain why the realities of working women's lives made the vote so important. According to the *Times*, the audience that filled the hall consisted "largely" of "women from the shops," who responded enthusiastically to the speakers, all of whom "knew by hard experience the work of the trade she represented." While the workers assembled in the hall would have been familiar with these labor organizers, their names and ideas would have been new to most readers of the daily papers. Even before they spoke, the appearance of these forceful wage-earning women on stage rebutted the senators' descriptions of women as domestic creatures, too fragile to enter the hurly-burly world of politics.

Maggie Hinchey, the Irish immigrant leader of the laundry workers, who had recently been imprisoned during a strike, was greeted with "thundering applause." She responded to Senator McLellan's contention that "the family and family relations" mattered more to women than "lawmaking or holding office." Hinchey corrected the middle-class notion of the home as the antithesis of work. For female workers, home was not a vocation, but a place "where we go at night to rest our weary bones for six or seven hours." Employed women did not have the luxury of staying out of the paid labor force. Most men did not earn enough to support their families on their own, and even those who did left their families with no savings to fall back on if they died. Widowed mothers with children who found work in the laundries faced fourteen- to sixteen-hour days, making it impossible for them to put their children in nurseries, which kept more regular hours. As a result, working mothers either left their children alone or put them in the care of a neighbor, whose negligence might lead to illness and even death. Laundry workers demanded shorter hours so that mothers could secure decent childcare and see their children in the evenings. Hinchey insisted on working women's need to combine paid employment with care for others; these women deserved the ballot to represent their interests as workers and as heads of families.[81]

Lillian Hefferly, a neckwear maker who spoke on behalf of a union of 1,400 workers who had endorsed suffrage, amplified Hinchey's theme of working women's family responsibilities. A married woman herself, Hefferly was keenly aware of the economic insecurities working-class families faced. Women whose husbands were killed in industrial accidents seldom collected any damages, since all-male juries did not take them seriously.

Entering the workforce, they faced long hours, making it almost impossible to find adequate childcare.[82] The demand for shorter hours was not just a means of protecting the health of working women themselves, as middle-class reformers claimed, but of enabling them to fulfill their family responsibilities.

Melinda Scott, a native-born hat trimmer, forcefully addressed the differences between the sentimental view of motherhood advanced by the men of the state legislature and the harsh realities of working mothers' lives. Invoking Roman history, one senator had described "Cornelia's jewels" as her children. According to Scott, "the modern Cornelia" was an Italian immigrant laboring nearby in a dark tenement house apartment, where she sewed pants alongside her eight "jewels." Together, she and her children sewed seven pairs of pants a day, earning just forty-nine cents. Nearby, another immigrant mother and her children made artificial violets. This Cornelia and her jewels earned three cents for every 144 artificial flowers they produced. Toiling until midnight, they earned sixty cents a day. These facts revealed the senators' invocation of "sacred motherhood" to be a complete "farce." Today's mother was "powerless to save her children from the juggernaut of the present economic system." Scott saw women's legal disabilities and their poor economic status as closely linked, concluding, "Men legislating as a class for women and children . . . have done exactly what every other ruling class has done since the history of the world began—they have discriminated against the class with no legal voice." If women had the vote, Scott argued, they would have protected "Cornelia and her jewels" by passing the fifty-four-hour bill without exempting canneries, which relied on child labor. With the vote, Scott promised, women would substitute enforcement of child labor legislation for "all this sickening sentiment about motherhood and the home."[83]

Mollie Schepps, an immigrant shirtwaist maker, sketched out an egalitarian vision of working women's relationships with working men based on their shared status as breadwinners. "Since economic conditions force us to fight our battles side by side with men in the industrial field we do not see why we should not have the same privileges in the political field," she explained. Working-class women regarded working-class men as partners: "We are not angels nor are they Gods. We are simply in business together and we refuse to play the silent partner any longer." The audience responded with laughter and applause. Acknowledging that some men objected to equal pay for equal work, fearing that it would keep women from getting married, Schepps commented: "If long miserable hours and starvation wages are the only means men can find to encourage marriage it is a very poor complement to themselves." She urged working women to work for the ballot themselves, not just to rely on their middle-class sisters to win it for them; invoking the Triangle Shirtwaist Factory fire, she explained that the ballot "as we mean to use it will abolish the burning and crushing of our bodies for the profit of a very few."[84] Schepps advocated suffrage from a distinctly working-class point of view, harboring no illusions about women sharing a universal set of interests regardless of class and urging her working-class listeners to become politically active on their own behalf.

While working women may have felt they had every right to be considered men's equals, the structure of the labor market continually drove them into unequal relationships. Clara Lemlich did not sugarcoat working-class women's often bitter experiences of marriage and motherhood. With no effective child labor legislation, young girls went into factories "full of hope and courage." After a few years of long hours and grinding work routines, they had lost both. Marriage seemed to be a way out, but young women who made hasty marriages soon discovered that their husbands could not support them. They remained stuck in the shop, their long hours of wage work compounded by their new duties as mothers and housekeepers. Old age brought no respite or respect. In New York state, 31,000 women over the age of sixty-five still worked to support themselves. Unable to find factory jobs, many cleaned offices at night, scrubbing on their hands and knees. Younger women who lost their husbands and had children to support often turned to prostitution, which, as Maggie Hinchey had remarked, paid better than "honest labor."[85]

In short, the state served men's interests and provided no real protection for working women. As Rose Schneiderman, a former cap maker and fiery public speaker, concluded, working women needed votes so that they could protect themselves. Rejecting the prevalent assumption that all women would be better off at home, Schneiderman explained: "We want to work, but we want to do it under humane conditions, to benefit the community, not just the very few." Like the previous speakers, Schneiderman pointed to the class bias contained in broad generalizations about women's nature. "Perhaps working women are not regarded as women, because it seems to me, when they talk all this trash of theirs about finer qualities . . . they can not mean the working woman." As a recent strike of laundry workers revealed, owners of commercial laundries reserved the worst work for women because they could be hired more cheaply and would work longer hours than men. Surely, casting a ballot would not compromise women's charm or beauty more than standing for fourteen hours a day "in the terrible steam and heat with their hands in hot starch." Schneiderman concluded: "We are going to push for 'Votes for Women' among working women everywhere. Those of you who want to be on the winning side of this abolition movement better join right now."[86] Like Maggie Hinchey, Schneiderman used the language of wage slavery to find points of connection among female workers divided by occupation and ethnicity, and to invoke a powerful example of the positive use of state power.

The WESL found support among British as well as American suffragists. When the labor organizers finished, Elizabeth Freeman, a suffragist visiting from England, presented O'Reilly with a green, white, and crimson banner stating "Give Women Citizenship" for the WESL to carry in the upcoming suffrage parade; "there was great applause as Miss O'Reilly took it." A band that had been playing outside Cooper Union before the meeting marched into the hall playing "The Wearing of the Green" in O'Reilly's honor. A collection was taken, yielding $77, mostly in coins and small bills, "gathered by the college women in their mortarboards."[87] According to Mary Ritter Beard, the presentations were so effective that "the membership of the League was greatly increased."[88] In a letter to O'Reilly the next day, Mary Ware Dennett, the director of NAWSA's publications department, described the meeting as "without exception the best suffrage meeting I have seen yet in this town!" With her help, the WESL reprinted the speeches given that evening, selling the series for twenty cents. Orders came in from around the country when advertisements ran in *Life and Labor*, the WTUL's monthly magazine, which appealed to working women through its lively mix of news, poems, photographs, and fiction.[89]

Mary Ritter Beard moved to New Milford, Connecticut, shortly after the meeting, "for the family's sake," depriving the WESL of an important ally. In a letter to O'Reilly, she apologized for having "to leave the fight so early," but she expressed the hope that there were "enough people interested in the wage-earners side of it now to make it go." In New Milford, she worked on a book of facts for suffrage advocates to use in their speeches.[90] Fact-finding and social investigation continued to be linked to social reform. The WTUL joined the General Federation of Women's Clubs and the National Consumers' League in lobbying for Congressional sponsorship of a nineteen-volume investigation of the conditions of women and children in industry. They planned to use the investigation to bolster the passage of labor legislation protecting women and children and to demonstrate the economic costs of women's political powerlessness.[91]

Given "the fact that such an *army* of tenement mothers and working women marched" in the May 1912 suffrage parade, Beard believed that working-class women's campaign for the vote had been launched.[92] O'Reilly, who led a delegation of women who "worked for a living" behind her new banner, surely must have agreed. The WESL, the WSP, the WTUL, and the College Equal Suffrage League marched in close formation, symbolizing their alliances.[93]

As the most prominent working-class woman to support suffrage, Leonora O'Reilly became nationally known. *McClure's* magazine described her as "gaunt and Irish and pale with the burden of her destiny." O'Reilly's class identity shaped her portrayal in the media, as the reporters exaggerated her slimness for the sake of drama and contrast with more ample, elite leaders of the movement, such as Harriot Stanton Blatch and Anna Howard Shaw. As O'Reilly's audience grew larger, she refused to moderate her message. At the annual meeting of the NAWSA held in Philadelphia, she advised college women in the audience "not to correct the grammar of working girls." Instead, she urged the middle-class women to "let the girls do things in their own way," explaining that those who attended meetings of working women should not "come to talk," but to listen. She advised them not to be afraid of working women when they went on strike, explaining, "We must protect ourselves."[94] Increasingly, O'Reilly was called upon to speak on behalf of the nation's working girls and women. As a young woman, she had resisted being cast as a representative of working women, but in middle age she embraced this identity as a source of power. In 1912 she testified in favor of suffrage before the U.S. Congress, speaking for the nation's 8 million female wage workers.[95]

O'Reilly continued to combine her activism on behalf of suffrage and labor, viewing the "Votes for Women question and the Women's Labor Movement" as "absolutely inseparable."[96] In 1912 she traveled to Kansas City for the WTUL to manage a strike of laundry workers, and to Kalamazoo, Michigan, where she organized corset workers and urged middle-class women to boycott the Kabo Corset Company. In New York City, she was a featured speaker at events sponsored by the Socialist Party and the Central Labor Federation. She continued to travel frequently, addressing suffrage and labor groups in Connecticut, New Jersey, Pennsylvania, Maryland, and Washington, D.C. As she became well-known, her fees increased from ten dollars per speech to twenty-five dollars plus expenses. O'Reilly's speaking fees put her in a considerably higher income bracket than the female workers she addressed. At this point, a female sewing machine operator earned an average woman's wage of about six dollars for a sixty-hour week; outworkers, finishers, and trimmers earned as little as three dollars a week.[97] However, O'Reilly's earnings were on a par with the salaries the ILGWU paid its full-time organizers. Pauline Newman, who had gone to work for the

ILGWU after the 1909 shirtwaist makers' strike, quit when she discovered that the men were earning forty-two dollars a week while she was making thirty-five dollars for the same work.[98] Like Newman, many female labor organizers went to work for the WTUL or for suffrage organizations rather than remain in trade unions where they earned less than male organizers and found themselves shut out of leadership positions.

O'Reilly used her salary and her speaking fees to contribute to the suffrage and labor movements and to support herself and her family. A small annuity from Mary Dreier allowed her to leave her teaching position at the Manhattan Trade School for Girls and to work full time as an organizer for the WTUL and the WESL. She took out a mortgage to purchase a new home in Bath Bay Beach, Brooklyn, where she moved with her mother, Winifred, and Victory Drury, an aging anarchist and veteran of the Paris Commune who had once been the most powerful leader of the Knights of Labor in New York City. O'Reilly's own father had died when she was an infant, and Drury, who was forty-five years her senior, recognized her potential as a leader and became like a father to her. As he aged, he required considerable care from both Leonora and Winifred O'Reilly. Leonora never married, but she wanted a child, so she adopted a daughter, Alice. Sadly, Alice lived for only a few years.[99] Despite her somewhat unconventional family, O'Reilly, like most working women, mixed care for others with paid labor, deepening her appreciation of working women's need for wages and free time adequate for family support.

O'Reilly worked tirelessly to educate the public about the negative consequences of women's low wages and lack of political rights. She used popular debates about urban working women's style of dress and self-presentation to raise economic issues.[100] In a debate with Annie Nathan Meyer, the founder of Barnard College, O'Reilly defended working women's rights to support themselves and to buy "finery" with any money they had left over. After all, working-class women had a right to aspire to beauty, even if middle-class reformers such as Meyer found the results "tawdry."[101] However, O'Reilly cautioned female workers against going into debt to buy clothes, despite pressures to dress like a "lady" in order to secure a job in a store or office. O'Reilly explained to a newspaper reporter: "Working women go to work to secure food, clothes, and shelter. Where her wages are too small to secure all three of these necessities, the working woman must sacrifice the one which to her seems less important." The woman who worked in a store or office could "be hungry without any visible sign." She urged the public to consider whether the working woman "received full return for services rendered. If not, why not?"[102] Her question pointed obliquely toward socialism and more directly toward the importance of securing a living wage for female workers.

In January 1913 Leonora O'Reilly helped lead a strike of white goods workers that lasted for several months. Like many of the strikers, she was arrested and charged with disorderly conduct, allegedly for harassing scabs. Middle-class suffragists whom O'Reilly had addressed in Westchester and Connecticut sent in contributions and offered to come to WTUL offices to work on behalf of the strike and to join the picket lines.[103] However, two of the many allies who showed up, "dressed in velvet and a little fur and jewelry," found the police reluctant to arrest them. As one suffragist who joined the picket lines with her friend explained in an article for *Life and Labor*, "the officer refused our right to ride in the patrol wagon, simply because of the way we were dressed. Infuriating!" Determined not to be left out of the action, the two suffragists climbed into the wagon anyway, where O'Reilly announced, "The Night Court, girls" and led them in singing the "Marseillaise," the anthem of the French Revolution and a staple of socialist labor rallies.[104] To suffragists, labor radicals, and their sympathizers, the revolution seemed imminent in 1913, and wage-earning women were at the center of it.[105]

O'Reilly's personal experience of being arrested may not have been so glorious. In her own article for *Life and Labor*, she described the terror of "feeling the hand of the law on her shoulder when she tried to keep a thoughtless sister" from taking the place of a striking worker, as well as "the officer's club upon her ribs" when she and other strikers were herded into the patrol wagon. The arresting officer taunted her "for the whiteness of her face and the style of her hat." In the night court, she and the other strikers were arraigned alongside prostitutes, whom the judge found guilty of soliciting plainclothes officers. While her upper-class allies were thrilled by the novelty of arrest, O'Reilly found the experience humiliating, in part because the police treated working-class women with considerably less respect than they accorded the ladies, whom they were reluctant to touch, much less insult. She marked an important difference between those who acted as observers in social struggles and those who participated in the great human drama directly, whether it turned out to be "farce, comedy, or tragedy." While far from triumphant, O'Reilly's experiences leading the strike and being arrested strengthened her conviction that "the whole body politic" was badly in need of "a breath of pure air" to be supplied by "votes for women."[106] Her vision of the changes to be achieved by women winning the vote extended to reforming the gender and class biases embedded in the way the police, the courts, and the prisons treated women.

While Leonora O'Reilly was willing to endure arrest to defend striking workers, she never courted arrest in pursuit of suffrage. By January 1913, 2 million women in ten states had won the right to vote. In New York state, the suffrage campaign went into high gear under the direction of Carrie Chapman Catt, who united the WSP, the College Equal Suffrage League, and the New York State Woman Suffrage Association into the Empire State Campaign Committee, which also won the cooperation of the WESL and the WTUL.[107] Later that year, however, the American suffrage movement divided over questions of tactics and strategy. Alice Paul, a graduate of Swarthmore College who had recently returned to the United States after working with the WSPU in England, established the Congressional Committee, a new group within the NAWSA, devoted to winning suffrage through a federal constitutional amendment. In April 1913 Paul broke away from the NAWSA to form the Congressional Union for Woman Suffrage, renamed the National Women's Party a few years later. In 1917 the National Women's Party adopted "militant" tactics by picketing in front of the White House. Although Paul and her colleagues remained committed to nonviolence, the women were arrested, staged a hunger strike, and were subjected to forced feedings.[108] The shock value of their arrest stemmed in part from their privileged social class, and their actions gained national publicity.

As in Great Britain, most working-class women in the United States who supported suffrage were reluctant to risk arrest because of their family responsibilities and fear of losing their jobs.[109] The arrest of Paul and other members of the National Women's Party challenged widespread assumptions of female weakness, passivity, and propriety. Arrest had different, less desirable social connotations for working-class women. First, it played into negative stereotypes of working-class women as savage and undisciplined, advanced by opponents of woman suffrage such as Mary Dean Adams. Second, it tarnished working-class women's hard-won respectability by associating them with prostitutes. Third, it may have been counter-productive to winning the support of organized working-class men, many of whom had conservative ideas of proper behavior for women. Pauline Newman, who campaigned for suffrage in New York state along with Leonora O'Reilly, recalled "a lot of opposition" to suffrage "among the labor men, even among the trade union men," who often interrupted her speeches to ask her why she was not home doing the dishes.[110] Working-class women's willingness to risk arrest during labor conflicts showed their determination to win rights as workers. For most of these women, suffrage must have seemed like a less pressing goal; leaders such as O'Reilly and Newman recognized that arrest would not serve the interests of working women or increase the respect of working men, whom they hoped to gain as allies in labor organization and in campaigns for suffrage.

O'Reilly remained loyal to Carrie Chapman Catt, who viewed Paul as an interloper. Here O'Reilly parted ways with her friend Mary Ritter Beard, who left the WSP to join the Congressional Union in 1913, perhaps out of loyalty to her friend Emmeline Pankhurst, whose militance Catt refused to defend.[111] Beard attempted to gain O'Reilly's support for the Congressional Union, which recognized the political value of claiming to have support from women of all classes, but she had limited success. O'Reilly refused to organize a delegation of working women from New York state to march in the large parade the Congressional Union staged in Washington, D.C., to coincide with Woodrow Wilson's inauguration in March 1913. She did, however, agree to march in the parade after she received a long letter from Beard explaining "the blind folly of ignoring political action." While Beard assumed that O'Reilly had been convinced by her reasoning, it seems more likely that O'Reilly felt indebted to Beard for the assistance Beard had offered in organizing the WESL.[112] Soon after, O'Reilly declined Alice Paul's invitation to teach at the Suffrage School sponsored by the Congressional Union, and she steadfastly refused to lend her name to the group for the purposes of publicity.[113] O'Reilly may have judged Paul's group to be a less promising vehicle for working-class women's participation than the WSP, which aligned itself with Catt and remained a firm ally of the WESL.

Campaigns focused on national political leaders offered limited space for working-class women to participate, except as a symbolic presence. In February 1914 Mary Ritter Beard orchestrated a visit of four hundred working-class women to the White House, where they demanded an audience with President Wilson, who agreed to meet with twenty-five of them. Beard presented the story to the press as "a spontaneous uprising of the proletariat," but in fact wealthy supporters of the Congressional Union had funded the event. Beard complained privately to Paul that members of the delegation from New York were "spoiled," since they expected the Congressional Union to cover the costs of their meals on the train.[114]

In contrast, Catt presided over a grassroots campaign in New York state that employed such female labor leaders as Leonora O'Reilly, Pauline Newman, Maggie Hinchey, and Rose Schneiderman, and integrated working-class women into its campaigns.[115] O'Reilly's schedule on a swing through upstate cities and towns early in the spring of 1913 suggests the Empire State Campaign Committee's multipronged approach. In Rochester, a socialist stronghold, she led three sets of gatherings: an open-air meeting aimed at women leaving work; a parlor meeting of middle-class suffragists; and a large public meeting of several thousand men and women who sympathized with socialism, labor, and women's rights.[116]

Mary Ritter Beard would later assess women's grassroots organizing as more significant to their development as a "force in history" than their winning of formal political rights. The accomplishments of the WESL can best be appreciated from this vantage point. By organizing to demand full political rights, women who participated in the group articulated a sense of themselves as workers and as citizens. By speaking and marching in public, they sought positive recognition for their status as wage earners, and gained a new sense of collective power. From 1913 to 1917, however, conflicting personal loyalties, class identifications, and political convictions divided O'Reilly and Beard in their approach to winning votes for women.[117]

On 4 May 1913, between ten and twenty thousand women marched in the annual suffrage parade (depending on whether opponents or proponents of suffrage were counting the marchers). Even the conservative *New York Times* conceded that since the first suffrage parade, woman suffrage had passed "the experimental stage." Indeed, votes for women could no "longer be debated as a theory," since it had "become a fact" in California, Oregon, Washington, Idaho, Wyoming, Utah, Arizona, Colorado, Kansas, and Michigan.[118] Although divisions within the movement caused friction between friends and former allies, they did not seem to be detracting from the movement's success in winning converts.

As president of the WESL and director of the Industrial Division of the WSP, O'Reilly rallied the city's working women to join the parade. She convinced Mary Dreier to pay for a band to lead the wage earners, and she either visited or wrote to the leaders of all the city's trade unions with female members. She also contacted socialist women's groups and working girls' clubs. In a typical note, she urged Ethel Greenberger, an organizer in the white goods strike, to press her fellow workers to march: "those of us who believe in Votes for Women ought to make as big a showing as possible this year to prove to the politicians that the Working Girl has arrived and that she knows she has rights as well as duties, and means to fight for them."[119] Maggie Finn, an old friend from the WWS who now worked as a New York state factory inspector, promised O'Reilly that she had been "working like a beaver" for suffrage, but feared she would not recruit many marchers, since "working girls have to work on Saturdays until June."[120] Midtown department stores lent their store windows for displays of suffrage hats, but they did not give their employees the day off to march in the parade, which organizers insisted must be held on Saturday.[121] Despite these strictures, hundreds of working women turned out, with a particularly large delegation of white goods workers.[122] O'Reilly was one of many speakers addressing the crowd from automobiles before the rally at the Metropolitan Opera House, where the WESL proudly occupied a box of seats.[123] That year, New York state passed a referendum to put the issue before the state's voters in 1915.

In many industrial states, suffrage faced an uphill battle. Middle-class suffrage leaders attributed some of their difficulties to working-class men, some of whom opposed woman suffrage as compromising their manly prerogatives as voters. The liquor industry fanned these fears by warning that woman suffrage would lead to legislation banning alcohol, and it financed antisuffrage campaigns across the nation.[124] In October 1914 O'Reilly responded to an urgent plea from the Ohio Woman Suffrage Association to visit their state to explain the difference between temperance and suffrage to working-class men.[125] Appearing at the annual meeting of the state labor federation, O'Reilly urged the men to include women in their ranks, not just in auxiliaries or in label leagues, but as workers.[126] Ironically, the *Cleveland Federationist* reprinted O'Reilly's speech as an "Address for Women," although she began her speech by commenting on the paucity of women in the audience.[127] Despite giving O'Reilly a chilly reception, the state labor federation voted to support equal rights for women. However, the weakness of rank-and-file male workers' support for women's suffrage was revealed in the general election when the amendment granting women the right to vote failed.[128]

O'Reilly's concern for realizing the ideals of democracy and ensuring a more equitable future extended beyond suffrage and the labor movement. In 1915 she became increasingly involved in the antiwar movement, having been concerned by the escalation of tensions between European powers since 1911. She saw the war as destroying international solidarity, arguing that workers around the world should be building an international movement rather than killing one another "at the command of King, Czar, Kaiser, Emperor, or President."[129] She objected to the fact that the men in power in the United States spent seventy-three cents out of every dollar they collected in taxes on preparations for war, when the funds could be better used to equalize the educational opportunities of working-class children.[130] Her concerns were widely shared among progressive men and women in Europe and in the United States, who saw the war as "a tragic interruption" of their most pressing challenge, "the realization of a more satisfactory economic order."[131] Socialists and suffragists had nurtured international connections since the nineteenth century. Members of both groups mobilized their social networks in opposition to the war. Women voiced especially strong support for the peaceful resolution of this and all future international conflicts, but socialist groups soon broke apart along national lines.[132]

In April 1915 O'Reilly joined a delegation of forty-two American women, many of them college-educated labor reformers associated with the WTUL and with college settlement houses, who sailed aboard the *Noordam* through the mine-filled waters of the North Atlantic to The Hague to attend the

International Congress of Women.[133] Aletta Jacobs, a Dutch physician and suffrage leader, called the meeting. Jane Addams, the director of Hull House, the famous Chicago social settlement, led the American delegation and presided over the international gathering, which included over one thousand women from twelve nations, some neutral and others already at war, who converged to express "their opposition to war and to consider ways of preventing it in the future."[134] O'Reilly represented the WTUL, and her address before the convention gained wide attention.[135] However, the WTUL could not afford to fund her trip, so she paid her own way with the savings she had accumulated as a popular public speaker, indicating her strong commitment to the cause.[136] O'Reilly was deeply affected by the voyage, which affirmed her allegiance to the women's movement and to the international movement on behalf of peace.[137] She incorporated her antiwar stance into her work on behalf of suffrage, arguing that women needed votes to establish an "Industrial Democracy" in which wealth was more equally shared, and all who worked for a living received "the full fruit of their labors," regardless of sex or nationality.[138]

Shortly after she returned from Europe, O'Reilly helped lead an energetic campaign for woman suffrage in New York and New Jersey, embarking on an unremitting schedule of appearances from August through October 1915. Although her doctor advised her not to make any more outdoor speeches because of a recent heart attack, O'Reilly presented the case for women's suffrage to more than thirty central labor associations, including the state federation of labor, and city federations in Gloversville, Utica, and Little Falls, and she attended union meetings of printers, machinists, boiler makers, and stone cutters. She helped secure pledges from the retail clerks' union and the waitresses' union to support suffrage. Her fellow organizers, Maggie Hinchey and Melinda Scott, won converts in New Jersey, making special appeals to Irish societies, Catholic clergymen, and union members. Hinchey wrote letters to twenty-seven labor journals appealing for the right to vote, and O'Reilly wrote editorials for *Life and Labor* and the *American Federationist,* the official AFL publication. The two friends also traveled upstate, establishing a labor committee to work for suffrage and presenting their case to skeptical union leaders in Rochester. Hinchey described a noontime rally she led in front of a factory: "I got upon a chare and started holl[er]in and in 10 minutes we had 150 people." By the time Hinchey finished, she was sweating, and "and the men took of[f] there hats and [yelled] hurray votes for women."[139] The campaign culminated with a mass meeting at Cooper Union, organized by O'Reilly and jointly sponsored by the WTUL and the WSP, where Carrie Chapman Catt and James Holland, the president of the state federation of labor, both addressed the crowd.[140]

In October and November the voters of New York, New Jersey, Pennsylvania, and Massachusetts all had the question of woman suffrage on the ballot. In an editorial addressed to union men, O'Reilly urged them to stand by their working-class sisters, reminding them: "We work side by side with you in the factories. We vote with you in our trade unions. We strike with you when you strike." Pointing out that the working men of New York were unable to vote until 1826, she argued that the working women of the state "need the ballot today as much as their disenfranchised brothers needed it up to 1826." Together, she insisted, working men and working women could make their political demands heard more clearly by electing candidates who would serve their interests as workers and by supporting legislation mandating "decent" working conditions in factories, abolition of sweatshops, and an end to child labor. O'Reilly presented union men with a vision of workers "united" across lines of gender, working together to secure "a larger, freer inheritance" for succeeding generations of workers "than has been ours until today."[141]

Despite this optimistic vision of increasing workers' power by including women as union members and as voters, suffrage was defeated in all these states; in New York, the measure lost by less than 200,000 votes.[142] Although she did not show it publicly, O'Reilly's faith in trade unions as vehicles for working women's emancipation was seriously shaken during the campaign. Returning from the annual meeting of the state federation of labor at the end of August, she wrote to Mary Dreier resigning from the WTUL, declaring, "I shall leave the movement for the movement's good." She did not doubt the necessity of trade unions, believing that "women must be organized better than men are organized." But she was frustrated by her attempts to work with "the powers that be in the labor movement of New York State," which refused to recognize the WTUL's right to help organize female workers and, worse still, attributed "their own shortcomings" to the WTUL. Most intolerably, the unions dismissed the WTUL as controlled by outsiders, as an excuse "to cover up their own crookedness."[143] Because of these irreconcilable differences, the WTUL began shifting its attention from organizing women workers to implementing protective labor legislation on their behalf.[144]

Mary Dreier and the other members of the executive board of the New York WTUL tabled O'Reilly's resignation until after the election. They urged her to reconsider, but she proved severely disillusioned, despite the fact that suffrage had come closest to passing in the working-class districts in New York City where she and the WESL had been most active.[145] Her participation in the WTUL became sporadic, and she became depressed, refusing to answer the telephone or to see friends. She withdrew from politics and organizational work to care for Victor Drury during his final illness. While old friends helped pay Drury's medical bills and contributed an occasional duck or case of claret to buoy his spirits, O'Reilly and her mother, Winifred, bore the burden of his care.[146]

O'Reilly contributed to the victory lap for woman suffrage in New York state in November 1917, but she did not lead the charge. In an article for the *Union Printer,* she reiterated an argument she had made for at least a decade: "The antique notion that man is the sole producer of wealth must take a back seat in the face of those 800,000 women in our own state who tread the lock step through life for their daily bread." As she saw it, the world needed a new motive power: "social motherhood," which she defined as care for others rather than the profit principle as the sole governing idea. Harking back to Henry George, she diagnosed the results of "modern industry" as a world divided between "Wealth, Luxury, Privilege," and "Fatigue, Poverty, Degradation." Without the vote, women were powerless "to remedy these wretched conditions we find about us." She presented women's votes as a strike against militarism and as a step toward constructing a new, "more humane order of social life." Enfranchised, women would be able to protect themselves as workers, while contributing more fully to the well being of the nation and the world.[147] Seeking social recognition of women's work as caregivers as well as wage earners, she integrated her commitments to class and gender equity into her call for women's political power.

While O'Reilly remained true to her ideals, the radical coalition of feminists, suffragists, and labor activists that had supported her activism fell apart. The suffrage campaign of 1917 was a sober and businesslike affair compared to the enthusiasm of 1913 and 1915. Despite pacifist opposition, the United States had joined the European conflict. With the nation now fighting in the Great War, suffragists watched their step, knowing they were subject to government censorship. Pacifism and socialism, two ideals dear to O'Reilly's heart, both became suspect as dangerous and potentially "un-American." In New York City, the Socialist Party withdrew its official support for woman suffrage in 1915, deeming it a distraction from the real work of class struggle. In 1917 the Russian Revolution split the party between Bolsheviks and those determined to chart a more independent course. American socialism lay in disarray and lost power as a popular movement.[148]

O'Reilly wanted nothing to do with the war, but many members of the WTUL viewed government service as an opportunity to expand women's access to skilled industrial positions and to lay the groundwork for a stronger state presence in regulating women's working conditions. Margaret Dreier Robins, the president of the national WTUL, supported this shift, and women's labor reform became institutionalized within the federal government. Leaders of the WTUL and the National Consumers' League exercised considerable power over the policies of the Women's Bureau of the Department of Labor through the 1940s, launching a series of national investigations of women's work and wages, and advocating protective labor legislation in order to limit the hours and set minimum wages for women in industry.[149]

Many suffrage leaders, too, viewed the war as an opportunity for women to prove their patriotism through government service, thereby adding weight to their demands for full citizenship. Carrie Chapman Catt abandoned her pacifist ideals once the United States declared war on Germany. Catt took a leading role in shifting NAWSA toward a new strategy of winning suffrage through an amendment to the U.S. Constitution. While historians have celebrated Catt's "winning plan," they have not considered the degree to which earlier, grassroots campaigns empowered and included working-class women, who had little role to play in national lobbying efforts.[150] In 1920 the Nineteenth Amendment granted all women the right to vote. However, middle-class leaders of the movement, such as Catt, disavowed its radical past, presenting suffrage as an essentially moderate reform, erasing the collaborations among socialists, labor leaders, and feminists that had helped win the vote in New York and in other states with high concentrations of industrial workers.[151] Ironically, women won the vote at a moment when they seemed unlikely to achieve the radical transformation of their political and economic position to which Leonora O'Reilly had devoted her life.

O'Reilly found a bright spot amid these darkening prospects for change in the First International Congress of Working Women, which met in Washington, D.C., in October 1919. The group was the outgrowth of conversations among women's labor leaders at the Paris Peace Conference, who bonded together over their exclusion from the International Labor Organization, a new international group charged with making recommendations on labor policy for members of the League of Nations. O'Reilly was moved by the spirit of female trade unionists from around the world, who had pledged "to labor faithfully until the human family shall know and enjoy an all inclusive freedom—no member of the family outcast anywhere on this earth." Looking forward to the new decade dawning in January 1920, she offered a tribute to these workers for peace and economic justice, declaring: "Here's to the world that is to be! And to the brave souls that shall dare to make it free and just!"[152]

O'Reilly herself was no longer in the vanguard of these struggles. As her mother, Winifred, became senile, O'Reilly devoted herself exclusively to her care, becoming a virtual prisoner in her own house. Mary Dreier, one of many friends who continued to visit, noted that even as Mother O'Reilly's grasp on reality slipped away, "her busy fingers, folded and cut and made attempts at sewing."[153] In contrast to Leonora O'Reilly's diaries and letters from the 1880s through the 1910s, which were bursting with activity, a single notecard from 1922 reads simply, "Home with mother." O'Reilly, an only child, had always been close to her mother; the two women had pooled their income, split the housework, and shared commitments to women's rights and the labor movement. Clearly, O'Reilly felt an intense sense of obligation for her mother's care, and she had accumulated enough savings to support both of them if she budgeted carefully. We have no way of knowing whether O'Reilly regarded her care for her mother as "labor," although it took up all of her time and energy and precluded public activity. Meanwhile, O'Reilly's own health remained shaky. Her weak heart often left her dizzy and short of breath, but there was no one to care for her as she cared for Victor Drury and her mother.

During this period, O'Reilly took on only one sustained engagement, teaching a course at the New School on the "Problems and Progress of Labor." Her ambitious syllabus surveyed the history of labor from the Middle Ages through the present, discussing the "impact of machinery, steam, and electricity to production," the organization of workers, and women's place in the labor market and the labor movement.[154] Teaching the course must have given O'Reilly the opportunity to draw together her thoughts on where women fit in the history of capitalist development and their prospects for gaining power as workers. In 1927 Leonora O'Reilly succumbed to the heart disease that had plagued her for years. Aside from an obituary in *Life and Labor,* her death received little public notice, marking the degree to which she had receded from public life during the previous decade.[155]

Leonora O'Reilly spent most of her life searching for ways for working women to realize their desires for economic independence. Like the female labor activists who preceded her, such as Jennie Collins and Leonora Barry, O'Reilly embraced collective solutions to the challenges individual women faced negotiating the labor market, leading female workers into labor unions and into the suffrage movement. She envisioned working women organized in unions, enjoying full political rights, and creating a new, more just social order.[156] As O'Reilly promised one of the many audiences she addressed, "When we women have economic independence we are going to change the character of the human race."[157] Indeed, as Charlotte Perkins Gilman might have added, if women were to become economically independent, fundamental changes in marriage, motherhood, the workplace, and politics would ensue.

From their position in the vanguard of women's entry into occupations beyond domestic service, O'Reilly and the women she organized proudly pointed to their wage earning as evidence of their entitlement to be treated as adults, with full citizenship rights. Echoing generations of working-class women, O'Reilly insisted that women's wage earning be treated as morally equivalent to men's wage earning. By referring to themselves as breadwinners, these women invoked their self-support and their responsibility for dependent family members. Subscribing to a labor theory of value popular among working women since the 1860s, O'Reilly argued that women, like men, deserved just compensation for the value they produced—not the paltry earnings employers, reformers, and male trade unionists defined as a woman's wage. Equal pay for equal work was not just a matter of equity; it would pave the way for stronger alliances between working women and working men, overcoming the sex-based antagonism created by employers who used female workers to cut labor costs. O'Reilly urged working men and working women to "make common cause in their unions and at the *ballot box*."[158] The moments when working women had allied with working men, as in the Knights of Labor, had provided important opportunities for women to organize and to begin to participate in labor politics.

Political rights, as O'Reilly and other working-class suffragists imagined them, were not a substitute for workers' organization, but a means of furthering a labor agenda that arose from within the working class and took the interests of men, women, and children into account. The associations O'Reilly established and led, from the Working Women's Society in the 1880s to the Wage-Earners' Suffrage League in the 1910s, provided forums for working women to use their own words to give voice to their own interests. Although mindful of the need to make alliances with working men and middle-class women, O'Reilly refused to subordinate the groups she led to outside leadership, insisting on working women's superior understanding of their own conditions and their estimation of the best means to remedy the problems they faced. Here she resembled the members of the Boston Working Women's League, who asserted their authority over the problems faced by the city's working women in the 1860s and insisted on their need to define remedies to those problems themselves.

Just as O'Reilly sought to educate labor men and well-to-do women about the lives and labors of the female wage earners she represented, so, too, did she seek to dispel the myth that a government dominated by men and run in the interests of business owners protected working women. Speaking before the U.S. Senate in 1912 on behalf of the nation's 8 million women "who must earn our daily bread," she invoked the Triangle fire to expose the fallacy that the state protected working women. Not only did state agencies fail to save women from being "burned alive," the courts failed to dispense justice to the perpetrators of the crime. Enfranchised, working women could stop pleading for mercy from the government and begin demanding justice.[159] She retained faith in the positive potential of the state to remedy social injustice if it could be disentangled from its gender and class biases. As O'Reilly confessed, "We women have dreamed of democracy but we have never enjoyed it."

In seeking full citizenship, the working-class women who joined the battle for suffrage envisioned a world in which their wage earning would be evidence of their power, not their debility. While middle-class jurists, legislators, and social reformers cast women who worked for wages as imperiled by their departure from "the home," working women themselves articulated an alternative set of understandings of both home and work. By calling themselves breadwinners, these women proudly asserted that they earned money in order to support themselves and their families. Establishing and maintaining their own households emerged as hard-won victories, achieved through the money they earned and the labor they gave. Ideally, they saw work as a route to social adulthood. By earning wages, they would have more power to decide if, when, and whom to marry. Laboring among other women, they became part of a female collective, drawing on their relationships with their coworkers to resist the coercion of their employers and, in some instances, to organize. Jobs as domestic servants blocked working women's aspirations in both arenas, impinging on their ability to establish their own households and offering them little chance to work with other women.

In claiming independence, working-class women affirmed their ability to establish their own households and to be treated with respect and dignity at work. They rejected the notion that women were best suited for domestic occupations, and they cast domestic service as a form of gender and class oppression akin to slavery. In claiming citizenship based on their status as independent wage earners, they sought a political means of representing their economic interests. The state they imagined was not paternalist or maternalist, but just: recognizing the social and economic value of their labor and helping to ensure fair compensation and reasonable hours for men and women, enabling them to form egalitarian relationships and to care for dependents. Working women's claims for independence encompassed new demands for selfhood, laying the groundwork for families, communities, and workplaces built on a new, more egalitarian basis.

NOTES

ABBREVIATIONS

AHR	*American Historical Review*
APS	American Periodicals Series
AQ	*American Quarterly*
AWWA	Annie Ware Winsor Allen
DAB	*Dictionary of American Biography*
ILWCH	*International Labor and Working-Class History*
JAH	*Journal of American History*
LOR	Leonora O'Reilly
MDR	Margaret Dreier Robins
NAW	*Notable American Women*
NEQ	*New England Quarterly*
PQHN	*ProQuest Historical Newspapers*
SL	Schlesinger Library, Radcliffe Institute, Harvard University

INTRODUCTION

1. Alice S. Rossi, ed., *The Feminist Papers: From Adams to de Beauvoir* (Boston: Northeastern University Press, 1988), 413–21; Eleanor Flexner, *Century of Struggle: The Woman's Rights Movement in the United States* (Cambridge, Mass.: Belknap Press, 1975). Seneca Falls is the best known but not the only women's rights convention held during the mid-nineteenth century; see Nancy Isenberg, *Sex and Citizenship in Antebellum America* (Chapel Hill: University of North Carolina Press, 1998); Lori D. Ginzberg, *Untidy Origins: A Study of Women's Rights in Antebellum New York* (Chapel Hill: University of North Carolina Press, 2005).

2. Christine Stansell, *City of Women: Sex and Class in New York, 1789–1860* (Urbana: University of Illinois Press, 1987); Thomas Dublin, *Women at Work: The Transformation of Home and Community in Lowell, Massachusetts, 1826–1860* (New York: Columbia University Press, 1979).

3. For discussion of the complex class identities of labor activists, see Elizabeth Faue, *Writing the Wrongs: Eva Valesh and the Rise of Labor Journalism* (Ithaca, N.Y.: Cornell University Press, 2002).

4. Here I build on scholarship by Meredith Tax, *The Rising of the Women: Feminist Solidarity and Class Conflict, 1880–1917* (New York: Monthly Review Press, 1980); and Mari Jo Buhle, *Women and American Socialism, 1870–1920* (Urbana: University of Illinois Press, 1983).

5. Leon Fink, *Workingmen's Democracy: The Knights of Labor and American Politics* (Urbana: University of Illinois Press, 1983); Kim Voss, *The Making of American Exceptionalism: The Knights of Labor and Class Formation in the Nineteenth Century* (Ithaca, N.Y.: Cornell University Press, 1993); Susan Levine, *Labor's True Woman: Carpet Weavers, Industrialization and Labor Reform in the Gilded Age* (Philadelphia: Temple University Press, 1984); Eileen Boris, *Home to Work: Motherhood and the Politics of Industrial Homework in the United States* (New York: Cambridge University Press, 1994); Ileen A. DeVault, *United Apart: Gender and the Rise of Craft Unionism* (Ithaca, N.Y.: Cornell University Press, 2004); Kathryn Kish Sklar, *Florence Kelley and the Nation's Work: The Rise of Women's Political Culture* (New Haven, Conn.: Yale University Press, 1995).

6. William Leach, *True Love and Perfect Union: The Feminist Reform of Sex and Society* (Middletown, Conn.: Wesleyan University Press, 1989); Karen J. Blair, *The Clubwoman as Feminist: True Womanhood Redefined, 1868–1914* (New York: Holmes and Meier, 1980); Linda Gordon, "Social Insurance and Public Assistance: The Influence of Gender in Welfare Thought in the United States, 1890–1935," *AHR* 97, no. 1 (February 1992): 19–54; Nancy Woloch, *Muller v. Oregon: A Brief History with Documents* (Boston: Bedford Books, 1996).

7. Gail Bederman, *Manliness and Civilization: A Cultural History of Gender and Race in the United States, 1880–1917* (Chicago: University of Chicago Press, 1995); Louise Michele Newman, *White Women's Rights: The Racial Origins of Feminism in the United States* (New York: Oxford University Press, 1999); Allison L. Sneider, *Suffragists in an Imperial Age: U.S. Expansion and the Woman Question, 1870–1929* (New York: Oxford University Press, 2008).

8. Daniel T. Rodgers, *The Work Ethic in Industrial America, 1850–1920* (Chicago: University of Chicago Press, 1974); Alice Kessler-Harris, *Out to Work: A History of Wage-Earning Women in the U.S.* (New York: Oxford University Press, 1982); Patricia Hill Collins, *Black Feminist Thought: Knowledge, Consciousness, and the Politics of Empowerment* (New York: Routledge, 1990).

9. Jacqueline Jones, *Labor of Love, Labor of Sorrow: Black Women, Work, and the Family from Slavery to the Present* (New York: Vintage, 1986); Paula Giddings, *When and Where I Enter: The Impact of Black Women on Race and Sex in America* (New York: Bantam, 1985); Linda Gordon, ed., *Women, the State, and Welfare* (Madison: University of Wisconsin Press, 1990).

10. Kathy Peiss, *Cheap Amusements: Working Women and Leisure in Turn-of-the-Century New York* (Philadelphia: Temple University Press, 1986); Nan Enstad,

Ladies of Labor, Girls of Adventure: Working Women, Popular Culture, and Labor Politics at the Turn of the Twentieth Century (New York: Columbia University Press, 1999).

11. Mary Blewett, *Men, Women and Work: Class, Gender and Protest in the New England Shoe Industry, 1780–1910* (Urbana: University of Illinois Press, 1990); Wendy Gamber, *Female Economy: The Millinery and Dressmaking Trades, 1860–1930* (Urbana: University of Illinois Press, 1997); and Dorothy Sue Cobble, *The Other Women's Movement: Workplace Justice and Social Rights in Modern American* (Princeton, N.J.: Princeton University Press, 2004). Each of these sources offers a compelling account of working-class women's self-conceptions and political ideas.

12. The Boston Conference, 27 September 1908, *Union Labor Advocate* (December 1908), 42–43. In the 1920s Casey would alienate her former colleagues in the WTUL by supporting the Equal Rights Amendment and by characterizing protective labor legislation as impeding women's progress in the workforce. Nancy F. Cott, *The Grounding of Modern Feminism* (New Haven, Conn.: Yale University Press, 1987), 126, 325n15.

13. Ava Baron, ed., *Work Engendered: Toward a New History of American Labor* (Ithaca: Cornell University Press, 1991). Nancy Hewitt, *Southern Discomfort: Women's Activism in Tampa, Florida, 1880s–1920s* (Urbana: University of Illinois Press, 2001); Tera W. Hunter, *To 'Joy My Freedom: Southern Black Women's Lives and Labors after the Civil War* (Cambridge, Mass.: Harvard University Press, 1997); David M. Katzman, *Seven Days a Week: Women and Domestic Service in Industrializing America* (Urbana: University of Illinois Press, 1981); Joanne J. Meyerowitz, *Women Adrift: Independent Wage Earners in Chicago, 1880–1930* (Chicago: University of Chicago Press, 1988); Carole Turbin, *Working Women of Collar City: Gender, Class and Community in Troy, New York, 1864–86* (Urbana: University of Illinois Press, 1992).

CHAPTER I. THE DAILY LABOR OF OUR OWN HANDS

1. Helen L. Sumner, *History of Women in Industry in the U.S.* (Washington, D.C.: Government Printing Office, 1910), 31; Thomas Dublin, *Transforming Women's Work: New England Lives in the Industrial Revolution* (Ithaca, N.Y.: Cornell University Press, 1994), 77–85.

2. Jennie Collins, *Nature's Aristocracy; or, Battles and Wounds in Time of Peace* (Boston: Lee and Shepard, 1871), 313–14; Anne Phillips and Barbara Taylor, "Sex and Skill: Notes toward a Feminist Economics," *Feminist Review* 6 (1980): 79–88.

3. Barbara Welter, "The Cult of True Womanhood: 1820–1860," *American Quarterly* 18, no. 2 (Summer 1966): 151–74; Jeanne Boydston, *Home and Work: Housework, Wages, and the Ideology of Labor in the Early Republic* (New York: Oxford University Press, 1990).

4. Jacqueline Jones, *Labor of Love, Labor of Sorrow: Black Women, Work, and the Family from Slavery to the Present* (New York: Vintage, 1986).

5. Collins, *Nature's Aristocracy,* 314, 180–81.

6. Quoted in Sumner, *Women in Industry,* 111; Collins, *Nature's Aristocracy,* 181.

7. Teresa Anne Murphy, "Bagley, Sarah George," *ANB Online* (February 2000); Murphy, *Ten Hours Labor: Religion, Reform and Gender in Early New England* (Ithaca, N.Y.: Cornell University Press, 1992).

8. Dublin, *Women's Work,* 125.

9. Resolutions Denouncing Mass. Legislative Report, *Voice of Industry,* 9 January 1846, 3, reprinted in *Women and Social Movements in the United States, 1600–2000,* ed. Kathryn Kish Sklar and Thomas Dublin (Alexandria, Va.: Alexander Street Press, 2007).

10. Jennie Collins, "New England Factories," *The Revolution,* 31 January 1870; Paul R. Dauphinais, "Être à l'Ouvrage ou Être Maîtresse de Maison: French-Canadian Women and Work in Late Nineteenth-Century Massachusetts," in *Women of the Commonwealth: Work, Family and Social Change in Nineteenth-Century Massachusetts,* ed. Susan L. Porter (Amherst: University of Massachusetts Press, 1996), 63–83.

11. Dublin, *Women's Work,* 155–58, 187.

12. Marilynn Wood Hill, *Their Sisters' Keepers: Prostitution in New York City, 1830–1870* (Berkeley: University of California Press, 1992), 64–65; Barbara Meil Hobson, *Uneasy Virtue: The Politics of Prostitution and the American Reform Traditions* (New York: Basic Books, 1987), 92–93.

13. Collins Obituary, *Boston Evening Transcript,* 21 July 1887; "John Lowell," *Dictionary of American Biography,* Base Set, American Council of Learned Societies, 1928–1936. Reproduced in Biography Resource Center (Farmington Hills, Mich.: Thomson Gale, 2006).

14. Collins, *Nature's Aristocracy,* 103–4; Sumner, *Women in Industry,* 183.

15. "Good Servants," *Workman's Advocate,* 19 June 1869; Jennie Collins, "Why Women Avoid Housework," clipping from *The Woman's Journal* 3, issue 10 (n.d.),74, The Gerritsen Collection of Aletta H. Jacobs (ProQuest, Chadwyck-Healey, 2002–2009).

16. Collins, *Nature's Aristocracy,* 105.

17. NEWC, *Report of the Committee on Needlewomen* (Boston: John Wilson and Son, 1869), 19.

18. Hobson, *Uneasy Virtue,* 96–97; Hill, *Sister's Keeper,* 84.

19. Ruth Rosen, *Lost Sisterhood: Prostitution in America, 1900–1918* (Baltimore: Johns Hopkins University Press, 1982).

20. Timothy Gilfoyle, *City of Eros: New York City, Prostitution, and the Commercialization of Sex, 1790–1920* (New York: W. W. Norton, 1992), 287.

21. Hasia R. Diner, *Erin's Daughters in America: Irish Immigrant Women in the Nineteenth Century* (Baltimore: Johns Hopkins University Press, 1983), xiv, 71, 81, 90, 93, 94; Carol Lasser, "The Domestic Balance of Power: Relations between Mistress and Maid in Nineteenth-Century New England," in *History of Women in the U.S.: Historical Articles on Women's Lives and Activities,* ed. Nancy F. Cott,

(Munich; New York: K.G. Saur, 1992–1993), 20 volumes, vol. 4, 123–24; Diane M. Hotten-Somers, "Relinquishing and Reclaiming Independence: Irish Domestic Servants, American Middle-Class Mistresses, and Assimilation, 1850–1920," *Éire-Ireland* 36, nos. 1–2 (Spring–Summer 2001): 185–201.

22. Stanley Nadel, *Little Germany: Ethnicity, Religion, and Class in New York City, 1845–1880* (Urbana: University of Illinois Press, 1990), 76, 192n60.

23. Quoted in Lasser, "Mistress and Maid," 125.

24. "The Bell Goes A-ringing for Sai-rah," *American Workman*, 5 June 1869.

25. Christine Stansell, *City of Women: Sex and Class in New York, 1789–1860* (Urbana: University of Illinois Press, 1987), 111.

26. Report of the Working-women's Convention of 21 April 1869, *American Workman*, May 1869; Wendy Gamber, "Tarnished Labor: The Home, the Market, and the Boardinghouse in Antebellum America," *Journal of the Early Republic* 22, no. 2 (Summer 2002): 184, 195–96; "The Death of a Noble Woman," *Journal of United Labor*, 30 July 1887.

27. Dublin, *Women's Work*, 158–59.

28. *New York Times*, 2 March 1869, reprinted in *The Black Worker: A Documentary History from Colonial Times to the Present*, ed. Philip S. Foner and Ronald L. Lewis, vol. 2 (Philadelphia: Temple University Press, 1978), 360–61; Brown, "The Negro Woman Worker," in *Black Women in White America: A Documentary History*, ed. Gerda Lerner (New York: Vintage, 1972), 251; Leon F. Litwack, *North of Slavery: The Negro in the Free States, 1790–1860* (Chicago: University of Chicago Press, 1961), 155.

29. *National Standard*, 11 November 1871, reprinted in *The Black Worker*, ed. Foner and Lewis, 2:281.

30. Quoted in Paula Giddings, *When and Where I Enter: The Impact of Black Women on Race and Sex in America* (New York: Bantam, 1985), 69.

31. Elizabeth F. Hoxie, "Collins, Jennie," in *Notable American Women: A Biographical Dictionary*, ed., Edward T. James, (Cambridge, Mass.: Belknap Press of Harvard University Press, 1971), 3 volumes, 1:362–63; Catherine Clinton, *The Other Civil War: American Women in the Nineteenth Century* (New York: Hill and Wang, 1999), 81.

32. Jeanie Attie, "Warwork and the Crisis of Domesticity in the North," in *Divided Houses: Gender and the Civil War*, ed. Catherine Clinton and Nina Silber (New York: Oxford University Press, 1992), 243–59.

33. Jonathan Grossman, *William Sylvis, Pioneer of American Labor* (New York: Columbia University Press, 1945), 49–50.

34. Collins, *Nature's Aristocracy*, 285–86.

35. Daniel T. Rodgers, *The Work Ethic in Industrial America, 1850–1920* (Chicago: University of Chicago Press, 1979), xiii–xiv.

36. Norman J. Ware, *The Labor Movement in the United States, 1860–1895: A Study in Democracy* (1929; reprint, Gloucester, Mass.: Peter Smith, 1959), 1–2, 4–5.

37. "Death of a Noble Woman."

38. David Montgomery, *Beyond Equality: Labor and the Radical Republicans, 1862–1872* (1967; reprint, Urbana: University of Illinois Press, 1981), 136, 412–14; Martin Henry Blatt, "Heywood, Ezra Hervey," *ANB Online* (February 2000); "Working Men's and Women's Labor Reform Convention," *American Workman,* 21 August 1869.

39. Grossman, *Sylvis,* 191, 222, 224, 227, 229, 238.

40. "My Laundress," *American Workman,* 1 May 1869.

41. Sumner, *Women in Industry,* 31.

42. Jamie L. Bronstein, *Land Reform and Working-Class Experience in Britain and the United States, 1800–1862* (Stanford, Calif.: Stanford University Press, 1999), 2–6, 8, 78–81, 173–85.

43. "The Wail of the Women," *Workingman's Advocate,* 24 April 1869, 1; Paul Goodman, "The Emergence of the Homestead Exemption in the United States: Accommodations and Resistance to the Market Revolution, 1840–1880," *Journal of American History* 80, no. 2 (September 1993): 470–98; Alice Kessler-Harris, *Out to Work: A History of Wage-Earning Women in the United States* (Oxford: Oxford University Press, 1982), 80–81.

44. "The Homestead Question—What and Why?" *American Workman,* May 1869.

45. "The Work-woman," *American Workman,* 26 June 1869.

46. Virginia Penny, *Think and Act; A Series of Articles Pertaining to Men and Women, Work and Wages* (Philadelphia: Claxton, Remsen, and Haffelfinger, 1869), 29, 83, 98, 189.

47. Robert E. Reigel, "Livermore, Mary," in *NAW,* 2:410–13; Letter from Mary Livermore, *American Workman,* May 1869.

48. Penny, *Think and Act,* 29.

49. "Go West, Young Girl," *Boston Daily Globe,* 24 March 1875, 3, *ProQuest Historical Newspapers.*

50. "White Slaves of New England," *Workingman's Advocate* 5, no. 4 (8 May 1869).

51. "Wail of the Women."

52. "Homestead Question—What and Why?"

53. "The Working-Women's League," *American Workman* 2, no. 4 (May 1869).

54. Parker Pillsbury, "How the Working Women Live," *The Revolution,* 13 May 1869; William Leach, *True Love and Perfect Union: The Feminist Reform of Sex and Society* (Middletown, Conn.: Wesleyan University Press, 1989), 134–36.

55. "The Working Women in Council," *American Workman,* May 1869.

56. Monday, 12 April 1869, "N.E.W.C. Meetings, 1868–1870," New England Women's Club Records, Schlesinger Library, Radcliffe Institute, Harvard University, Folder 40.

57. "Working Women in Council."

58. *Workingman's Advocate* 5, no. 41 (8 May 1869); Rosalyn Baxandall, Linda Gordon, and Susan Reverby, "Boston Working Women Protest, 1869," *Signs* 1, no. 3 (1976): 803–8.

59. "Death of a Noble Woman."

60. "Working Women in Council"; Sumner, *Women in Industry,* 149.

61. Penny, *Think and Act,* 197. For discussion of antebellum uses of this motto, see Karen Sánchez-Eppler, *Touching Liberty: Abolition, Feminism, and the Politics of the Body* (Berkeley: University of California Press, 1993); and Jean Fagan Yellin, *Women and Sisters: The Antislavery Feminists in American Culture* (New Haven, Conn.: Yale University Press, 1989).

62. Louisa May Alcott, *Work: A Story of Experience,* ed. Joy S. Kasson (1873; reprint, New York: Penguin, 1994), 336–41.

63. David R. Roediger, *The Wages of Whiteness: Race and the Making of the American Working Class* (London: Verso, 1993); Gunther Peck, "White Slavery and Whiteness: A Transnational View of the Sources of Working-Class Radicalism and Racism," *Labor* 1, no. 2 (June 2004): 41–63. Scholarly study of "whiteness" has recently come under critical scrutiny. See Eric Arnesen, "Whiteness and the Historian's Imagination," and responses by James Barrett, David Brody, Barbara Fields, Eric Foner, Victoria Hattam, and Adolph Reed; Peter Kolchin, *International Labor and Working-Class History* 60 (October 2001): 3—92; Peter Kolchin, "Whiteness Studies: The New History of Race in America," *JAH* 89, no. 1 (June 2002): 154–73. However, Roediger's insights remain useful for understanding the intersections of race and class.

64. NEWC, *Report of the Committee on Needlewomen,* 19–20.

65. "Working Women in Council."

66. "Working Women Again," *The Revolution,* May 1869.

67. Sarah Deutsch, "Learning to Talk More Like a Man: Boston Women's Class-Bridging Organizations, 1870–1940," *American Historical Review* 97 (April 1992): 379–404.

68. Alcott, *Work,* 330–31.

69. "The Working Women's League," *American Workman* 2, no. 4 (May 1869).

70. "The Boston Workingwoman," *American Workman,* 21 August 1869.

71. Mary H. Blewett, *Men, Women and Work: Class, Gender and Protest in the New England Shoe Industry, 1780–1910* (Urbana: University of Illinois Press, 1990), 167–70.

72. Collins, *Nature's Aristocracy,* 196–97.

73. Thomas Dublin, *Women at Work: The Transformation of Work and Community in Lowell, Massachusetts, 1826–1860* (New York: Columbia University Press, 1979), 120.

74. "Jennie Collins and the Dover Strike," *The Revolution,* 30 December 1869.

75. "Jennie Collins and the Dover Strike," *The Revolution,* 30 December 1869.

76. Jennie Collins, "New England Factories," *The Revolution,* 13 January 1870.

77. Hoxie, "Collins, Jennie," in *NAW,* 362–63.

78. Paulina W. Davis, *A History of the National Woman's Rights Movement for Twenty Years* (New York: Journeymen Printers' Co-Operative Association, 1871), 30.

79. "Jennie Collins in Washington," *The Revolution*, 10 February 1870; "Death of a Noble Woman."

80. Margaret Andrews Allen, "Jennie Collins and Her Boffin's Bower," *Charities Review* 2 (December 1892): 106.

81. "Boffin's Bower," *Woman's Journal*, 25 March 1871.

82. Allen, "Jennie Collins and Her Boffin's Bower," 105.

83. Lilian Whiting, "Jennie Collins," *Chautauquan* 8, no. 3 (December 1887), 159.

84. Collins, *Nature's Aristocracy*, 296–97, 300.

85. Blewett, *Men, Women, and Work*, 173; Ellen Carol DuBois, *Feminism and Suffrage: The Emergence of an Independent Women's Movement in America, 1848–1869* (Ithaca, N.Y.: Cornell University Press, 1978), 121–24.

86. Collins, *Nature's Aristocracy*, 304–5, 306, 309–10, 314.

87. Ibid., 103–4.

88. Ibid., 222.

89. Quoted in Allen, "Jennie Collins and Her Boffin's Bower," 111.

90. Daniel T. Rodgers, *Atlantic Crossings: Social Politics in a Progressive Age* (Cambridge, Mass.: Harvard University Press, 1998).

91. Quoted in Allen, "Jennie Collins and Her Boffin's Bower," 115.

92. Mary A. Livermore, "Jennie Collins' Work," *Boston Daily Globe*, 31 July 1887, 5, *PQHN*.

93. Mary H. Blewett, *Constant Turmoil: The Politics of Industrial Life in Nineteenth-Century New England* (Amherst: University of Massachusetts Press, 2000), 102–3.

94. Azel Ames, *Sex in Industry: A Plea for the Working Girl* (Boston: Osgood, 1875), 20. For further discussion, see Lara Vapnek, "The Politics of Women's Work in the United States, 1865–1909," (Ph.D. diss, Columbia University, 2000), 89–93.

95. Collins, *Sixth Annual Report of Boffin's Bower*, 11–13.

96. Richard Hofstadter, *Social Darwinism in American Thought*, with a new introduction by Eric Foner (Boston: Beacon, 1992), 31–35.

97. Mary Livermore, "Jennie Collins," *Woman's Journal*, 6 August 1887; Collins, *Sixth Annual Report of Boffin's Bower*, 16–17; "Boffin's Bower: Miss Jennie Collins' Report for the Past Year—The Bower in Prosperous Condition," *Boston Daily Globe*, 18 June 1873, 8, *PQHN*.

98. "Jennie Collins and Boffin's Bower—What the Newspaper-Men Think of Her," *Chicago Daily Tribune*, 19 December 1875, 10, *PQHN*.

99. "School for Housekeepers: Jennie Collins' Latest Project for the Education of the Working Girls," *Boston Daily Globe*, 3 February 1873, 8, *PQHN*.

100. Hoxie, "Collins, Jennie," in *NAW*, 1:362–63; "[History of the] Work Committee," 1938, 3–4, NEWC Records, SL, folder 95; Eric Foner, *The Story of American Freedom* (New York: W. W. Norton, 1998), 113–20.

101. "Local Miscellany," *Boston Daily Globe*, 23 May 1874, *PQHN*.

102. Carole Turbin, *Working Women of Collar City: Gender, Class, and Com-

munity in Troy, New York, 1864–1886 (Urbana: University of Illinois Press, 1992), 163–164.

103. "Aurora," *New York Times,* 28 October 1873, 4, *PQHN;* "Suburban Notes," *Boston Daily Globe,* 27 November 1873, 5, *PQHN;* "A Community of Women Only," *Saturday Evening Post* 53, no. 21 (20 December 1873), 8 "Death of Noted Character," *Boston Daily Globe,* 6 January 1876, 5.

104. "The Working-Women's League," *American Workman* 2, no. 4 (May 1869).

CHAPTER 2. WORKING GIRLS AND WHITE SLAVES

1. Joseph A. Hill, *Women in Gainful Occupations 1870 to 1920,* vol. 9, Census Monographs (Washington, D.C.: U.S. Government Printing Office, 1929), 16–19, 31, 36, 40.

2. Ellen Ross, *Slum Travelers: Ladies and London Poverty, 1860–1920* (Berkeley: University of California Press, 2007), introduction, 1–39 and Seth Koven, *Slumming: Sexual and Social Politics in Victorian London* (Princeton: Princeton University Press, 2004).

3. Daniel T. Rodgers, *Atlantic Crossings: Social Politics in a Progressive Age* (Cambridge, Mass.: Harvard University Press, 1998), 26, 35–36; Helene Silverberg, "Introduction: Toward a Gendered Social Science History," Nancy Folbre, "The 'Sphere of Women' in Early Twentieth-Century Economics," and Kathryn Kish Sklar, "Hull House Maps and Papers: Social Science as Women's Work in the 1890s," all in *Gender and American Social Science: The Formative Years,* ed. Helene Silverberg (Princeton, N.J.: Princeton University Press, 1998); Alice O'Connor, *Poverty Knowledge: Social Science, Social Policy, and the Poor in Twentieth-Century U.S. History* (Princeton, N.J.: Princeton University Press, 2001), 25–26.

4. Kathryn Kish Sklar, *Florence Kelley and the Nation's Work: The Rise of Women's Political Culture* (New Haven, Conn.: Yale University Press, 1995), 237–39; Elizabeth Faue, *Writing the Wrongs: Eva Valesh and the Rise of Labor Journalism* (Ithaca, N.Y.: Cornell University Press, 2002), 39–40.

5. James Leiby, *Carroll Wright and Labor Reform: The Origin of Labor Statistics* (Cambridge, Mass.: Harvard University Press, 1960), 28–29, 48, 54, 56–57, 61, 63, 67–68, 75; Wendell D. MacDonald, "The Early History of Labor Statistics in the U.S.," *Labor History* 13, no. 2 (1972): 270; Daniel Horowitz, "Genteel Observers: New England Economic Writers and Industrialization," *New England Quarterly* 48, no. 1 (March 1975): 66.

6. Alice Kessler-Harris, *A Women's Wage: Historical Meanings and Social Consequences* (Lexington: University Press of Kentucky, 1990), 6–7.

7. Mary H. Blewett, *Constant Turmoil: The Politics of Industrial Life in Nineteenth-Century New England* (Amherst: University of Massachusetts Press, 2000), 129.

8. Helen Campbell, *Women Wage Workers: Their Past, Their Present, and Their*

Future (Boston: Roberts, 1893); Robert H. Bremmer, *From the Depths: The Discovery of Poverty in the U.S.* (New York: New York University Press, 1972), 75–76.

9. Massachusetts Bureau of Statistics of Labor, *Fifteenth Annual Report*, "The Working Girls of Boston" (1884), 3–4, 48. Hereafter cited as MA, BSL 15 (1884). Lack of certainty over categories of analysis characterized investigations of male workers, too; see Mary O. Furner, "The Republican Tradition and the New Liberalism: Social Investigation, State Building and Social Learning in the Gilded Age," in *The State and Social Investigation in Britain and the United States,* ed. Michael J. Lacey and Mary O. Furner (Cambridge: Cambridge University Press, 1993), 171–241.

10. Elizabeth Pleck, *Black Migration and Poverty, Boston, 1865–1900* (New York: Academic Press, 1979), 158–59; Sarah Deutsch, *Women and the City: Gender, Space and Power in Boston, 1870–1940* (New York: Oxford, 2000), 19, 55, 419.

11. Pleck, *Black Migration and Poverty,* 158–59.

12. Deutsch, *Women and the City,* 19, 55, 419.

13. Mari Jo Buhle, *Women and American Socialism, 1870–1920* (Urbana: University of Illinois Press, 1983), 57–58; Alice Rhine, "Woman in Industry," in *Woman's Work in America,* ed. Annie Nathan Meyer (New York: Henry Holt, 1891), 303.

14. Fourth Annual Report of the Commissioner of Labor, *Working Women in Large Cities* (Washington, D.C.: Government Printing Office, 1889), 10.

15. Sklar, "Hull House Maps and Papers," 127–36.

16. Barbara Meil Hobson, *Uneasy Virtue: The Politics of Prostitution and the American Reform Tradition* (Chicago: University of Chicago Press, 1990), 93–94, 100, 106.

17. MA, BSL 15 (1884), 48.

18. Jennie Collins, *Fourteenth Annual Report of Boffin's Bower* (Boston: Franklin Press, 1884), 8–10.

19. Leonora Barry, "Report of the General Instructor and Director of Women's Work," published with *Proceedings of the General Assembly of the Knights of Labor* (n.p., 1889), 5.

20. Approximately two-thirds of the women surveyed lived at home; those who lodged or boarded were likely to live with relatives or friends. MA, BSL 15 (1884), 36. On women living alone, see Joanne Meyerowitz, *Women Adrift: Independent Wage-Earners in Chicago, 1880–1930* (Chicago: University of Chicago Press, 1988).

21. MA, BSL 15 (1884), 33, 35, 40.

22. Nancy Folbre, "The Unproductive Housewife: The Evolution of Nineteenth-Century Economic Thought," *Signs* 16, no. 3 (Spring 1991): 463–84.

23. MA, BSL 15 (1884), 35, 127.

24. Ibid., 58–62.

25. Ibid., 66–69, 72.

26. Claudia Goldin, "The Work and Wages of Single Women, 1870–1920," in *History of Women in the U.S.,* ed. Nancy F. Cott (New York: K. G. Saur, 1992–93), vol. 7, part 1, 258.

27. MA, BSL 15 (1884), 70–75.

28. Quoted in Collins, *Fourteenth Annual Report of Boffin's Bower,* 9.

29. Rhine, "Woman's Work in Industry," 305.

30. Ida M. Van Etten, *The Condition of Women Workers under the Present Industrial System* (New York: Concord Co-Operative Print, 1891), 11.

31. Claudia Goldin, *Understanding the Gender Gap: An Economic History of American Women* (Oxford: Oxford University Press, 1990), Table 3.1.

32. Series Ba4283–4289, "Daily Wages in Manufacturing Establishments, by Occupation: 1860–1880," in *Historical Statistics of the United States, Millennial Edition Online* (Cambridge University Press), available at https://hsus.cambridge.org .arugula.cc.columbia.edu:2443/HSUSWeb/indexes/indexTablePath.do?id=Ba4283 –4289 (accessed 5 January 2007).

33. Goldin, *Understanding the Gender Gap,* Table 3.1.

34. Pleck, *Black Migration and Poverty,* 127–28, 135, 213.

35. This holds true even when income is held constant. Goldin, "Female Labor Force Participation," 174–75.

36. MA, BSL 15 (1884), 109, 113.

37. This figure is from 1875, but it probably had not changed substantially, since wages stayed fairly steady from 1870 to 1900. MacDonald, "Early History of Labor Statistics," 272.

38. MA, BSL 15 (1884), 110. Laws were soon developed punishing men for their failure to support their families. Michael Willrich, "Home Slackers: Men, the State, and Welfare in Modern America," *JAH* 87, no. 2 (September 2000): 460–89.

39. David Montgomery, *Beyond Equality: Labor and the Radical Republicans, 1862–1872* (1967; reprint, Urbana: University of Illinois Press, 1981), 40; Alexander Keyssar, *Out of Work: The First Century of Unemployment in Massachusetts* (New York: Cambridge University Press, 1986), 45–46.

40. Anne Phillips and Barbara Taylor, "Sex and Skill: Notes Toward a Feminist Economics," *Feminist Review* 6 (1980): 79–88.

41. Jeanne Boydston, *Home and Work: Housework, Wages, and the Ideology of Labor in the Early Republic* (New York: Oxford University Press, 1990), 45–47.

42. Julie A. Matthaei, *An Economic History of Women in America: Women's Work, the Sexual Division of Labor, and the Development of Capitalism* (New York: Schocken Books, 1982), 211–15.

43. MA, BSL 15 (1884), 129.

44. The California commissioner complained of his lack of state support compared to eastern bureaus and described his difficulties gathering statistics. CA, BLS, 3d Biennial Report (1888), 1–13.

45. The Colorado report included investigation of employment offices and advertisements for domestic service to uncover fraudulent business practices and fronts for prostitution rings. However, it did not look into conditions of women working as domestics. CO, BLS, 1st Biennial Report (1887–88), 364–68.

46. CA, BLS, 3d Biennial Report (1888), 15.

47. CO, BLS, 1st Biennial Report (1887–88), 334–43.

48. CA, BLS, 3d Biennial Report (1888), 80.

49. Kessler-Harris, *A Woman's Wage,* 8–9; Matthaei, *Economic History of Women,* 215; Rhine, "Woman in Industry," 306.

50. MA, BSL 15 (1884), 92–98.

51. Joan Wallach Scott, *Gender and the Politics of History* (New York: Columbia University Press, 1988), 113–38.

52. Boydston, *Home and Work.* Folbre, "The Unproductive Housewife."

53. Leiby, *Carroll Wright,* 75.

54. As quoted in Carroll D. Wright, "An Historical Sketch of the Knights of Labor," *Quarterly Journal of Economics* 1, no. 1 (January 1887): 139–43; Kim Voss, *The Making of American Exceptionalism: The Knights of Labor and Class Formation in the Nineteenth Century* (Ithaca, N.Y.: Cornell University Press, 1993), 82.

55. Leon Fink, *Workingmen's Democracy: The Knights of Labor and American Politics* (Urbana: University of Illinois Press, 1983), 4–5, 7; Victoria Hattam, *Labor Visions and State Power: The Origins of Business Unionism in the U.S.* (Princeton, N.J.: Princeton University Press, 1993), 205–7.

56. Donna L. Van Raaphorst, *Union Maids Not Wanted: Organizing Domestic Workers, 1870–1940* (New York: Praeger, 1988), 156–60.

57. Gerald Grob, *Workers and Utopia: A Study of Ideological Conflict in the American Labor Movement, 1865–1900* (Chicago: Quadrangle, 1961), 52, 54–56.

58. Susan Levine, "Domesticity and Equal Rights in the Knights of Labor," *JAH* 70, no. 2 (September 1983): 337; Robert E. Weir, *Knights Unhorsed: Internal Conflict in a Gilded Age Social Movement* (Detroit: Wayne State University Press, 2000), 143.

59. John B. Andrews and W. D. P. Bliss, *History of Women in Trade Unions,* vol. 10 of U.S. Senate, *Report on Condition of Woman and Child Wage-Earners in the U.S.* (Washington, D.C.: Government Printing Office, 1911), 114–16. This pay rate was about one dollar a week less than Wright estimated for the "working girls" of Boston; Leonora Barry and Nell Nelson's investigations found even lower average earnings.

60. Leonora Barry, "A New Year's Resolution: No More Unlabeled Goods for Knights," *Journal of United Labor,* 31 January 1889.

61. Norman J. Ware, *The Labor Movement in the United States, 1860–1895* (1929; reprint, Gloucester, Mass.: Peter Smith, 1959), 342–43.

62. John L. Rury, *Education and Women's Work: Female Schooling and the Division of Labor in Urban America, 1870–1930* (Albany: State University of New York Press, 1991), 49–51.

63. Eleanor Flexner, "Barry, Leonora Marie Kearney," in *NAW,* 1:101–2; Mrs. Barry, "What the Knights Are Doing for Women," *The Woman's Tribune,* 30 March 1888.

64. Rhine, "Woman in Industry," 311.

65. Eleanor Flexner, *Century of Struggle: The Woman's Rights Movement in the United States,* rev. ed. (Cambridge, Mass.: Harvard Belknap Press, 1977), 198–99.

66. Susan Levine, *Labor's True Woman: Carpet Weavers, Industrialization and*

Labor Reform in the Gilded Age (Philadelphia: Temple University Press, 1984), 108–9.

67. Leonora Barry, "Report of the General Investigator," Knights of Labor, *Proceedings of the General Assembly* (Philadelphia, 1887), 1581–97.

68. *Report of the Annual Convention of the Knights of Labor* (Philadelphia, 1887), 1857–58; Amy Dru Stanley, *From Bondage to Contract: Wage Labor, Marriage, and the Market in the Age of Slave Emancipation* (New York: Cambridge University Press, 1998), xiii, 219, 230–48, 258–68.

69. *Report of the Annual Convention,* 1857–58.

70. Weir, *Knights Unhorsed,* 149.

71. Rebecca Edwards, *New Spirits: Americans in the Gilded Age, 1865–1905* (New York: Oxford University Press, 2006), 218–19.

72. Weir, *Knights Unhorsed,* 155; Voss, *Making of American Exceptionalism,* 12; Hattam, *Labor Visions and State Power,* 177.

73. Leonora Barry, "Report of the General Instructor and Director of Women's Work," published with *Proceedings of the General Assembly of the Knights of Labor* (n.p., 1889), 1.

74. Ibid., 1–6.

75. Ileen A. DeVault, *United Apart: Gender and the Rise of Craft Unionism* (Ithaca, N.Y.: Cornell University Press, 2004), 217–20.

76. Barry, "Report" (1889), 1–6.

77. Weir, *Knights Unhorsed,* 148–57.

78. "Barry, Leonora," in *NAW,* 1:101–2.

79. Andrews and Bliss, *History of Women in Trade Unions,* 120–21.

80. Levine, *Labor's True Woman,* 125.

81. William Leach, *True Love and Perfect Union: The Feminist Reform of Sex and Society* (Middletown, Conn.: Wesleyan University Press, 1989), 316–17.

82. Bremmer, *From the Depths,* 76; Henry George, *Progress and Poverty: An Inquiry into the Cause of Industrial Depressions and of Increase of Want with Increase of Wealth* (1879; reprint, New York: Schalkenbach Foundation, 1937).

83. Helen Campbell, "The Working Women of Today," *The Woman's Tribune,* 29 March 1888.

84. Campbell's beliefs in evolutionary socialism were widely shared among those interested in the "social question" during the 1880s; see Buhle, *Women and American Socialism,* 90.

85. Ross E. Paulson, "Campbell, Helen Stuart," in *NAW,* 1:280–81.

86. U.S. Census Bureau, Tenth Census, Table VI, 422.

87. Helen Campbell, *Prisoners of Poverty: Women Wage Workers, Their Trades and Their Lives* (Boston: Roberts, 1887; reprint, Westport, Conn.: Greenwood Press, 1970), 9–10.

88. Campbell, *Prisoners of Poverty,* 76–77.

89. Ibid., 31. Mass-produced, ready-made clothing crept slowly up through the social strata; see Michael Zakim, *Ready-Made Democracy: A History of Men's Dress in the American Republic, 1760–1860* (Chicago: University of Chicago Press, 2003).

90. Alan Trachtenberg, *The Incorporation of America: Culture and Society in the Gilded Age* (New York: Hill and Wang, 1982), 121, 129–30.

91. Tenth Census, Table XXXVI, 892.

92. Campbell, *Prisoners of Poverty*, 103.

93. Eileen Boris, *Home to Work: Motherhood and the Politics of Industrial Homework in the United States* (New York: Cambridge University Press, 1994), 88.

94. Campbell, *Prisoners of Poverty*, 32–33, 81–82.

95. Ibid., 52, 67, 68.

96. Wright, *The Working Girls of Boston*, 129.

97. Campbell, "The Working Women of Today."

98. Campbell, *Prisoners of Poverty*, 236.

99. Ibid., 73–74.

100. Ruth Schwartz Cowan, *More Work for Mother: The Ironies of Household Technology from the Open Hearth to the Microwave* (New York: Basic Books, 1983), 122. Faye E. Dudden, *Serving Women: Household Service in Nineteenth-Century America* (Middletown, Conn.: Wesleyan University Press,1983), 44–47. Mary Romero, *Maid in the U.S.A.* (New York: Routledge, 1992), 55.

101. Jeremy Brecher, *Strike!* (Boston: South End Press, 1972), 37–39; Campbell, *Prisoners of Poverty*, 224–29.

102. Campbell, *Prisoners of Poverty*, 226, 228, 229.

103. Stanley Nadel, *Little Germany: Ethnicity, Religion, and Class in New York City, 1845–1880* (Urbana: University of Illinois Press, 1990), 76–77, 192n60. The Tenth Census breaks down occupations only by nativity, not by race; the total number of 56,255 servants included 6,316 men and 49,939 women (Table XXXVI, 892). The majority of these male servants were African Americans who worked as butlers or coachmen.

104. Campbell, *Prisoners of Poverty*, 236.

105. Quoted in David M. Katzman, *Seven Days a Week: Women and Domestic Service in Industrializing America* (New York: Oxford University Press, 1978), 69.

106. Campbell, *Prisoners of Poverty*, 239–41.

107. Ibid., 246–49.

108. Rhine, "Women in Industry," 318–19.

109. "City Slave Girls," *Chicago Times*, 14 August 1888.

110. Faue, *Writing the Wrongs*, 96–101.

111. Eric Shocket, "Undercover Explorations of the 'Other Half,' Or the Writer as Class Transvestite," *Representations* 64 (Autumn 1998): 109–12. Koven, *Slumming*, 142, 155.

112. *Journalist* 8, no. 4 (13 October 1888): 2, 13; *Journalist* 8, no. 19 (26 January 1889): 2; *Current Literature* 1, no. 5 (November 1888): 3851; all *APS Online*.

113. Nell Nelson, "City Slave Girls," *Chicago Times*, 31 July 1888.

114. "City Slave Girls," *Chicago Times*, 6 August 1888; Richard Schneirov, *Labor and Urban Politics: Class Conflict and the Origins of Modern Liberalism in Chicago, 1864–1897* (Urbana: University of Illinois Press, 1998), 270–72.

115. Bessie Louise Pierce, *A History of Chicago*, vol. 3 (New York: Knopf, 1957), 408–09, 413–14; Lloyd Wendt, *The Chicago Tribune: The Rise of a Great American Newspaper* (Chicago: Rand McNally, 1979), 23, 36, 292–93, 313; John Tebbel, *An American Dynasty: The Story of the McCormicks, Medills and Pattersons* (New York: Doubleday, 1947), 32–35, 51–55; David Paul Nord, "The Public Community: The Urbanization of Journalism in Chicago," *Journal of Urban History* 11 (August 1985): 416–18.

116. For discussion of freedom as a progressive story, see Eric Foner, *Story of American Freedom* (New York: W. W. Norton, 1998).

117. *Chicago Times*, 27 August 1888.

118. Gunther Peck, "White Slavery and Whiteness: A Transnational View of the Sources of Working-Class Radicalism and Racism," *Labor* 1, no. 2 (June 2004): 46.

119. "The Ethical Society Discusses City Slave Girls," *Chicago Times*, 13 August 1888.

120. James R. Grossman, *Land of Hope: Chicago, Black Southerners, and the Great Migration* (Chicago: University of Chicago Press, 1989), 127–29.

121. "City Slave Girls," *Chicago Times*, 5 August 1888.

122. Richard C. Wade and Harold M. Mayer, *Chicago: Growth of a Metropolis* (Chicago: University of Chicago Press, 1969), 152.

123. Mary, "Slave Girls of Chicago," *Chicago Times*, 31 July 1888.

124. Mary Bularzik, "Sexual Harassment at the Workplace, Historical Notes," in *History of Women in the U.S.*, ed. Cott, vol. 7, part 1 (Industrial Wage Work), 95, 97, 99, 116.

125. "Fixing Wages by Law," *Chicago Times*, 8 August 1888; Frances E. Willard, "Miss Willard's Views," *Chicago Times*, 19 August 1888.

126. *Chicago Times*, 12 August 1888.

127. "The Public Voice," 3 August 1888. For more examples, see the following *Chicago Times* articles: "Degrading Female Labor," 1 August 1888; A Constant Reader, "Restaurant and Hotel Girls," 5 August 1888; "Applauding the Work," 10 August 1888.

128. Meredith Tax, *The Rising of the Women: Feminist Solidarity and Class Conflict, 1880–1917* (New York: Monthly Review Press, 1980), 49–50.

129. L. M. H., "An Ex-Shop Girl Who Has Endured All That Miss Nelson Has Described," *Chicago Times*, 10 August 1888.

130. Nell Nelson, "City Slave Girls," *Chicago Times*, 27 August 1888.

131. "Phelps, Dodge and Palmer," *Chicago Times*, 18 August 1888. The letter may have been encouraged, or even written, by the women's employer. For further discussion of working women's pride in their identities as consumers, see Nan Enstad, *Ladies of Labor, Girls of Adventure: Working Women, Popular Culture, and Labor Politics at the Turn of the Twentieth Century* (New York: Columbia University Press, 1999).

132. Mary Kenney O'Sullivan, "Autobiography," Papers of the Women's Trade Union League and Its Principal Leaders. Microfilm, Edward T. James, ed. (Woodbridge, Conn.: Research Publications, 1981), Collection VIII, Reel 1, 30–31.

133. "A Bread Winner's Protest," *Chicago Times*, 8 August 1888.

134. Corinne S. Brown, "Unions for Workingwomen," *Chicago Times*, 18 August 1888. For other suggestions that working women should organize, see the following *Chicago Times* articles: "Let the Pulpit Join the Press," 5 August 1888; Mary Hering, "Let Them Join the Assemblies," 6 August 1888; "A Bread Winner's Protest," 8 August 1888; "A Possible Remedy" reprinted from the *Burlington (Wisconsin) Standard Democrat,* 6 August 1888; "The Ethical Society Discusses City Slave Girls," 13 August 1888.

135. "Brown, Mrs. Corinne Stubbs," in *A Woman of the Century,* ed. Frances E. Willard and Mary A. Livermore (1893; reprint, Detroit: Gale Research Co., 1967), 126; Tax, *Rising of the Women,* 65–89; Sklar, *Florence Kelley,* 211–15.

136. Nelson, "City Slave Girls," *Chicago Times*, 24 August 1888.

137. Abraham Bisno, *Union Pioneer* (Madison: University of Wisconsin Press, 1967), 212.

138. "City Slave Girls," *Chicago Times*, 24 August 1888. About 20 percent of all marriages in Chicago ended in divorce. Mrs. May (Wood) Simons, *Woman and the Social Problem* (Chicago: Charles H. Kerr, 1890), 19.

139. Pater Familias, "The Attractions of Domestic Service," *Chicago Times*, 5 August 1888.

140. D. R., "Girls Out of Their Proper Sphere," *Chicago Times*, 5 August 1888; Workman, "A Few Questions Asked," *Chicago Times*, 7 August 1888.

141. "Four Dollars Wages and $4 Board," *Chicago Times*, 12 August 1888.

142. Kathy Peiss, *Cheap Amusements: Working Women and Leisure in Turn-of-the-Century New York* (Philadelphia: Temple University Press, 1986), 4–6.

143. Foner, *American Freedom,* 111–22; Lawrence B. Glickman, *A Living Wage: American Workers and the Making of Consumer Society* (Ithaca, N.Y.: Cornell University Press, 1997), 64–65, 100.

144. J. J. H., "A Shop Girl's Experiences," *Chicago Times*, 8 September 1888.

145. M. H. S., "Anything Better Than Housework," *Chicago Times*, 8 August 1888.

146. Mrs. A. C. W., "Those 'Good Homes' for Domestics," *Chicago Times*, 8 September 1888.

147. "The Public Voice," *Chicago Times*, 3 August 1888; "Go to the Country," reprinted from the *Watseka (Illinois) Times*, 6 August 1888; "Go to Dakota and Get Married," *Chicago Times*, 19 August 1888.

148. Mrs. J. S. R., "One Woman's Life in the Country," *Chicago Times*, 5 August 1888.

149. J. M. W., "Hard Work Everywhere," *Chicago Times*, 7 August 1888.

150. M. H. S., "Anything Better Than Housework," *Chicago Times*, 8 August 1888.

151. L. M. H., "Too Deep for Shallow Remedies," *Chicago Times*, 5 August 1888.

152. S. P. Porter, "Reform in the Kitchen," *Chicago Times*, 11 August 1888.

153. "Domestic Service," *Chicago Times,* 12 August 1888. See also Mary E. Breedy, "The Kitchen Drudge," *Chicago Times,* 1 September 1888.

154. "The Times Crusade," *Chicago Times,* 13 August 1888.

155. "Chicago Workingwomen," *Journal of United Labor,* 16 August 1888.

CHAPTER 3. GENDER, CLASS, AND CONSUMPTION

1. Mary J. Bularzik, "The Bonds of Belonging: Leonora O'Reilly and Social Reform," *Labor History* 24, no. 1 (Winter 1983): 61, 64, 67.

2. Alice Henry, "Mrs. Winifred O'Reilly," *Life and Labor* (May 1911): 132–34.

3. Edward T. James, "Leonora O'Reilly," in *Papers of the WTUL and Its Principal Leaders: Guide to the Microfilm Edition,* ed. Nancy Schrom Dye, Robin Miller Jacoby, and Edward T. James (Woodbridge, Conn.: Research Publications, 1981), 211.

4. [Mary Dreier?], "Winifred O'Reilly," Leonora O'Reilly [hereafter, LOR] Papers, Schlesinger Library, Radcliffe Institute, Harvard University, series 2, reel 3.

5. Letter from Mary S. Wolfe to Mary Dreier, c. 1927, LOR Papers, reel 3, series 2.

6. Henry, "Winifred O'Reilly," 135–36; Mary E. Dreier, "Leonora O'Reilly, A Chapter of Memories," 3–4, Mary Elisabeth Dreier Papers, Schlesinger Library, Radcliffe Institute, Harvard University, folder 57.

7. Charles Shively, "Leonora O'Reilly," in *NAW,* 2:651.

8. Maureen Fitzgerald, *Habits of Compassion: Irish Catholic Nuns and the Origins of New York's Welfare System, 1830–1920* (Urbana: University of Illinois Press, 2006), 4–5, 92–95, 109–10.

9. The African American population in New York City remained small, rising to just 60,000 in a city of over 1 million souls by the turn of the century. Gilbert Osofsky, *Harlem, The Making of a Ghetto: Negro New York, 1890–1930,* 2d ed. (New York: Harper, 1971), 4–6.

10. Jacob Riis, *How the Other Half Lives* (New York: Charles Scribner's Sons, 1890), hypertext edition, chap. 20, para. 8: http://www.cis.yale.edu/amstud/inforev/riis/chap20.html.

11. Ruth Huntington Sessions, *Sixty-Odd: A Personal History* (Brattleboro, Vt.: Stephen Daye Press, 1936), 287.

12. Ronald Mendel, "Workers in Gilded Age New York and Brooklyn, 1886–1898" (Ph.D. diss., City University of New York, 1989), 10.

13. Addresses can be gleaned from correspondence in LOR Papers.

14. "Working Women of Today as Viewed by Miss O'Reilly," *Utica Daily Press,* 29 March 1899, LOR Papers, reel 9, series 5.

15. Leonora O'Reilly, "Misguided Charity," *American Press Association,* Labor Page, 1896, LOR Papers, reel 9, series 5.

16. James, "Leonora O'Reilly," 211.

17. Sessions, *Sixty-Odd,* 288.

18. "Dear Honor," 11 January 1896, diary entries for 22 May 1898 and "Monday," LOR Papers, reel 1, series 1, vol. 2; 13 and 20 February [1898], Appointment Book, reel 1, series 1, vol. 4.

19. Henry, "Winifred O'Reilly," 136.

20. Jean-Baptiste Hubert to Leonora O'Reilly, 3 March 1886, LOR Papers, reel 4, series 4.

21. Henry, "Winifred O'Reilly," 136; Jean-Baptiste Hubert to Leonora O'Reilly, 3 March 1886. It seems likely that Leonora and Winifred joined Local 2234, a mixed assembly composed of workers from different trades. Robert Weir, "'Here's to the Men Who Lose!' The Hidden Career of Victor Drury," *Labor History* 36, no. 4 (Fall 1995): 538.

22. Edward Thomas O'Donnell, "Henry George and the 'New Political Forces': Ethnic Nationalism, Labor Radicalism, and Politics in Gilded Age New York City" (Ph.D. diss., Columbia University, 1995), 191.

23. Jean-Baptiste Hubert to Leonora O'Reilly, 1 December 1886, LOR Papers, reel 4, series 4.

24. Robert E. Weir, "Drury, Victor S.," *ANB Online* (February 2000); Mari Jo Buhle, *Women and American Socialism, 1870–1920* (Urbana: University of Illinois Press, 1983), 11–12.

25. Letter from J.-B. Hubert, 3 March 1886, LOR Papers, reel 4, series 4.

26. Gregory Weinstein, *The Ardent Eighties* (reprint, New York: Arno Press, 1975), 40.

27. "Better Wages for Women," *New York Times*, 10 October 1888; Maud Nathan, *The Story of an Epoch-Making Movement* (New York: Doubleday, 1926), 16; Shively, "O'Reilly, Leonora," in *NAW*, 2:651–53.

28. William Rhinelander Stewart, *The Philanthropic Work of Josephine Shaw Lowell* (New York: Macmillan, 1911), 334–35; Alice Henry, *Trade Union Woman* (1915; reprint, New York: Burt Franklin, 1973), 43.

29. Edward King to Leonora O'Reilly, undated [c.1889], LOR Papers, reel 4, series 4; Stewart, *Lowell*, 334; Leon Fink, *Workingmen's Democracy: The Knights of Labor and American Politics* (Urbana: University of Illinois Press, 1983), 11.

30. Letter from Maggie Finn to Leonora O'Reilly, 9 July 1912, LOR Papers, reel 6.

31. Robert D. Cross, "Grace Hoadley Dodge," in *NAW*, 1:490.

32. Priscilla Murolo, *The Common Ground of Womanhood: Class, Gender, and Working Girls' Clubs, 1884–1928* (Urbana: University of Illinois Press, 1997), chap. 2.

33. *Annual Report of the Working Women's Society, 1892* (New York: Freytag Printing Co., 1893).

34. Gerald Grob, *Workers and Utopia: A Study of Ideological Conflict in the American Labor Movement, 1865–1900* (Chicago: Quadrangle Books, 1969), 164–65; Bruce Laurie, *Artisans into Workers: Labor in Nineteenth-Century America* (Urbana: University of Illinois Press, 1997), 165, 174–75.

35. Unidentified clipping, Church Association for the Advancement of the Interests of Labor Scrapbook, vol. 1, Archives of the Episcopal Diocese of New York.

36. Frank Sugeno, "Huntington, James Otis Sargent," *ANB Online* (February 2000); Edwin G. Burrows and Mike Wallace, *Gotham: A History of New York City to 1898* (New York: Oxford University Press, 1999), 1171–72; Clyde Griffen, "Christian Socialism Instructed by Gompers," *Labor History* 12, no. 2 (1971): 197–202; Vida Dutton Scudder, *Father Huntington, Founder of the Order of the Holy Cross* (New York: E. P. Dutton, 1940), 96, 98, 134–35, 138–39, 159.

37. Sessions, *Sixty-Odd,* 287–89; Helen Lefkowitz Horowitz, *Rereading Sex: Battles over Sexual Knowledge and Suppression in Nineteenth-Century America* (New York: Vintage Books, 2002), 412–13.

38. Kathryn Kish Sklar, *Florence Kelley and the Nation's Work: The Rise of Women's Political Culture, 1830–1900* (New Haven, Conn.: Yale University Press, 1995), 148–49, 146.

39. Robert H. Bremner, "Lowell, Josephine Shaw," in *NAW,* 2:437–38.

40. Stewart, *Lowell,* 334–35.

41. Edward King to Leonora O'Reilly, 29 May 1888, LOR Papers, reel 4, series 4.

42. Grob, *Workers and Utopia,* 167–68.

43. Ileen A. DeVault, *United Apart: Gender and the Rise of Craft Unionism* (Ithaca, N.Y.: Cornell University Press, 2004), 4–5.

44. Sklar, *Florence Kelley,* 150–51.

45. Quoted in Eleanor Flexner, *Century of Struggle: The Woman's Rights Movement in the United States,* rev. ed. (Cambridge, Mass.: Belknap Press, 1976), 212.

46. Stewart, *Lowell,* 372.

47. Alice L. Woodbridge, "Woman's Labor," *American Federationist* 1, no. 4 (June 1894): 66–67.

48. *Annual Report of the Working Women's Society, 1892.*

49. Stewart, *Lowell,* 373–74. Lowell's reasoning echoed that of Ira Steward and George McNeil, leading proponents of shorter hours for all workers; see Lawrence B. Glickman, *A Living Wage: American Workers and the Making of Consumer Society* (Ithaca, N.Y.: Cornell University Press, 1997), 100, 106–7.

50. Stewart, *Lowell,* 375–79.

51. "A Woman Worker's Plea for Her Sex," *New York World,* 30 May 1899.

52. As Maud Nathan recalled, "To have such a character at the head of a humanitarian movement was to insure its success" (*Epoch-Making Movement,* 17).

53. "Working Women of Today as Viewed by Miss O'Reilly," *Utica Daily Press,* 29 March 1899.

54. Henry, *Trade Union Woman,* 44; *New York Times,* 10 October 1888.

55. "A Paper Read before the Working Women's Society of New York," printed in the *Evening Post,* 8 March [n.d.], LOR Papers, reel 13.

56. "Better Wages for Women," *New York Times,* 10 October 1888.

57. Stewart, *Lowell,* 335.

58. "Bedlam at Cooper Union," *New York Times,* 27 March 1890, PQHN.

59. Ida M. Van Etten, *Condition of Women Workers under the Present Industrial System: An Address . . . at the National Convention of the American Federation of Labor . . . Detroit, Michigan, December 8th, 1890* (New York: Concord Co-operative Print, c.1891), microfilm (New Haven, Conn.: Research Publications, 1977), 6–7; Sklar, *Florence Kelley,* 142; Helen Campbell, *Women Wage Workers: Their Past, Their Present, and Their Future* (Boston: Roberts, 1893), 234–35.

60. Alice Kessler-Harris, *A Woman's Wage: Historical Meanings and Social Consequences* (Lexington: University of Kentucky Press, 1990), 33–40.

61. Roy Lubove, "Jacobi, Mary Putnam," in *NAW,* 2:264.

62. Flexner, *Century of Struggle,* 212–13.

63. Nathan, *Epoch-Making Movement,* 16–21; Robert D. Cross, "Maud Nathan," in *NAW,* 2:608.

64. "To Better the Shop Girls Lot," *New York Sun,* 7 May 1890.

65. Susan Porter Benson, *Counter Cultures: Saleswomen, Managers, and Customers in American Department Stores, 1890–1940* (Urbana: University of Illinois Press, 1988), 23–25, 139–40, 208–9.

66. Theodore Dreiser, *Sister Carrie* (1900; unexpurgated ed., New York: Penguin, 1981), 22–23, 69–71.

67. Benson, *Counter Cultures,* 128, 130, 135–36.

68. "You are earnestly requested to attend a mass meeting," n.d. [May 1890], Gerritsen Collection.

69. "To Help Women Who Work," *New York Daily Tribune,* 7 May 1890; "The Interests of Working Girls," *New York Times,* 7 May 1890.

70. Riis, *How the Other Half Lives,* hypertext edition, chap. 20, paras. 3–4.

71. "To Better the Shop Girls Lot," *New York Sun,* 7 May 1890.

72. Mona Domosh, "The 'Gorgeous Incongruities': Polite Politics and Public Space on the Streets of Nineteenth-Century New York City," *Annals of the Association of American Geographers* 88, no. 2 (June 1998): 209–26; David Scobey, "Anatomy of the Promenade: The Politics of Bourgeois Sociability in Nineteenth-Century New York," *Social History* 17, no. 2 (May 1992): 214–15.

73. "To Help Women Who Work," *New York Daily Tribune,* 7 May 1890. Nathan claimed (inaccurately) that Woodbridge took the unprecedented step of addressing the audience; *Epoch-Making Movement,* 21–22.

74. Olive Hoogenboom, "Wheeler, Everett Pepperrell," *ANB Online* (accessed February 2000).

75. "To Help Women Who Work," *New York Daily Tribune,* 7 May 1890.

76. Paul Boyer, *Urban Masses and Moral Order in America, 1820–1920* (Cambridge, Mass.: Harvard University Press, 1978), 126.

77. Alice L. Woodbridge, *Report on the Condition of Working Women in New York Retail Stores* (New York: Freytag Printing Co., 1893), 3.

78. Riis, *How the Other Half Lives,* hypertext edition, chap. 20, paras. 3–4.

79. Woodbridge, *Working Women in New York Retail Stores,* 7.

80. Ibid., 3–6.

81. Timothy J. Gilfoyle, *City of Eros: New York City, Prostitution, and the Commercialization of Sex, 1790–1920* (New York: W. W. Norton, 1992), 270–74, 283–91.

82. Woodbridge, *Working Women in New York Retail Stores,* 8.

83. Griffen, "Christian Socialism," 202.

84. Burrows and Wallace, *Gotham,* 1171–72; Sugeno, "Huntington, James Otis Sargent."

85. "To Help Women Who Work," *New York Daily Tribune,* 7 May 1890.

86. "The 'White List' Association," *Washington Post,* 18 January 1890, *PQHN.*

87. "The Interests of the Working Girls," *New York Times,* 7 May 1890; Nathan, *Epoch-Making Movement,* 22.

88. Nathan, *Epoch-Making Movement,* 130–31; "The 'White List' Association," *Washington Post,* 18 January 1890, 4, *PQHN.*

89. Sklar, *Florence Kelley,* 222.

90. Glickman, *Living Wage,* 95–98, 108–28.

91. Robert D. Cross, "Nathan, Maud," in *NAW,* 2:609.

92. Diary entry, 18 December 1898, LOR Papers, reel 1, series 1, vol. 6.

93. David C. Hammack, *Power and Society: Greater New York at the Turn of the Century* (New York: Columbia University Press, 1982), 60–63.

94. Joan Waugh, "Unsentimental Reformer: The Life of Josephine Shaw Lowell" (Ph.D. diss, University of California—Los Angeles, 1992), 468.

95. "The Boycott," *Harper's Weekly,* 4 April 1886, 258, "HarpWeek"; David Scobey, "Boycotting the Politics Factory: Labor Radicalism and the New York City Mayoral Election of 1886," *Radical History Review* 28 (1984): 282.

96. "Ida Van Etten Dead in Paris," *New York Times,* 7 March 1894, 8, *PQHN.*

97. Elizabeth Faue, *Righting the Wrong: Eva Valesh and the Rise of Labor Journalism* (Ithaca, N.Y.: Cornell University Press, 2002), 152.

98. Van Etten, *Condition of Women Workers.*

99. Grob, *Workers and Utopia,* 171–74; Laurie, *Artisans into Workers,* 181–82.

100. Meredith Tax, *The Rising of the Women: Feminist Solidarity and Class Conflict, 1880–1917* (New York: Monthly Review Press, 1980), 61; De Vault, *United Apart,* 217.

101. Griffen, "Christian Socialism," 202–3.

102. *Annual Report of the Working Women's Society,* 1892.

103. Mary F. Seymour, "The Bill for the Enfranchisement of Self-Supporting Women," *Business Woman's Journal* 4, no. 4 (January 1892): 29.

104. O'Donnell, "Henry George," 580.

105. "Ida Van Etten Dead in Paris," *New York Times,* 7 March 1894, 8; "Ida Van Etten's Death Abroad," *New York Times,* 8 March 1894, 5; "Hunger Hastened Her Death," *Washington Post,* 8 March 1894, 1; "The Late Ida Van Etten," *Washington Post,* 25 March 1894, 22; all *PQHN.*

106. Letter from Louise Perkins to Leonora O'Reilly, March 21 [1894], LOR papers, reel 4, series 4.

107. *Annual Report of the Working Women's Society, 1892;* "To Benefit the Workingwomen," "Will Sit Many Months," unidentified clippings, Maud Nathan Papers, Schlesinger Library, Radcliffe Institute, Harvard University, Scrapbooks, vol. 2.

108. Campbell, *Woman Wage-Earners,* 23–24.

109. "The Shop Girl's Grievance," unidentified clipping, Nathan Scrapbooks, vol. 2.

110. Waugh, "Unsentimental Reformer," 464.

111. Maud Nathan, "The Consumers' League—Its Birth and Development," unidentified clipping from *Harpers,* Nathan Scrapbooks, vol. 2. A pamphlet prepared by Josephine Shaw Lowell in 1898 reflected similar reasoning; see Stewart, *Lowell,* 337–38.

112. See, for example, "High Society to Aid Overworked Shopgirls," *New York Evening Journal,* 10 December 1898, Nathan Scrapbooks, vol. 2.

113. Nathan, *Epoch-Making Movement,* 25–26.

114. Nathan recalled the list as including Aitken, Son & Co.; B. Altman & Co.; Arnold, Constable & Co.; Lord & Taylor & Co.; James McCreery & Co.; E. A. Morrison & Son; The New York Exchange for Women's Work; and The Society of Decorative Art. The stores were concentrated in the prime retail shopping district of Broadway and Sixth Avenue between Eleventh and Twenty-Third Streets. The last two stores were women's cooperatives. Nathan, *Epoch-Making Movement,* 26–29.

115. Consumers' League, *Annual Report, 1895,* 13.

116. Kessler-Harris, *A Woman's Wage,* 8–10, 12, 15, 20–21; Glickman, *Living Wage,* 52. In the early 1900s, economists calculated the minimum level for individual subsistence at eight dollars a week; David Montgomery, *The Fall of the House of Labor: The Workplace, the State, and American Labor Activism, 1865–1925* (New York: Cambridge University Press, 1987), 69–70, 135–36.

117. Nathan, *Epoch-Making Movement,* 26–27; "Carpenters to Work Again," *New York Tribune,* 4 May 1890; "The Strike Fever Raging" and "Gaining an Easy Victory," *New York Tribune,* 7 May 1890.

118. Campbell, *Women Wage-Earners,* 262–63.

119. Nathan, *Epoch-Making Movement,* 31–32.

120. Consumers' League, *Annual Report, 1895,* 18–22.

121. David R. Roediger, *The Wages of Whiteness: Race and the Making of the American Working Class* (New York: Verso, 1993), 145–47; Matthew Frye Jacobson, *Whiteness of a Different Color: European Immigrants and the Alchemy of Race* (Cambridge, Mass.: Harvard University Press, 1998), 48–49.

122. "Prof. Munsterberg" [1873–88], 12, Mary Putnam Jacobi Papers, Schlesinger Library, Radcliffe Institute, Harvard University, folder 30.

123. "The Enemy of Sweatshops," *Commercial Advertiser,* November 1897, Nathan Scrapbooks, vol. 2. See also Irwin Yellowitz, *Labor and the Progressive Movement in New York State, 1897–1916* (Ithaca, N.Y.: Cornell University Press, 1965), 44–49.

124. These included seats, a ten-hour day, "fair compensation," equal pay for equal work, and no child labor; Consumers' League, *Annual Report, 1895,* 6–9.

125. John B. Andrews and W. D. P. Bliss, *History of Women in Trade Unions,* vol. 10 of U.S. Senate, *Report on the Condition of Woman and Child Wage-Earners in the U.S.* (Washington, D.C., 1911), 191–92; Benson, *Counter Cultures,* 269–70.

126. "Women and Their Work," unidentified clipping, 5 January 1898, Nathan Scrapbooks, vol. 2.

127. Stewart, *Lowell,* 343–44.

128. "The Shop Girl's Grievance," unidentified clipping, Nathan Scrapbooks, vol. 2.

129. "Women Might Be Inspectors," unidentified clipping, Nathan Scrapbooks, vol. 1.

130. "Retail Stores' Employés," *New York Times,* 23 December 1898, 8, PQHN.

131. New York State Legislature, Assembly, Special Committee Appointed to Investigate the Condition of Female Labor in the City of New York, *Report and Testimony* (Albany: Wynkoop, Hallenbeck, Crawford, 1896), 787.

132. Assembly, *Report and Testimony,* 98.

133. "Small Riot of Shop Girls," unidentified clipping, Nathan Scrapbooks, vol. 2.

134. John M. Goodale to Leonora O'Reilly, 3 December 1896; "Rules and Regulations, Siegel-Cooper, Sixth Ave, 18th & 19th St."; Siegel-Cooper Co. Beneficial Association, Inc., Constitution and By-Laws, September 1896, Annie Ware Winsor Allen [hereafter AWWA] Papers, Schlesinger Library, Radcliffe Institute, Harvard University, box 8, folder 81.

135. During the first two decades of the twentieth century, store managers turned to corporate welfare as a means of improving their public image and creating a more tractable workforce. Benson, *Counter Cultures,* 132–37, 142–45.

136. Alice Kessler-Harris, "Where Are the Organized Women Workers?" *Feminist Studies* 3, nos. 1–2 (Autumn 1975): 92–110.

137. Louise Perkins to Leonora O'Reilly, 25 July [1892], LOR Papers, reel 4, series 4; Mary K. O'Sullivan Autobiography, Schlesinger Library, Radcliffe Institute, Harvard University, 84–85; "An Organizer of Women," unidentified clipping from New York *World* [1892], Mary Kenney O'Sullivan Papers, Schlesinger Library, Radcliffe Institute, Harvard University, folder 8; Kathleen Banks Nutter, *The Necessity of Organization: Mary Kenney O'Sullivan and Trade Unionism for Women, 1882–1912* (New York: Garland, 2000), 11–12.

138. Burrows and Wallace, *Gotham,* 1185–90.

139. Appointment book, LOR Papers, reel 1, series 1, vol. 3.

140. "Dear Honor," 11 January 1896, LOR Papers, reel 1, series 1, vol. 2.

141. "Dearest Kate," 24 January 1896, LOR Papers, reel 9, series 5.

142. "Dear Honor," 11 January 1896, LOR Papers, reel 1, series 1, vol. 2; diary entry, Monday, 24 January, LOR Papers, reel 1, series 1, vol. 4.

143. Diary entries, 22 May and 19 June 1898, LOR Papers, reel 1, series 1, vol. 2.

144. Weinstein, *Ardent Eighties,* 40–41, 166, 169.

145. "Dear Honor," 11 January 1896, LOR Papers, reel 1, series 1, vol. 2.

146. L. S. W. Perkins to Leonora O'Reilly, 21 December [1894], LOR Papers, reel 4, series 4.

147. The SRC met at 28 East Fourth Street until September 1898; it then moved to 45 University Place near Ninth Street. "Report of Meeting May 7, 1901," SRC of New York, Calendars, 1896–1902, New York Public Library.

148. Sessions, *Sixty-Odd,* 322.

149. SRC, *Annual Report/Constitution/List of Members,* pamphlet, 1898, AWWA Papers, Schlesinger Library, Radcliffe Institute, Harvard University, box 4, folder 38.

150. Yellowitz, *Labor and the Progressive Movement,* 51–54.

151. "Report of September 28, 1897," SRC Calendars, New York Public Library.

152. Leonora O'Reilly to AWWA, 29 April 1896, AWWA Papers, box 5, folder 61.

153. I would distinguish this shared goal from "a common ground of womanhood" as described by Priscilla Murolo, *Common Ground of Womanhood,* 2–3, 37–38. O'Reilly's and Lowell's divergent class positions gave them quite different identities and experiences of womanhood.

154. "New York Association of Working Girls Societies," 1893; "38th Street Working Girls' Society, Tuesday Evening Practical Talks, 1893–1894"; "The Working Girls Clubs, Second National Convention, Boston, May 9, 10 and 11, 1894," all in LOR Papers, reel 13.

155. "Dear Honor," 11 January 1896, LOR Papers, reel 1, series 1, vol. 2; SRC, *Annual Report,* 4–6, AWWA Papers, box 4, folder 38.

156. Assembly, *Report and Testimony,* 60; printed circular from Mercantile Inspection Committee dated 13 November 1896, AWWA Papers, box 8, folder 81.

157. "The State Pays the Bills," *New York Times,* 15 April 1895, PQHN; "Sweating Abuses," undated clipping from the *Evening Post,* Nathan Scrapbooks, vol. 2.

158. "Not Controlled by Women," *New York Times,* 12 May 1895, PQHN.

159. Assembly, *Report and Testimony,* 966–68.

160. Ibid., 1796.

161. Ibid., 777–84.

162. Ibid., 1826–29, 1835.

163. Ibid., 1821.

164. Printed circular from Mercantile Inspection Committee dated 13 November 1896, AWWA Papers, box 8, folder 81.

165. "Not Controlled by Women; Chairman Reinhardt's [*sic*] Reply to Mornay Williams," *New York Times,* 12 May 1895, PQHN.

166. Assembly, *Report and Testimony,* 779–80. This opinion had been developed in *In re. Jacobs,* 98 N.Y. 98 (1885) and *Ritchie v. People,* 155 Ill. 98, 40 N.E. 454 (1895).

Eileen Boris, *Home to Work: Motherhood and the Politics of Industrial Homework in the U.S.* (New York: Cambridge University Press, 1994), 21–22, 50.

167. Assembly, *Report and Testimony*, 41.

168. Sarah S. Whittelsey, "Tendencies of Factory Legislation and Inspection in the United States," in *Social Legislation and Social Activity*, ed. American Academy of Political and Social Science of Philadelphia (New York: McClure, Phillips, 1902), 242–43, 246–47.

169. Sklar, *Florence Kelley*, 142–43.

170. "Women Might Be Inspectors," unidentified clipping, Nathan Scrapbooks, vol. 1; Assembly, *Report and Testimony*, 29.

171. Printed circular from the Mercantile Inspection Committee dated 13 November 1896, AWWA Papers, box 8, folder 81.

172. Consumers' League, *Annual Report, 1896*, 8.

173. Maud Nathan spoke on the problems of enforcement at the SRC, Tuesday, 20 December 1898, AWWA, box 4, folder 38. Leonora O'Reilly attended the meeting; diary entry, 29 December [1898], LOR Papers, reel 1, series 1, vol. 6. Nathan, *Epoch-Making Movement*, 52–53.

174. Glickman, *Living Wage*, 95–98.

175. Dana Frank, "Where Are the Workers in Consumer-Worker Alliances? Class Dynamics and the History of Consumer-Labor Campaigns," *Politics and Society* 31, no. 3 (September 2003): 366; "Consumers' Trade and Label Circle," [c. 1896], pamphlet with examples of union labels, LOR Papers, series 6, reel 11.

176. M. E. J. Kelley, "Women and the Labor Movement," *North American Review* 166, no. 497 (April 1898): 417.

177. Nutter, *Necessity of Organization*, 79.

178. Description and subscription form for Union Label Leaflets, 1897, AWWA Papers, box 9, folder 91.

179. Nancy Tomes, "The Private Side of Public Health: Sanitary Science, Domestic Hygiene, and the Germ Theory," *Bulletin of the History of Medicine* 64, no. 4 (Winter 1990): 526–27.

180. "Church Workers Endorse Strikers," "Striking Ladies' Tailors," and "Consumers' League to Aid Strikers," unidentified clippings, Nathan Scrapbooks, vol. 2.

181. Boris, *Home to Work*, 23, 36, 47, 50, 70–80, 85.

182. AWWA Papers, box 4, folder 38.

183. Daniel E. Bender, *Sweated Work, Weak Bodies: Anti-Sweatshop Campaigns and Languages of Labor* (New Brunswick, N.J.: Rutgers University Press, 2004), 48–52.

184. AWWA Papers, box 4, folder 38.

185. "The Enemy of Sweatshops," *Commercial Advertiser*, November 1897, Nathan Scrapbooks, vol. 2.

186. Sklar, *Florence Kelley*, 309–10.

187. Yellowitz, *Labor and the Progressive Movement*, 47.

CHAPTER 4. SOLVING THE SERVANT PROBLEM

1. Paul S. Boyer, "Howe, Julia Ward," in *NAW*, 2:225–29. The significance Howe attached to women's growing field of labor can be seen in her introduction to *Woman's Work in America*, ed. Annie Nathan Meyer (New York: Henry Holt, 1891), 1–2.

2. "Woman's Work," "Woman's Great Work," "Twenty Years of Existence," all in Women's Educational and Industrial Union, Clippings, Schlesinger Library, Radcliffe Institute, Harvard University, vol. 4; Sarah Deutsch, *Women and the City: Gender, Space, and Power in Boston, 1870–1940* (New York: Oxford University Press, 2000), 144–45.

3. Many women remained active in both organizations. Sarah Deutsch, "Learning to Talk More Like a Man: Boston Women's Class-Bridging Organizations, 1870–1940," *AHR* 97, no. 2 (April 1992): 388–89. For evidence of the elite nature of the membership through the 1880s, see notice of the Kirmess in WEIU Clippings, vol. 3.

4. Barbara Burns, "Newest Program Is Companionship," *Sunday Herald Traveler,* 5 November [1967?], WEIU Clippings, vol. 1; "Woman's Work," "Women's Great Work," "Twenty Years of Existence," WEIU Clippings, vol. 4.

5. Jane Johnson Bernardete, "Diaz, Abby Morton," in *NAW*, 1:471–73.

6. "Social Economy," letter to the editor of the *Transcript*, n.d. [c. 1892], signed "One Woman," WEIU Clippings, vol. 4.

7. Robert Sklar, "Kehew, Mary Morton," in *NAW*, 2:313–15.

8. Mary K. O'Sullivan Autobiography, Schlesinger Library, Radcliffe Institute, Havard Univeristy, 125–27. Kathleen Banks Nutter, *The Necessity of Organization: Mary Kenney O'Sullivan and Trade Unionism for Women, 1892–1912* (New York: Garland, 2000), 41–42.

9. Glenna Matthews, *Just a Housewife: The Rise and Fall of Domesticity in America* (New York: Oxford University Press, 1987), 153, 156.

10. One of Florence Kelley's first projects at Hull House was to organize a bureau to place immigrant women as domestics in wealthy homes. Kathryn Kish Sklar, *Florence Kelley and the Nation's Work* (New Haven, Conn.: Yale University Press, 1995), 177.

11. Violet Barbour, "Salmon, Lucy," in *NAW*, 3:223–25.

12. Lucy Salmon, *Domestic Service* (New York: Macmillan, 1897), vii–xiv, 129, 275–81.

13. Faye E. Dudden, *Serving Women: Household Service in Nineteenth-Century America* (Middletown, Conn.: Wesleyan University Press, 1983), 237–238.

14. Ibid., 75–80; Browen Walter, *Outsiders Inside: Whiteness, Place and Irish Women* (London: Routledge, 2001), 34–39, 54–57.

15. In 1890 the U.S. Census recorded the proportions of servants who were "colored": Pacific Coast, 26.59 percent; Eastern, 5.67 percent; Middle, 10.67 percent;

Western, 6.91 percent; Border 61.73 percent; Southern, 80.18 percent. The designation "colored" included African American as well as Asian servants, who were more common in California and Oregon. Salmon, *Domestic Service,* Table II, 76.

16. Salmon, *Domestic Service,* 172–76.

17. W. E. B. DuBois, *The Philadelphia Negro: A Social Study, with a New Introduction by Elijah Anderson* (1899; reprint, Philadelphia: University of Pennsylvania Press, 1996), xvi–xix, 1–3.

18. Ibid., 136–37, 141; David M. Katzman, *Seven Days a Week: Women and Domestic Service in Industrializing America* (Urbana: University of Illinois Press, 1981), 206.

19. Fannie Barrier Williams, "The Problem of Employment for Negro Women" (1903), in *Major Problems in Women's History,* ed. Mary Beth Norton (Ithaca, N.Y.: Cornell University Press, 1989), 289–92; Victoria W. Wolcott, "Bible, Bath, and Broom: Nannie Helen Burroughs's National Training School and African-American Racial Uplift," *Journal of Women's History* 9, no. 1 (Spring 1997): 88–110.

20. For biographical information on Ruffin, see Rodger Streitmatter, "Josephine St. Pierre Ruffin: A Nineteenth-Century Journalist of Boston's Black Elite Class," in *Women of the Commonwealth: Work, Family, and Social Change in Nineteenth-Century Massachusetts,* ed. Susan L. Porter (Amherst: University of Massachusetts Press, 1996), 154–55; Roger A. Shuppert, "Ruffin, Josephine St. Pierre," *ANB Online* (February 2000).

21. Tera Hunter, "Historical Note," and Isabel Eaton, "Special Report on Negro Domestic Service in the Seventh Ward, Philadelphia," in DuBois, *Philadelphia Negro,* 425–29.

22. Eaton, "Negro Domestic Service," 428, 446–49, 459–62, 464–67; Mary Jo Deegan, "W. E. B. DuBois and the Women of Hull House, 1895–1899," *American Sociologist* 19 (Winter 1988): 307–8.

23. Unidentified clipping from *Bulletin of the DRL* (May 1905), WEIU Clippings, vol. 7.

24. Elizabeth Hafkin Pleck, *Black Migration and Poverty: Boston, 1865–1900* (New York: Academic Press, 1979), 32–33.

25. Salmon, *Domestic Service,* 109–10; Eaton, "Negro Domestic Service," 480.

26. Eaton, "Negro Domestic Service," 480–89.

27. Salmon, *Domestic Service,* 111.

28. Ibid., 228.

29. Ibid., 200.

30. Ibid., 212–15, 223.

31. In industry, according to David Montgomery, "laborers and operatives alike engaged in unprecedented levels of collective protest during the period of prewar prosperity," *The Fall of the House of Labor: The Workplace, the State, and American Labor Activism, 1865–1925* (New York: Cambridge University Press, 1987), 240.

32. "Report of the Employment Committee for the Year Ending May, 1898,"

Women's Educational and Industrial Union Papers, Schlesinger Library, Radcliffe Institute, Harvard University, box 1, folder 6; "History of the DRL," 1903, WEIU Papers, box 1, folder 5.

33. Ibid.

34. Dolores Hayden, *The Grand Domestic Revolution: A History of Feminist Designs for American Homes, Neighborhoods and Cities* (Cambridge, Mass.: MIT Press, 1981), 186–87. These ideas had become commonplace by 1895; see "The Servant Question," *New York Times,* 17 March 1895, 25, *PQHN.*

35. Letter from Ada M. Child, 25 August 1897, WEIU Papers, box 1, folder 5.

36. "Boston Women's E. and I. Union," unidentified clipping from the *Woman's Journal,* WEIU Clippings, vol. 4, reel 1; Barbara Balliet, "What Shall We Do with Our Daughters? Middle-Class Women's Ideas about Work, 1840–1920" (Ph.D. diss., New York University, 1988), 252–54.

37. For information on Gardener (1853–1925), Evans (1856–1937), and Kehew (1859–1918), see Alden Whitman, ed., *American Reformers* (New York: Wilson, 1985), 280–81, 330–32, 488–89. Also "Abby Morton Diaz," in *National Cyclopedia of American Biography* (New York: White, 1901), 11:169–70. Also see entries in *NAW*; and Erica Harth, "Founding Mothers of Social Justice," *Historical Journal of Massachusetts* (Summer 1999), 152, 154, 158.

38. WEIU Clippings, vol. 4, reel 1.

39. Ibid.

40. "History of the DRL," 1903, WEIU Papers, box 1, folder 5.

41. Deutsch, "Learning to Talk More Like a Man," 390–92. WEIU members had made contact with Wright by 1880, when they called on him to discuss the problem of saleswomen's long hours spent standing. Harth, "Founding Mothers of Social Justice," 155.

42. Elizabeth Glendower Evans, *Report of the Committee on Domestic Reform, No. 1, The Effort to Attract the Workers in Shops & Factories to Domestic Service* (Cambridge: Co-Operative Press, 1898), WEIU Papers, box 1, folder 5.

43. Ibid., 11–12.

44. "Report of the WEIU," 1888, quoted in Salmon, *Domestic Service,* 126n1.

45. "Housework Not in Favor," *New York Times,* 8 December 1898, 20, *PQHN.*

46. Evans, *Effort to Attract the Workers,* 12–16.

47. "The Committee of the DRL of the WEIU," Molly Dewson Papers, Schlesinger Library, Radcliffe Institute, Harvard University, series II, folder 14, reel 2.

48. "The Hours of Labor in Domestic Service," reprinted from *Massachusetts Labor Bulletin* 8 (October 1898) (Boston: Wright and Potter, 1898), 10, 14–21; "Servant Girl Science," *Boston Daily Globe,* 10 September 1899, 30, *PQHN.*

49. "Hours of Labor in Domestic Service," 3.

50. Ibid., 25, 28–29.

51. "Social Conditions in Domestic Service," prepared by the Massachusetts Bureau of Statistics of Labor in Collaboration with WEIU of Boston, reprinted from

Massachusetts Labor Bulletin 13 (February 1900) (Boston: Wright and Potter, 1900), 1–4.

52. Tera W. Hunter, "Domination and Resistance: The Politics of Wage Household Labor in New South Atlanta," *Labor History* 34 (Spring–Summer 1993): 205–20.

53. Pleck, *Black Migration and Poverty,* 134–37.

54. This figure is based on the U.S. Census for 1900. "Nationalities of Women Wage-Earners in Domestic Service in Mass.," WEIU Papers, box 7, folder 47.

55. Eaton, "Special Report," 484–89.

56. Clipping from the *Bulletin of the DRL* (May 1905), WEIU Clippings, vol. 7, reel 1. African American men who worked as butlers, porters, and waiters in New York City faced increased competition from European immigrants during the first decade of the twentieth century, leading some recent migrants to return to the South; African American women had an easier time finding domestic positions in the city. Marcy Sacks, "'To be a Man and Not a Lackey': Black Men, Work, and the Construction of Manhood in Gilded Age New York City," *American Studies* 45, no. 1 (2004): 47–48, 52–53.

57. Gail Bederman, *Manliness and Civilization: A Cultural History of Gender and Race in the U.S., 1880–1917* (Chicago: University of Chicago Press, 1996), 198–201.

58. "Mary Esther Trueblood (b. 1872)," in *Woman's Who's Who of America,* ed. John William Leonard (1914; reprint, New York: Commonwealth, 1976), 825.

59. Dorothy Sue Cobble, *Dishing It Out: Waitresses and Their Unions in the Twentieth Century* (Urbana: University of Illinois Press, 1991), 19, 21.

60. "Social Statistics of Working Women," prepared by the Massachusetts Bureau of Labor Statistics from information collected by the School of Housekeeping, reprinted from the *Massachusetts Labor Bulletin* 18 (May 1901): 22–23, WEIU Papers, box 1, folder 9.

61. *Bulletin of the DRL* 3, no. 2 (January 1909), WEIU Papers, box 1, folder 5; "Exhibit A," "Domestic Service—A Belated Industry," conference held at Horticultural Hall, Boston, 11 April 1907, WEIU Papers, box 7, folder 47.

62. M. H. S., "Anything Better Than Housework," *Chicago Times,* 8 August 1888; Bettina Berch, "'The Sphinx in the Household': A New Look at the History of Household Wage Workers," *Review of Radical Political Economics* 16 (Spring 1984): 105–21.

63. Female workers who lived with their parents often did not have to pay board. At the turn of the twentieth century, immigrant women living in Boston and boarding with relatives paid about $2.70 a week. An older female relative generally did the cooking. "Report of an Investigation of 500 Immigrant Women in Boston Conducted by the Research Department of the Women's Educational and Industrial Union," 11, WEIU Papers, box 7, folder 48. As historian Faye E. Dudden has pointed out, payment for room and board implied that someone else would be doing the cleaning, cooking, and laundry; the domestic servant did her own work. *Serving Women,* 221.

64. These earnings figures assume that domestic servants worked 85 hours for the equivalent of $7.50, textile workers worked 58 hours for $7.00, and saleswomen worked 60 hours for $6.00.

65. "Report of the Employment Committee for the Year Ending May, 1898," 49, WEIU Papers, box 1, folder 6.

66. Dudden, *Serving Women,* 79–85.

67. "Domestic Reform League Report Is Full of Facts," unidentified clipping, WEIU Clippings, vol. 5, reel 1.

68. DRL Contract, WEIU Papers, box 1, folder 5.

69. "History of the DRL," 1903, WEIU Papers, box 1, folder 5.

70. *Bulletin of the DRL* 1 (January 1907); "The Law of Employer and Domestic Employee," WEIU Papers, box 1, folder 5.

71. "History of the DRL," 1903, WEIU Papers, box 1, folder 5.

72. DRL Report, 1898–99, WEIU Papers, box 1, folder 5.

73. "History of the DRL," 1903, WEIU Papers, box 1, folder 5.

74. "Associations Which the Inter-Municipal Committee Represents," unidentified clipping, c. 1905, WEIU Clippings, reel 1, vol. 7. In 1902 the DRL served 4,540 employers and 1,866 employees. In 1901 it made $58; in 1902 it earned more than of $600. "Report of the Employment Committee for the Year Ending April, 1902," 43, 46, WEIU Papers, box 1, folder 6.

75. Salmon, *Domestic Service,* 115–16.

76. Ellen Fitzpatrick, *Endless Crusade: Women Social Scientists and Progressive Reform* (New York: Oxford University Press, 1990), 132–33; Nancy Schrom Dye, *As Equals and As Sisters: Feminism, the Labor Movement, and the Women's Trade Union League of New York* (Columbia: University of Missouri Press, 1980), 36.

77. "History of the DRL," 1903, WEIU Papers, box 1, folder 5.

78. "Servants Who Like to Sue," unidentified clipping from the *New York Sun,* c. 1905, WEIU Clippings, vol. 7, reel 1.

79. Mary Esther Trueblood, "The Boston School of Housekeeping," reprinted from *Good Housekeeping,* April 1900, WEIU Clippings, vol. 5, reel 1.

80. Montgomery, *Fall of the House of Labor,* 240–41; Phyllis Palmer, *Domesticity and Dirt: Housewives and Domestic Servants, 1920–1945* (Philadelphia: Temple University Press, 1989), 90–91.

81. Wolcott, "Bible, Bath, and Broom," 96–98.

82. *School of Housekeeping,* booklet published by WEIU, 1899, Dewson Papers, series II, folder 14, reel 2.

83. Trueblood, "The Boston School of Housekeeping."

84. "Home Life Science," *Boston Herald,* 27 December 1899, WEIU Clippings, vol. 5, reel 1.

85. Trueblood, "The Boston School of Housekeeping."

86. Circular for Employees, WEIU Papers, box 1, folder 9; Trueblood, "The Boston School of Housekeeping."

87. "A School of Housekeeping," *Cambridge Tribune,* 23 June 1900, WEIU Clippings, vol. 5, reel 1.

88. Balliet, "What Shall We Do with Our Daughters?" 225. Cooks earned the highest wages among female domestic workers. Eaton, "Negro Domestic Service," 448–49.

89. Salmon, *Domestic Service,* 186.

90. Wolcott, "Bible, Bath, and Broom," 98.

91. "A School of Housekeeping," *Cambridge Tribune,* 23 June 1900, WEIU Clippings, vol. 5, reel 1.

92. *School of Housekeeping,* 31, Dewson Papers, series II, folder 14, reel 2.

93. *Bulletin of the DRL* 3, no. 1 (October 1908), WEIU Papers, box 1, folder 5.

94. Bellamy recommended solving the problem through the establishment of cooperative housekeeping and the development of "scientific cuisine." Quoted in Matthews, *Just a Housewife,* 99.

95. Sylvia E. Bowman, *Edward Bellamy* (Boston: Twayne Publishers, 1986), 101; William Leach, "Looking Forward Together: Feminists and Edward Bellamy," *Democracy* 2, no. 1 (1982): 123–34.

96. Ruth Levitas, "'Who Holds the Hose?' Domestic Labour in the Work of Bellamy, Gilman, and Morris," *Utopian Studies* 6, no. 1 (1995): 66–70.

97. The high cost of electricity and gas limited the new appliances to the wealthy until after 1900. Susan Strasser, *Never Done: A History of American Housework* (New York: Pantheon, 1982), 73, 76, 78, 163.

98. Unidentified clipping from *The Outlook,* 31 August [1901?], WEIU Clippings, vol. 5, reel 1.

99. Matthews, *Just a Housewife,* 134. Gilman was strongly influenced by Bellamy's Nationalism, an American form of socialism. Mark W. Van Wienan, "A Rose by Any Other Name: Charlotte Perkins Stetson (Gilman) and the Case for American Reform Socialism," *AQ* 55, no. 4 (2003): 603–34.

100. Charlotte Perkins Gilman, *The Home: Its Work and Influence* (New York: McClure, 1903), 83–84, 117–18, 122, 330.

101. "Co-Operative Housekeeping," *The Revolution,* 29 July 1869; Barbara Ryan, *Love, Wages, Slavery: The Literature of Servitude in the United States* (Urbana: University of Illinois Press, 2006), 148–49.

102. Cowan, *More Work for Mother,* 104–5.

103. Kate Gannett Wells, "The Servant Girl of the Future," *North American Review* (December 1893), 719. For further discussion of collective approaches, see Cowan, *More Work for Mother,* 111–19.

104. "Is Bought Cake Too Costly?" WEIU Clippings, vol. 5, reel 1.

105. Unidentified clipping from *The Outlook,* 31 August [1901?], WEIU Clippings, vol. 5, reel 1.

106. "No Cooking at Home," WEIU Clippings, vol. 5, reel 1.

107. "A Possible Alleviation of Present Difficulties in Domestic Service," *Bulletin of the DRL* 1 (January 1907), WEIU Papers, box 1, folder 5.

108. "Concerning the Domestic Problem," *Woman's Journal,* 13 February [n.d.], WEIU Clippings, vol. 5, reel 1.

109. Palmer, *Domesticity and Dirt,* 68–69.

110. "Exhibit A," "Domestic Service—A Belated Industry," Horticultural Hall, Boston, 11 April 1907, WEIU Papers, Box 7, Folder 47. Day work would not become the norm until World War I, when the severe shortage of labor gave many mistresses no choice but to accept day workers; Katzman, *Seven Days a Week*, 177. For discussion of the transition to day work, see Elizabeth Clark-Lewis, *Living In, Living Out: African American Domestics in Washington, D.C., 1910–1940* (Washington, D.C.: Smithsonian Institution Press, 1994).

111. *Trained and Supplemental Employees for Domestic Service*, report prepared by the Massachusetts Bureau of Statistics of Labor, in collaboration with the WEIU, reprinted from Part II of the *Annual Report* for 1906 (Boston: Wright and Potter, 1906).

112. Ibid., 2, 30–33.

113. Ibid., 30–35. Jane Addams would make a similar point in her 1916 book *Democracy and Social Ethics*. Susan Strasser, "Mistress and Maid, Employer and Employee: Domestic Service Reform in the United States, 1870–1920," *Marxist Perspectives* 1, no. 4 (Winter 1978): 62.

114. For further discussion of food delivery services, see Hayden, *Domestic Revolution,* chap. 10.

115. "Concerning the Domestic Problem." The DRL noted that commercial laundry facilities for "family washing" were increasing "constantly"; the Household Aid Co. lasted from 1903 to 1905. "Exhibit A," "Domestic Service—A Belated Industry," Horticultural Hall, Boston, WEIU Papers, box 7, folder 47.

116. "Concerning the Domestic Problem."

117. "Among the Women's Clubs," WEIU Clippings, vol. 5, reel 1.

118. Ibid.

119. "Work of Women," WEIU Clippings, vol. 5, reel 1.

120. "Sociological Study of the Family," *Transcript*, WEIU Clippings, vol. 5, reel 1.

121. Molly Ladd-Taylor, *Mother-Work: Women, Child Welfare, and the State, 1890–1930* (Urbana: University of Illinois Press, 1994), 139–41.

122. Geraldine Youcha, *Minding the Children: Child Care in America from Colonial Times to the Present* (New York: Scribner, 1995), 140–42, 243–44, 248–49.

123. *Bulletin of the DRL* (May 1905), WEIU Clippings, vol. 7, reel 1. "Colored" servants were rare in New England, making up only 5.7 percent of the total servant population. For a discussion of regional distribution of servants by nativity and race in 1890, see Salmon, *Domestic Service,* 76.

124. Eaton, "Negro Domestic Service," 479–89.

125. Despite its expansion, use of the DRL registry remained limited to WEIU members. Circular, September 1907, WEIU Papers, box 1, folder 5.

126. New York supporters of the organization included Lucy Salmon, Grace Dodge, Margaret Dreier, Frances Kellor, and Lillian Wald. Dudden, *Serving Women,* 239.

127. Fitzpatrick, *Endless Crusade,* 17, 18, 58, 64, 132; Christopher W. Diemicke, "Kellor, Frances Alice," *ANB Online* (accessed February 2000).

128. Fitzpatrick, *Endless Crusade,* 132–34.

129. Ibid., 132–37.

130. Ibid., 131–38; Diemicke, "Kellor, Frances Alice."

131. Frances Kellor, "The Immigrant Woman, I," [unidentified publication] 100, no. 3: 402, 406, WEIU Papers, box 7, folder 48.

132. Ryan, *Love, Wages, Slavery,* 150.

133. Campbell, *Prisoners of Poverty,* 236.

134. Kellor, "The Immigrant Woman," 402–4; Elizabeth Ewen, *Immigrant Women in the Land of Dollars: Life and Culture on the Lower East Side, 1890–1925* (New York: Monthly Review Press, 1985), 149–50.

135. Nancy Tomes, "The Private Side of Public Health: Sanitary Science, Domestic Hygiene, and Germ Theory, 1870–1900," *Bulletin of the History of Medicine* 64, no. 4 (Winter 1990): 509–39.

136. John Higham, *Strangers in the Land: Patterns of American Nativism, 1860–1925,* 2d ed. (New York: Athenaeum, 1963), 87–96, 149–57.

137. Kellor, "The Immigrant Woman," 402.

138. "Nationalities of Women Wage-Earners in Domestic Service in the United States," WEIU Papers, box 7, folder 47.

139. Kellor, "The Immigrant Woman," 403–4. As an agent from Hebrew Charities on Ellis Island explained in a letter to Kellor: "Domestic service presents unattractive outlook. Would not wish to work in Christian family and work is very hard and menial in Jewish family of moderate circumstances." Unidentified letter to Frances Kellor from Agent of Hebrew Charities, WEIU Papers, box 7, folder 48.

140. "Report of an Investigation of 500 Immigrant Women in Boston Conducted by the Research Department of the Women's Educational and Industrial Union," Table VI, 12, WEIU Papers, box 7, folder 4. A Boston employment agency found Irish immigrants to be the only ones willing to go into domestic service. Notes on Domestic Service, WEIU Papers, box 7, folder 48.

141. Ewen, *Immigrant Women in the Land of Dollars,* chap. 6; John Bodnar, *The Transplanted: A History of Immigrants in Urban America* (Bloomington: Indiana University Press, 1985), chap. 2.

142. *Advertiser,* 4 and 7 May 1910, WEIU Clippings, vol. 9, reel 1; "Employment Office Closed," *Boston Globe,* 3 May 1910; "Women Press Bill to Probe Labor Bureaus," unidentified clipping, 3 May 1910; "The Worker and the Chance to Work," *Boston Globe,* Sunday, 8 May 1910; "Licenses Held Up in Pique," *Post,* 4 May 1910, WEIU Clippings, vol. 11, reel 1.

143. "The Worker and the Chance to Work," *Boston Globe,* Sunday, 8 May 1910. President Mary Morton Kehew refused to discontinue the work of the field agent, describing it as essential to the DRL's mission; "Refuses Union a Public Hearing," *Journal,* 5 May 1910, WEIU Clippings, vol. 11, reel 1.

144. "Mary Boyle O'Reilly, The Union's New President," WEIU Clippings, vol. 13, reel 1.

CHAPTER 5. DEMOCRACY IS ONLY AN ASPIRATION

1. "A Woman Worker's Plea for Her Sex," clipping from New York *World*, 30 March 1899, LOR Papers, Schlesinger Library, Radcliffe Institute, Harvard University, reel 9; oral history interview of Pauline Newman by Barbara Wertheimer, 13, Pauline Newman Papers, Schlesinger Library, Radcliffe Institute, Harvard University, box 1, folder 13; Charles Shively, "O'Reilly, Leonora," in *NAW*, 2:652–53. Workers who assembled at the People's Home hissed, booed, and jeered Samuel Gompers, the president of the AFL, when he argued that organized labor should stay out of politics, and that only women and children needed the legal protection of an eight-hour day. "Audience Jeers Gompers," *New York Times*, 22 March 1899, 7, PQHN.

2. Elite suffrage activists, such as Harriot Stanton Blatch, assumed that working-class women needed "educated" women to explain their need for full rights. Ellen Carol DuBois, "Working Women, Class Relations, and Suffrage Militance: Harriot Stanton Blatch and the Woman Suffrage Movement, 1894–1909," *JAH* 74, no. 1 (June 1987): 36, 40.

3. James Weinstein, *The Decline of Socialism in America, 1912–1925* (New Brunswick, N.J.: Rutgers University Press, 1984), 22–25.

4. Marilyn J. Boxer, "Rethinking the Socialist Construction and International Career of the Concept 'Bourgeois Feminism,'" *AHR* 112 (February 2007): 131–58.

5. Meredith Tax, *The Rising of the Women: Feminist Solidarity and Class Conflict, 1880–1917* (New York: Monthly Review Press, 1980), 170–73, 175–77. Tax focuses on tensions between working-class suffragists and upper-class allies, but does not fully describe O'Reilly's work on behalf of suffrage. Annelise Orleck, *Common Sense and a Little Fire: Women and Working-Class Politics in the United States, 1900–1965* (Chapel Hill: University of North Carolina Press, 1995), 87–89, 94, 96–98, 100–105. Orleck describes working-class women's suffrage activism but does not focus on O'Reilly.

6. Here I depart from the interpretation of Leslie Woodcock Tentler, who presents working-class women's industrial employment as "conservative" and as "reinforc[ing] a self-image of dependence and passivity in the world outside the home" (*Wage-Earning Women: Industrial Work and Family Life in the United States, 1900–1930* [New York: Oxford University Press, 1979], 9). I seek to extend some of the insights of Sarah Eisenstein, who viewed working-class women's entry into the workforce as the beginnings of a collective consciousness, affirmed by their involvement in the suffrage movement; see her posthumously published book, *Give Us Bread, But Give Us Roses: Working Women's Consciousness in the United States, 1890 to the First World War* (London: Routledge, 1983), 42, 155.

7. Joseph A. Hill, *Women in Gainful Occupations, 1870–1920*, Census Monographs 9 (Washington, D.C.: Government Printing Office), 8–11.

8. Quoted in Philip Sheldon Foner, *History of the Labor Movement in the United States*, vol. 6 (New York: International Publishers, 1947), 139–49.

9. For discussion of the "family wage" as constitutive of respectable masculinity, see Michael Willrich, "Home Slackers: Men, the State, and Welfare in Modern America," *JAH* 87, no. 2 (2000): 460–89.

10. Nancy F. Cott, *The Grounding of Modern Feminism* (New Haven, Conn.: Yale University Press, 1987), 7, 40–41, 118–19.

11. Orleck, *Common Sense,* 97–99.

12. "Minutes of the First Meeting of the National Women's Trade Union League," Mary Kenney O'Sullivan Papers, Schlesinger Library, Radcliffe Institute, Harvard University, folder 6. Key works on the WTUL include the following: Robin Miller Jacoby, *The British and American Women's Trade Union Leagues, 1890–1925* (New York: Carlson Publishing, 1994); Elizabeth Anne Payne, *Reform, Labor and Feminism: Margaret Dreier Robins and the Women's Trade Union League* (Urbana: University of Illinois Press, 1988); Nancy Schrom Dye, *As Equals and As Sisters: Feminism, Unionism and the Women's Trade Union League of New York* (Columbia: University of Missouri Press, 1980); and Tax, *Rising of the Women.*

13. For material regarding individual strikes, see LOR Papers, reel 11.

14. Jon E. Gorse, "Strike Expert Leonora O'Reilly Advocates Unions for All Women," clipping from *St. Louis Post-Dispatch,* 8 June 1913, LOR Papers, reel 9.

15. Eleanor Flexner, *Century of Struggle: The Woman's Rights Movement in the United States* (Cambridge, Mass.: Harvard University Press, 1975), 253–54.

16. Dye, *As Equals and As Sisters,* 52–55.

17. Oral history interview of Pauline Newman by Barbara Wertheimer, 13.

18. Blatch was influenced by Fabian socialists, who carefully studied the meanings and possibilities of economic independence for women of different social classes. The Fabian Women's Group, "Summary of Six Papers and Discussions upon the Disabilities of Women as Workers" (n.p.: Issued for Private Circulation, 1909); Ellen Carol DuBois, *Harriot Stanton Blatch and the Winning of Woman Suffrage* (New Haven, Conn.: Yale University Press, 1997), 74–77.

19. DuBois, *Blatch,* 93–95.

20. "Talk Given Suffrage," 1907, LOR Papers, reel 9; Flier, "Mrs. Cobden Sanderson, to speak on the Militant Suffrage Movement," sponsored by League of Self-Supporting Women and the Collegiate Suffrage League Cooper Union, 12 December, LOR Papers, reel 12.

21. Nora Blatch de Forest, "Suffrage Politics in the State of New York," Papers of Harriot Stanton Blatch, Library of Congress, reel 1, container 1, scrapbooks, vol. 1.

22. Annual Report, 1908–9, WTUL of New York, LOR Papers, reel 9. This reel contains numerous fliers and newspaper clippings describing her appearances.

23. For an account of the strike, see Tax, *Rising of the Women,* chap. 8; oral history interview of Pauline Newman by Barbara Wertheimer, 13.

24. "A Working Woman's Plea," reprinted from *Life and Labor* (February 1915), by the National American Woman Suffrage Association.

25. Clipping from *Life and Labor* (September 1913), 264–65, LOR Papers, reel 3.

26. WESL, "Senators v. Working Women: Rose Schneiderman, Cap Maker," LOR Papers, reel 12.

27. "Woman Attacks the 'Antis,'" 1 March 1909, unidentified clipping, LOR Papers, reel 9; "Women in Albany in Ballot Battle," *New York Times,* 25 February 1909, 1, *PQHN.*

28. "N.Y. Suffragettes Invade the Capital," undated clipping from *Hearst's American,* Miller NAWSA Suffrage Scrapbooks, 1897–1911, Scrapbook 7, 76, Library of Congress Rare Books and Special Collections Division. Discussion of this older, elitist ideology can be found in DuBois, "Working Women, Class Relations, and Suffrage Militance," 37–40.

29. "Women in Albany in Ballot Battle."

30. "N.Y. Suffragettes Invade the Capital," Miller Scrapbooks, Scrapbook 7, 76; "Woman Attacks the 'Antis.'"

31. Temma Kaplan, "On the Socialist Origins of International Women's Day," *Feminist Studies* 11, no. 1 (Spring 1985): 166.

32. "Woman Attacks the 'Antis.'"

33. "Women Strike a Blow for the Ballot in All the Land," New York *World,* 1 March 1909; "Woman Attacks the 'Antis.'"

34. Unidentified clipping, Harriot Stanton Blatch Scrapbooks, vol. 1.

35. Helen Marot, "A Woman's Strike," in *Proceedings of the Academy of Political Science* (New York: Columbia University, 1910), 123–25.

36. DuBois, *Blatch,* 116–20.

37. Letter from Harriot Stanton Blatch to LOR, 6 February 1912, LOR Papers, reel 6.

38. Laura E. Nym Mayhall distinguishes *militance,* which included a wide range of public protest behaviors, from *violence,* and argues that the WSPU's use of violence and destruction of property was a point of division among British suffragists, some of whom saw these techniques as counterproductive. Laura E. Nym Mayhall, "Defining Militancy: Radical Protest, the Constitutional Idiom, and Women's Suffrage in Britain, 1908–1909," *Journal of British Studies* 39 (July 2000): 348–49, 369–70. While historians have used the term *militance* to cover a wide range of protest behaviors, contemporaries used it almost exclusively to describe violence and destruction of property. Mary Winsor, "The Militant Suffrage Movement," *Annals of the American Academy of Political and Social Science* 56 (November 1914): 134. For discussion of the American response to Sylvia Pankhurst and her daughters, Christabel and Sylvia, see Christine Bolt, "America and the Pankhursts," in *Votes for Women: The Struggle for Suffrage Revisited,* ed. Jean H. Baker (New York: Oxford University Press, 2002), 143–58.

39. Tax, *Rising of the Women,* 236.

40. Dye, *As Equals,* 96; "Leonora O'Reilly," 23–24, Mary Elisabeth Dreier Papers, Schlesinger Library, Radcliffe Institute, Harvard University, folder 57. The committee also proved to be an opportunity for Tammany Hall politicians to revise their public

image, identifying themselves as progressive and sympathetic to striking workers. David Von Drehle, *Triangle: The Fire That Changed America* (New York: Grove Press, 2003), 212–15, 218.

41. Nancy Woloch, *Muller v. Oregon: A Brief History with Documents* (New York: Bedford Books, 1996); Nancy S. Erickson, "*Muller v. Oregon* Reconsidered: The Origins of a Sex-Based Doctrine of Liberty of Contract," *Labor History* 30, no. 2 (Spring 1989): 228–50.

42. LOR, "Plea for 54–Hour Bill, Albany, May, 1911," LOR Papers, reel 9; Josephine Goldmark, *Fatigue and Efficiency* (New York: Charities Publications Committee, 1912).

43. O'Reilly, "Plea for 54–Hour Bill."

44. LOR, "Notes for Labor Suffrage Mass Meeting, March 22, 1911, Carnegie Hall," LOR Papers, reel 9.

45. Susan Lehrer, *Origins of Protective Labor Legislation for Women, 1905–1925* (Albany: State University of New York Press, 1987), 159, 177.

46. Editorial on May Day written for the *Call* on 22 April 1911, published 1 May 1911, LOR Papers, reel 9; newspaper clipping from the *Sun*, 1911, Harriot Stanton Blatch Scrapbooks, vol. 2.

47. "She Pleads for Votes for Women," 18 October 1913, newspaper clipping from Watertown, N.Y., LOR Papers, reel 9.

48. Letter from Valerie H. Parker to LOR, January 1912, LOR Papers, reel 6.

49. Letter from Rose Perkins Hale (Mrs. L. E. Hale) to LOR, April 1912, LOR Papers, reel 6.

50. Letters from Florence Woolston to LOR, 24 and 27 June 1912, LOR Papers, reel 6.

51. "Suffrage Talks in Vaudeville Near," *New York Times*, 30 August 1912, 3; and "Sidelights on the Smart Set," *Washington Post*, 30 August 1912, both *PQHN*.

52. Flier for the Vaudeville Show in Support of Suffrage, Hammerstein's Victoria Theatre, LOR Papers, reel 12; letter from LOR to MDR, 23 September 1912, Margaret Dreier Robins [hereafter MDR] Collection, George A. Smathers Libraries, University of Florida, reprinted in *Papers of the WTUL and Its Principal Leaders*, reel 22.

53. DuBois, *Blatch*, 136.

54. Women's Political Union, "Cards for March and Formation in Suffrage Parade of 5/3/1913," LOR Papers, reel 12. As described on the card, "Business Women" included industrial, retail, laundry, and domestic workers.

55. Letter from Daisy Byrnes to LOR, 9 June 1912, and letter from Katherine Dreier to LOR, June 1912, LOR Papers, reel 6, series 4.

56. Susan Englander, *Class Conflict and Coalition in the California Woman Suffrage Movement, 1907–1912: The San Francisco Wage Earners' Suffrage League* (Lewiston, N.Y.: Edwin Mellen Press, 1992), 85, 95–97, 112–13; Susan Englander, "Younger, Maud," and Nancy F. Cott, "Beard, Mary Ritter," both *ANB Online* (accessed February 2000).

57. Dorothy Sue Cobble, *Dishing It Out: Waitresses and Their Unions in the Twentieth Century* (Urbana: University of Illinois Press, 1991), 74–75; National Women's Trade Union League, "Proceedings of the Second Biennial Convention of the National Women's Trade Union League of America, Chicago, September 27 to October 1, 1909," 26, Harvard University Library, "Women Working, 1800–1930."

58. Mary Beard to LOR, c. 1912, LOR Papers, reel 6, series 4.

59. The school established close ties with organized labor and later became affiliated with Oxford University. Harold Pollins, *The History of Ruskin College* (Oxford: Ruskin College Library Occasional Publications, 1984), 9–17.

60. Ann J. Lane, *Mary Ritter Beard: A Sourcebook* (Boston: Northeastern University Press, 1988), 21; Nancy F. Cott, *Mary Ritter Beard through Her Letters* (New Haven, Conn.: Yale University Press, 1991), 5–7.

61. Although the school employed female teachers from the beginning, it did not admit women as students until World War I. Nick Kneale, "'The Science and Art of Man-Making': Class and Gender Foundation of Ruskin Hall Oxford, 1899," in *Ruskin College: Contesting Knowledge, Dissenting Politics,* ed. Geoff Andrews, Hilda Kean, and Jane Thompson (London: Lawrence and Wishart, 1999), 23, 25–26.

62. Cott, "Beard, Mary Ritter"; Lane, *Mary Ritter Beard,* 22–24.

63. M. R. B. [Mary Ritter Beard], "The Wage-Earners' League," unidentified clipping, c. 1912, LOR Papers, reel 12.

64. Tensions between Beard and Lemlich developed later. Orleck, *Common Sense,* 98–99.

65. "Constitution of the Wage Earners Suffrage League," LOR Papers, reel 12; letter from Mary Beard to LOR, 1 January 1912, LOR Papers, reel 6.

66. Letter from LOR to Hettie Sherman, 12 May 1913, LOR Papers, reel 6.

67. Letter from Rosalie Jones to LOR, 29 April 1912, LOR Papers, reel 6.

68. Mary White Ovington, *Half a Man: The Status of the Negro in New York* (New York: Longmans, Green, and Co., 1911), 161–63.

69. Correspondence between Harriet Laidlaw and LOR, 15 and 23 April 1913, LOR Papers, reel 6. No organizational records survive; estimates of membership are based on contemporary descriptions of the group by O'Reilly and Beard.

70. Letter from LOR to Ida Millkofsky, 12 May 1913, LOR Papers, reel 6.

71. Letter from LOR to Harriet Laidlaw, 7 May 1912, LOR Papers, reel 6.

72. Draft of letter from LOR to Miss Brody of Chicago WTUL, 23 January 1914, LOR Papers, reel 7.

73. See numerous letters regarding requests for speeches in LOR Papers, reel 12. Letter from Clara Schlingheyd to LOR, 11 October 1915, LOR Papers, reel 7.

74. Membership form for WESL; "Wage Earners to Be Suffragettes," undated clipping, LOR Papers, reel 12.

75. Letter from LOR to MDR, 23 September 1912, MDR Papers, reel 22.

76. Letter from MDR to LOR, 17 January 1912, LOR Papers, reel 6.

77. Letter from Miss Brody of Chicago WTUL to LOR, 13 January 1914; draft of letter from LOR to Miss Brody, 13 January 1914; letter from Emma Steghagen, Secretary WTUL of Chicago, 22 January 1914, LOR Papers, reel 7.

78. Beard, "The Wage-Earners League."

79. Letter from Mary Beard to LOR, April 1912, LOR Papers, reel 6.

80. Their approach resembled that of Marietta Holley, who used humor to under-cut opposition to women's rights in her writings as "Samantha Allen." Jane Curry, ed., *Marietta Holley: Samantha Rastles the Woman Question* (Urbana: University of Illinois Press, 1983).

81. "Suffrage Demanded by Working Women," *New York Times*, 23 April 1912, 24, *PQHN*; WESL, "Senators v. Working Women, Maggie Hinchey, Laundress." The text of the pamphlets, which are included on reel 12 of the LOR Papers, corresponds closely to the speeches reported in the *Times*.

82. WESL, "Senators v. Working Women: Lillian Hefferly, Neckwear Maker."

83. "Suffrage Demanded by Working Women," *New York Times*, 23 April 1912, 24, *PQHN*; WESL, "Senators v. Working Women: Melinda Scott, Hat Trimmer."

84. WESL, "Senators v. Working Women: Mollie Schepps, Shirt Waist Maker."

85. WESL, "Senators v. Working Women: Clara Lemlich, Shirt Waist Maker."

86. WESL, "Senators v. Working Women: Rose Schneiderman, Cap Maker."

87. "Suffrage Demanded by Working Women," *New York Times*, 23 April 1912, 24, *PQHN*.

88. Beard, "The Wage Earner's League."

89. Letters requesting the pamphlets can be found on reel 6 of the LOR Papers.

90. Letter from Mary Beard to LOR, May 1912, LOR Papers, reel 6.

91. S. P. Breckinridge, "Political Equality for Women and Women's Wages," in *American Academy of Political and Social Science, Women in Public Life* (Philadelphia, 1914), 123–24; Christine A. Lunardini, *From Equal Suffrage to Equal Rights: Alice Paul and the National Women's Party, 1910–1928* (New York: New York University Press, 1986), 38–39.

92. Letter from Mary Beard to LOR, May 1912, LOR Papers, reel 6.

93. Clipping from *N.Y. Evening Journal*, 3 May 1912, LOR Papers, reel 12.

94. "Suffragists Elect Anna H. Shaw Again," *New York Times*, 26 November 1912, 11, *PQHN*; Wallace Irwin and Inez Milholland, "Two Million Woman Vote," *McClure's Magazine* 60, no. 3 (January 1913): 249.

95. "Suffragists Invade National Capital to Plead Their Cause," New York *Call*, [14?] March 1912, LOR Papers, reel 9.

96. "The Incentive to Motherhood," 14 July 1912, LOR Papers, reel 9.

97. Dye, *As Equals*, 20–22.

98. Letter from Pauline Newman to Rose Schneiderman, Cleveland, 1911, Pauline Newman Papers, box 5, folder 77.

99. Charles Shively, "Leonora O'Reilly," in *NAW*, 2:652–53; papers relating to purchase of house at 6801 Seventeenth Avenue in Homewood, Brooklyn, June 1909, LOR Papers, reel 3; letters from Daisy Byrnes and Arthur Brisbane, LOR Papers, reels 6 and 7; Robert Weir, "'Here's to the Men Who Lose!' The Hidden Career of Victor Drury," *Labor History* 36, no. 4 (Fall 1995): 530–56.

100. Kathy Peiss, *Cheap Amusements: Working Women and Leisure in Turn-of-the-Century New York* (Philadelphia: Temple University Press, 1986), 63–67; Nan

Enstad, *Ladies of Labor, Girls of Adventure: Working Women, Popular Culture, and Labor Politics at the Turn of the Twentieth Century* (New York: Columbia University Press, 1999), 20, 29, 32–33, 38; and Enstad, "Fashioning Political Identities: Cultural Studies and the Historical Construction of Political Subjects," *American Quarterly* 50, no. 4 (December 1998): 745–82. Enstad argues that young working-class women asserted themselves through a distinctive and highly feminized style of dress that appeared tawdry to middle-class observers, but expressed their own sense of agency. However, middle-class commentators and journalists, such as Dorothy Richardson, may have exaggerated the appearance of working-class women for dramatic effect. O'Reilly was particularly critical of Richardson's demeaning caricatures of working-class women's appearance, speech, and dress in her book *The Long Day* (1905). See Tax, *Rising of the Women*, 117–18.

101. "The Working Girl Is Entitled to Wear Finery," *New York Evening World*, 3 May 1911, LOR Papers, reel 9.

102. "Working Girls Should Keep Out of Debt," unidentified clipping, LOR Papers, reel 9.

103. Letter from Mrs. A. C. Kellogg to LOR, 3 February 1917, LOR Papers, reel 7.

104. "On the Picket Line," *Life and Labor*, March 1913, 71–73.

105. These connections are illuminated in Mary Jane Treacy's "Reacting to the Past" game, "Greenwich Village 1913: Suffrage, Labor, and the New Woman."

106. LOR, "A Working Women's Plea," article reprinted from February 1915 issue of *Life and Labor* by the New York State Women Suffrage Association. For a discussion of class differences in the treatment of women arrested for suffrage militance in Great Britain, see June Purvis, "The Prison Experiences of Suffragettes in Edwardian Britain," *Women's History Review* 4, no. 1 (1995): 103–33.

107. Irwin and Milholland, "Two Million Woman Vote," 241. The WPU did not join this coalition. DuBois, *Blatch*, 161.

108. This commitment to nonviolence distinguished Paul from her British colleagues in the WSPU, who suspended their protests during the war, and drew on her Quaker background and her readings of Henry David Thoreau, Leo Tolstoy, and Mahatma Gandhi. Katherine H. Adams and Michael L. Keene, *Alice Paul and the American Suffrage Campaign* (Urbana: University of Illinois Press, 2008).

109. Jill Liddington and Jill Norris, *"One Hand Tied behind Us": The Rise of the Women's Suffrage Movement* (London: Virago, 1978; reprint, London: Rivers Oram Press, 2000), 206. There were exceptions to this rule, as Michelle Myall argues in "'No Surrender!' The Militance of Mary Leigh, a Working-Class Suffragette," in *The Women's Suffrage Movement: New Feminist Perspectives,* ed. June Purvis and Maroula Joannou (Manchester, 1998), 173–87.

110. Oral history interview with Pauline Newman by Barbara Wertheimer, 49.

111. Cott, *Woman Making History*, 14. Beard's evolution can be traced through her writings; see Lane, *Mary Ritter Beard*, 75–127.

112. Letter from Virginia Shoreham to LOR, c. 21 March 1913, LOR Papers, reel 7; letter from Mary Beard to Alice Paul [1913], reprinted in Cott, *Woman Making History*, 68–69.

113. Letter from Alice Paul to LOR, 29 October 1913, LOR Papers, reel; letter from Alice Paul to LOR, 12 June 1914, LOR Papers, reel 7.

114. Cott, *Woman Making History*, 71–76.

115. Newman expected Catt to be conservative, but found her pragmatic and unconcerned by the fact that Newman was a socialist; see oral history interview with Pauline Newman by Barbara Wertheimer, 49–50. Catt's negative remarks about immigrants and her eventual repudiation of socialism have overshadowed her collaboration with female labor leaders (many of them immigrants and socialists) to win the vote in New York state. Orleck, *Common Sense*, 92–93; DuBois, *Blatch*, 164–65; Mari Jo Buhle, *Women and American Socialism, 1870–1920* (Urbana: University of Illinois Press, 1981), 236.

116. Letters from Alice Clements to LOR, 26 December 1912 and 9 April 1913, LOR Papers, reel 6.

117. Cott, *Woman Making History*, 19–25.

118. "Great Advance of Suffrage Since Last Year's Parade," *New York Times*, 4 May 1913, SM3, *PQHN*.

119. Letter from LOR to Ethel Greenberger, 25 April 1913, LOR Papers, reel 6.

120. Letter to LOR from Maggie Finn, 28 April 1913, LOR Papers, reel 6.

121. DuBois, *Blatch*, 153–54.

122. Letter from LOR to Harriet Laidlaw, 28 April 1913, LOR Papers, reel 6.

123. "Great Advance of Suffrage Since Last Year's Parade," *New York Times*, 4 May 1913.

124. Letter from Mary O'Neill of Montana Equal Suffrage/State Central Committee to LOR, 20 June 1914, LOR Papers, reel 6.

125. Letter from Mary Gray Peck to LOR, 5 October 1914; telegram from MDR to LOR, 7 October 1914, LOR Papers, reel 6.

126. "Report of the Proceedings of the 31st Annual Convention of the Ohio State Federation of Labor," 13 October 1914, 9–11.

127. "Address to Women," *Cleveland Federationist*, 12 November 1914, 1.

128. "Suffrage Wins Labor Sanctions," *Youngstown Daily Vindicator*, 16 October 1914, LOR Papers, reel 12; Buhle, *Women and American Socialism*, 232.

129. LOR, "Construction, Not Destruction, Our Motto," New York *Call*, 4 September 1911.

130. LOR, Transcript of Speech Given in Rochester, N.Y., before the Political Equality Club, 6 May 1913, LOR Papers, reel 9.

131. Emily Greene Balch, as quoted in Mercedes M. Randall, *Improper Bostonian: Emily Greene Balch* (New York: Twayne Publishers, 1964), 134–35; Harriet Hyman Alonso, "Introduction" in Jane Addams, Emily G. Balch, and Alice Hamilton, *Women at the Hague: The International Congress of Women and Its Results* (1915; reprint, Urbana: University of Illinois Press, 2003), vii–xxi.

132. Leila J. Rupp, *Worlds of Women: The Making of an International Women's Movement* (Princeton, N.J.: Princeton University Press, 1997), 34–36.

133. In addition to O'Reilly and Addams, the American delegates included Grace Abbott, Emily Greene Balch, Sophonisba Breckinridge, Elizabeth Glendower Evans, and Alice Hamilton. "List of American Delegates to the Hague Conference," LOR Papers, reel 11.

134. Randall, *Improper Bostonian,* 141–43, 152.

135. Shively, "Leonora O'Reilly," in *NAW,* 2:653.

136. Letter from Stella Franklin to LOR, 5 January 1914 [1915], LOR Papers, reel 7.

137. She wrote daily letters to her mother, Winifred, describing the voyage and the proceedings of the conference; LOR Papers, reel 3, series 3.

138. LOR, "Industrial Democracy," *The Woman Voter* 6, no. 6 (June 1915), LOR Papers, reel 9.

139. Letter from Maggie Hinchey to LOR, Thursday, 29 [May 1913?], LOR Papers, reel 6.

140. Minutes of the Meeting of WTUL Suffrage Committee, 29 September 1915, LOR Papers, reel 12.

141. LOR, "Appeal to Organized Working Men," *Life and Labor* 5, no. 9 (September 1915), 141–42.

142. Buhle, *Women and American Socialism,* 232; DuBois, *Blatch,* 178.

143. Letter from LOR to MDR, 31 August 1915, LOR Papers, reel 7.

144. Jacoby, *British and American WTUL,* 130–31.

145. DuBois, *Blatch,* 179.

146. Letter from Alice S. Bean to LOR, 2 October 1915; letter from Harriet Wells to LOR, 20 March 1917; letter from Arthur Brisbane to LOR, 26 September 1917, LOR Papers, reel 7; Tax, *Rising of the Women,* 122–24.

147. "Why an Industrial Section for Votes for Women," manuscript of article for the *Union Printer,* 1917, LOR Papers, reel 9.

148. Buhle, *Women and American Socialism,* 235–37.

149. Dorothy Sue Cobble, *The Other Women's Movement: Workplace Justice and Social Rights in Modern America* (Princeton, N.J.: Princeton University Press. 2004), chap. 3, 147; Landon R. Y. Storrs, *Civilizing Capitalism: The National Consumer's League, Women's Activism and Labor Standards in the New Deal Era* (Chapel Hill: University of North Carolina Press, 2000), 178–86.

150. Robin Booth Fowler and Spencer Jones, "Carrie Chapman Catt and the Last Years of Struggle for Woman Suffrage: 'The Winning Plan,'" in *Votes for Women,* ed. Baker, 135–40.

151. Buhle, *Women and American Socialism,* 238–39.

152. LOR, Our Book of the Year, *Life and Labor* (January 1920), 12.

153. Mary E. Dreier, "Leonora O'Reilly, A Chapter of Memories," 1931, 3–4, Mary E. Dreier Papers, Schlesinger Library, Radcliffe Institute, Harvard University, folder 57.

154. Notecard and course catalog from The New School for Social Research, 1925–1926, 18, LOR Papers, reel 3, series 2.

155. Shively, "Leonora O'Reilly," in *NAW*, 2:653.

156. LOR, Transcript of Speech Given in Rochester, N.Y., before the Political Equality Club, 6 May 1913, LOR Papers, reel 9.

157. "Women Toilers to Better Our Race," 1 February 1909, unidentified clipping, LOR Papers, reel 9.

158. LOR, "Why the Working Woman Should Vote," *The Woman Voter* (October 1911), LOR Papers, reel 9.

159. "Silver-Tongued Suffragist Wins 29 Men to the Cause," *North American* (Philadelphia), 1912.

INDEX

Ladies Federal Labor Union, 60
Ladies Female Reform Association, 26
Ladies' Tailors Union, 99
Lake, Obadiah, 48
LaRue, Louise, 142
laundry workers, 45, 50, 112, 147, 149
Lease, Mary Elizabeth, 92
legislation. *See* protective legislation
legislative hearings, 24; in New York state,
  95–96, 135–37, 139; in U.S. Congress,
  151, 163–64
Lemlich, Clara, 131, 135, 143, 145, 146, 149
Life and Labor (magazine), 150, 153, 158,
  162
Livermore, Mary, 20, 31
Looking Backward (Bellamy), 69, 119
Lowell, Charles Russell, 73
Lowell, Francis Cabot, 13–14
Lowell, John, 13–14
Lowell, Josephine Shaw, 8, 93; class attitudes of, 67, 73–74, 81, 83; family back-
  ground of, 73; and Leonora O'Reilly,
  73–75, 94, 95; and NYCL, 8, 67, 83, 86,
  87, 88, 96; and WWS, 73–75, 77, 79
Lowell Female Labor Reform Association, 13

Manhattan Trade School for Girls, 144
marriage, 38, 47, 55–56, 148–49
Massachusetts Bureau of Statistics of Labor,
  30, 105, 110, 111, 112, 121–22, 127
Massachusetts State Federation of Women's
  Clubs, 123
McClellan, George B., 135
McClure's magazine, 151
McDonald, Eva. *See* Valesh, Eva McDonald
Meyer, Annie Nathan, 152
"middle class" (term), 2
middle-class status, 53
minimum wage laws, 76
Morgan, Elizabeth, 60
Morgan, Thomas J., 57–58
mothers, widowed, 6, 28–29, 56, 68, 147–48

nannies, 124
Nathan, Maud, 2, 77, 88, 90; and Consumers' League label, 98, 99, 100; elite
  background of, 2, 4, 9, 77, 87; as a leader
  of NYCL, 8–9, 82, 86, 87
National American Woman Suffrage Association (NAWSA), 136, 150, 151,
  161. *See also* National Woman Suffrage
  Association

National Consumers' League, 100–101,
  139, 150, 161
National Labor Union, 18
National Training School for Women and
  Girls, 117, 118
National Woman Suffrage Association, 27.
  See also National American Woman Suf-
  frage Association
National Women's Party, 154
Nature's Aristocracy (Collins), 28, 29
NAWSA. *See* National American Woman
  Suffrage Association
needle trades, 13, 22, 25, 51–52, 68, 126;
  deskilling of labor in, 19, 22, 24; ILGWU
  and, 138, 151–52; NEWC and, 23–24,
  102; piecework in, 84 (*see also* outworkers); strikes in, 1, 99 (*see also* shirtwaist
  strike of 1909–10); wages in, 22, 60
"Nelson, Nell." *See* Cusack, Nell
NEWC. *See* New England Women's Club
New England Labor Reform League, 18,
  26, 30
New England Women's Club (NEWC), 3, 4,
  7–8, 22, 23–24, 102, 109; and domestic
  service, 4, 8, 14, 23–24, 52–53; elite
  composition of, 4, 8, 25; gulf between,
  and working women, 25, 52–53, 102;
  and needle trades, 23–24, 102
Newman, Pauline, 133, 135, 140, 151–52;
  in suffrage movement, 131, 135, 154,
  155
New York Consumers' League (NYCL),
  8–9, 81–82, 86–90, 96, 97, 98; and
  domestic service, 4, 88–89; elite composition of, 4, 8–9, 67, 77, 82–83, 87; emphasis of, on protecting public health, 9, 100,
  101; Helen Campbell and, 55, 82–83,
  86–87, 89–90; Leonora O'Reilly and, 77,
  83; white label of, 67, 99–101; white list
  maintained by, 67, 82–83, 87–88, 98
New York State Factory Investigating Committee, 138–40
New York State Women's Suffrage Association, 132, 141
New York Times, 32, 79, 146–47, 156
NYCL. *See* New York Consumers' League

occupational health. *See* health, occupa-
  tional
Oliver, Henry K., 36
O'Reilly, John, 67–68, 69
O'Reilly, Leonora, 8, 9, 66, 67–70, 72; an-

ॐ

Lara Vapnek is an assistant professor of history at St. John's University in Queens, New York.

WOMEN IN AMERICAN HISTORY

Southern Single Blessedness: Unmarried Women in the Urban South,
    1800–1865   *Christine Jacobson Carter*
Widows and Orphans First: The Family Economy and Social Welfare
    Policy, 1865–1939   *S. J. Kleinberg*
Habits of Compassion: Irish Catholic Nuns and the Origins of the Welfare
    System, 1830–1920   *Maureen Fitzgerald*
The Women's Joint Congressional Committee and the Politics of
    Maternalism, 1920–1930   *Jan Doolittle Wilson*
"Swing the Sickle for the Harvest Is Ripe": Gender and Slavery in
    Antebellum Georgia   *Daina Ramey Berry*
Christian Sisterhood, Race Relations, and the YWCA, 1906–46
    Nancy Marie Robertson
Reading, Writing, and Segregation: A Century of Black Women Teachers
    in Nashville   *Sonya Ramsey*
Radical Sisters: Second-Wave Feminism and Black Liberation in
    Washington, D.C.   *Anne M. Valk*
Feminist Coalitions: Historical Perspectives on Second-Wave Feminism
    in the United States   *Edited by Stephanie Gilmore*
Breadwinners: Working Women and Economic Independence,
    1865–1920   *Lara Vapnek*

The University of Illinois Press
is a founding member of the
Association of American University Presses.

Composed in 10/13 Sabon
by Jim Proefrock
at the University of Illinois Press
Designed by Dennis Roberts
Manufactured by Cushing-Malloy, Inc.

University of Illinois Press
1325 South Oak Street
Champaign, IL 61820-6903
www.press.uillinois.edu